Your Godly Brand

Your Godly Brand

A Guide to Defining Your Faith-Based Brand

Daniel L. Rhodes

RESOURCE *Publications* • Eugene, Oregon

YOUR GODLY BRAND
A Guide to Defining Your Faith-Based Brand

Copyright © 2022 Daniel L. Rhodes. All rights reserved. Except for brief quotations in critical publications or reviews, no part of this book may be reproduced in any manner without prior written permission from the publisher. Write: Permissions, Wipf and Stock Publishers, 199 W. 8th Ave., Suite 3, Eugene, OR 97401.

Resource Publications
An Imprint of Wipf and Stock Publishers
199 W. 8th Ave., Suite 3
Eugene, OR 97401

www.wipfandstock.com

PAPERBACK ISBN: 978-1-6667-5796-5
HARDCOVER ISBN: 978-1-6667-5797-2
EBOOK ISBN: 978-1-6667-5798-9

12/22/22

All Scripture quotations, unless otherwise indicated, are taken from the Holy Bible, New International Version®, NIV®. Copyright ©1973, 1978, 1984, 2011 by Biblica, Inc.™ Used by permission of Zondervan. All rights reserved worldwide. www.zondervan.com The "NIV" and "New International Version" are trademarks registered in the United States Patent and Trademark Office by Biblica, Inc.™

To my father, Ernest Lee Rhodes II,
who always wanted me to enter God's ministry.

It was his reinforcement of the Scriptures from my earliest years that built the foundation for where I am today in my faith walk—and with God's help—enabled me to write this book.

Contents

Acknowledgements | ix
Preface | xi

Section 1: All About Branding
1. What You Need to Know About Branding | 3
2. Everything Has a Brand, Even Dogs | 18
3. Personal Branding Differs from Godly Branding | 30

Section 2: What Is Godly Branding
4. Your Body is a Temple (for Branding) | 55
5. Brand Attribute—Loves Others | 71
6. Brand Attribute—Shows Patience | 77
7. Brand Attribute—Demonstrates a Servant Mindset | 85
8. Brand Attribute—Demonstrates Trust and Obedience in God | 94
9. Brand Attribute—Forgives | 99
10. Brand Attribute—Glorifies God Through Thankfulness | 108
11. Brand Attribute—Is a Member of God's Community / Church | 116
12. Brand Attribute—Is an Agent of Change | 123
13. Strengthening the Frieze: How Your Actions Define You | 132
14. Things that Harm Your Godly Brand | 144

Section 3: Defining Your Godly Brand

- 15 Prep Work: Personality Tests, Spiritual Gifts, & Role of Diversity | 159
- 16 Defining Your Core Purpose and Values | 170
- 17 Defining Your Brand Messaging | 192
- 18 Verifying and Applying Your Godly Brand | 213
- 19 Aspirational Branding: Evolving Your Godly Brand | 220
- 20 The Final Word: Walk the Walk and Pray | 232

Acknowledgements

- The Triune God: Without all three's help, this book would not be possible.
- My wife Lori: Her amazing love and listening helped give me the strength to persevere and write this book.
- My three kids (Rebekah, Jesse, and Nathan): They supported me and understood when I was busy with work during my career and writing this book.
- Those who helped support me and this book over the years:
  - Terry Lambert: The only person who read my first draft cover to cover. His feedback was invaluable. Thank you!
  - Chris Perez, APR: My friend and colleague at Westbound Communications (where I currently work) who read and gave me feedback on my initial book proposal.
  - Katie Coates, APR: My friend and fellow author who served as an inspiration for me with her book and an open ear when we discussed mine.
  - Pastor Lon Wagner: Over several coffees and long talks, he supported my writing efforts and let me conduct the first-ever adult bible study based on this book's contents.
- Bible Study Fellowship (BSF): God has strengthened me immensely over the last 6 years that I have been involved in this global ministry. Thank you to all the leaders in my Leadership Circle at Cypress Class 210!

- The pastoral staffs at my last two churches, Bethany Christian Reform Church in Bellflower, CA, and Neighborhood Church of Cypress in Cypress, CA. God regularly inspired thoughts and insights for this book through their Sunday morning messages.

Preface

THIS BOOK IS MEANT to help guide those who profess to being a believer in God to live in a way that more clearly glorifies Him. The contents of this book pertain to believers of all walks of life, at any age, with any socioeconomic background, or during any stage of their personal faith.

When I originally conceived of this book, my intent was to write about personal branding and reputation management through a faith-based lens, creating a concept that I called Godly branding, which will be explained throughout this book. What seemed important at the onset was walking believers step-by-step through exercises to help them understand and define their personal (Godly) brand.

As God frequently does, He "flipped the script" on me. It didn't take much research for me to see that there were already plenty of books and educational resources published on the topic of personal branding. The step-by-step approach in this book for determining your personal brand isn't much different than what others have written. Many of us who write brand platforms for organizations and people use most of the same tools with the same elements. Brand platforms communicate your core values, core purpose, your differentiators, and so on. Some may add personal interests, passions, and skill sets. The process for determining your personal brand—the exercises in this book—are nothing especially new to those familiar with branding.

What is different is the way in which they are visually presented. This book will use a graphical depiction of your brand as a temple. The Scriptures tell us that your body is a temple for God. I use it to describe the firm *foundation* on which you should build your brand (i.e., eight brand attributes based on the life of Jesus and others in the Bible), *columns* that represent your core brand values, and the *frieze* that details the actions and significant achievements of your life. These elements will be covered in *Section 2: About Godly Branding* of this book. I cover how to change your brand once you've identified it and the harmful effects of sin on the structure of your temple.

Section 1: All About Branding provides a background about branding for those who are new to it. *Section 2: About Godly Branding* outlines those brand attributes that Jesus and God's followers in the Bible exhibited during their lives. The crux of this book is that the Scriptures gave us terrific examples of Godly branding through the lives of Jesus as well as David, Moses, Paul, Ruth, Mary, and dozens of others throughout the Old and New Testaments. *Section 3: Determining Your Godly Brand* offers a series of exercises to determine your individual or business' brand and how to live it.

Along the way, the book discusses purpose. So many books have been written on the topic; this book weighs in with a few insights about figuring out your purpose and how it relates to your Godly brand. But the more important thing is your brand helps define your God-given purpose.

One note: the terms "attributes" and "values" are used to describe a brand throughout this book. Regarding usage, an attribute describes a brand from an external perspective, while a value refers to the internal development of one's brand. For example, I can discern Paul the Apostle's brand attributes by studying his life and actions, but only he can determine his Core Values.

Last thing before we get started . . .

You may or may not be a believer in God and Christ as your Risen Savior. If you're not, that's okay. You should still derive a lot of meaning and practical application from the book. The book does contain a great many biblical references. Hopefully, they'll be clear as you read them. If they are not, please contact me at YourGodlyBrand@gmail.com.

If you are a believer, regardless of where you are in your spiritual walk with God, this book should help you identify your Godly brand values and how you may use them to carry out His will on this earth.

God bless you as you read this . . .

Section 1

All About Branding

A look at different types of branding, how to define a brand, successful corporate and faith-based brands, and what they all have in common. Also, a review of where branding fits with God-given purpose.

Chapter 1

What You Need to Know About Branding

IN FALL 2011, MY daughter's school, Valley Christian Middle School in Bellflower, California, instituted iPads to replace textbooks and promote new methods of interactive learning. The iPads did enhance the middle schoolers' education. But they also broadened the students' awareness and use of social media.

The following spring semester, the school was forced to take disciplinary action against a couple dozen students over a social media post on Instagram that made their 7th-grade teacher look bad. One 7th grader made the post. Another 25 or so kids liked or commented on the post. The specific details of the post and disciplinary action are less relevant than the fact that the incident reminded the entire middle school community—from teachers to students to their parents—about the potentially harmful effects of social media and the Internet when either medium is mis-used.

Social media's potential impact on people's feelings was nothing new. The concept of cyberbullying and sexting, along with their long-term effects, had been well publicized. As a marketing professional, I had represented a mobile app developer that released an app specifically meant to prevent these things.

After the school disciplined the students, the IT staff conducted an informational session for parents to better understand what it was doing about the students' use of social media on those iPads. During the session, several different app and network-filtering technologies were discussed to limit students' accessibility to social media and other offensive content on the Internet.

As I listened to the presentation, I realized that trying to employ technology as a means to limit and manage a teenager's social media use was fraught with pitfalls and—as King Solomon may have described it—a chasing of the wind. See, one can never underestimate a teenager's ability to circumvent technology meant to prevent him or her from doing something.

It dawned on me that the only way to make an impact on teenagers was to appeal to their reputation. What our middle schoolers seemed to need was training in reputation management and—more broadly—personal branding.

If middle schoolers defined their brand, then understood that their actions or inactions affected it, including improper social media posts and online activities, perhaps they would self-monitor and self-correct their behavior, even if just by a tiny bit. Just as major brands such as Coca-Cola or Google or Apple nurture and defend their brand, teens would care at some level about staying true to their core brand values. Now, trying to get teenagers to think about the effects of branding may seem like folly. But some may take it seriously enough to consider their actions and their long-term consequences.

To be clear, good branding is not just for middle schoolers. The fundamental principles of branding and reinforcing one's brand are applicable to people of all ages. It's never too late to define one's brand, although—based on one's life decisions and actions as well as the things that one says about him- or herself—shifting that brand may become challenging depending on the situation. For example, if a father divorces his wife, neglects his children, avoids paying child support, then tries to characterize himself as a good parent, his disingenuous actions counteract anything he may say about himself or have others say on his behalf.

The larger truth is that the world is a sinful place and most of us tend to be—as the Old Testament passages referred to the Israelites—a "rebellious, stick-necked" people. We are stubborn and willful about our sin. We frequently enter into sinful acts knowingly, but we do them anyway. How do we, as sinful creatures, overcome that? Then, how do we go one step further to *consistently* glorify God by our actions?

The *only* way is to commit to a "Godly brand," which—as we'll discuss throughout this book—mandates certain types of Christ-like behavior. It doesn't matter if you're man or woman, rich or poor, educated or not, or living in the city or on a farm, Godly branding applies to you, if you call yourself a person of faith. Godly branding spans all race, socioeconomic background, spiritual background, country of origin, or any other criteria that you can imagine.

When you call yourself a follower of God, you take on a responsibility and accountability to act, speak, and behave in a manner that glorifies God. That's the Godly part of your Godly brand, a concept that will be explained throughout this book.

In Paul's first letter to the church in Corinth, the apostle dealt with a severe disconnect between the believers whom he praised with thanksgiving in verses 4–9 of chapter 1 and their actions that dishonored Christ and harmed their reputation among the city's large unbelieving population.

Corinth was a major port city in the ancient world and a huge economic center. With the comings and goings of commerce through the city, it was an ideal place to spread the Word of God throughout the region. Paul arrived in the city and spent a year and a half getting to know people, talking to them about the saving grace of Jesus, and forming a strong church.

Then, Paul departed Corinth to spread the Word of God in other cities, continuing on his second mission journey. Problem is, he started to hear reports of sinful acts by the followers there. In chapter 1:11, he writes: "My brothers and sisters, some from Chloe's household have informed me that there are quarrels among you." Paul wrote the letter in response to these quarrels and other sinful behavior that were told to him.

The Book of 1 Corinthians addressed five main problems that the church was having, including divisions among the followers, issues involving both sex and food, how they conducted themselves when they gathered as a church, and the resurrection. The first four chapters of the letter concerned the divisions within the church. After Paul left Corinth, Acts 18 details that Apollos followed him there and spoke boldly. Some of the believers aligned with him. Scriptures tell us that there were followers of Cephas, who is Peter, too. Paul had his own following. And some said, "I follow Christ."

The believers divided into factions that followed each of these church leaders much in the same way that fans follow their favorite sports team. Even worse, the fans from one faction trash-talked and derided fans from other factions. The people had fallen into worldly considerations of popularity and celebrity, then let their own pride cause rifts in the church. It's what Prov 13:10 tells us: "Where there is strife, there is pride." And these rifts didn't just harm their fellow believers. Their pride damaged their witness in the city, as all of their feuding occurred in the public eye.

The rest of 1 Corinthians goes on to describe incidents where a son was openly sleeping with his step-mother in chapter 5, believers were taking other believers to secular court to adjudicate matters between them in chapter 6, sexual immortality was rampant in chapter 7, and so on. In all these matters, the believers were actually proud of their actions! They thought that God's boundless grace was their "get out of jail free" card and, if they merely repented, everything would be fine.

Paul tackles this issue head-on in chapter 10, starting in verse 23: "'I have the right to do anything,' you say—but not everything is beneficial. 'I have the right to do anything'—but not everything is constructive. No one should seek their own good, but the good of others." The believers weren't just hurting themselves with their sinful behavior, some of which led to sickness and death (11:30), but it affected how others perceived them and God's church. In chapter 10, Paul concludes: "So whether you eat or drink or whatever you do, do it all for the glory of God. Do not cause anyone to stumble, whether Jews, Greeks or the church of God—even as I try to please everyone in every way. For I am not seeking my own good but the good of many, so that they may be saved."

Two very important concepts jump out here: "whatever you do, do it all for the glory of God" and "Do not cause anyone to stumble." For the Corinthians, poor judgment led to bad behavior, which led to them being a horrible example for Christ. Simply put, they reflected a very bad Godly brand.

Most people have heard the term branding. It's hard to be a working professional in nearly any business sector without the term coming up at some point. If you watch television or listen to talk radio, the brands of celebrities, politicians, and sports stars are constantly discussed. However, most people do not clearly understand what branding is. Many equate the term with an organization's logo, tagline, messaging, advertising, or some form of corporate marketing. And yes, all of those things fit into branding, but it's far more involved than that.

The concept of branding originated with the Old Norse term "brandr," which means "to burn." The practice of branding began centuries ago when manufacturers burnt their mark (i.e., identifying symbol) onto their products or shipping containers to differentiate them. Many times, this was done to separate one's products or services from the competition or to more easily identify the product as it was being transported. Research indicates that this practice dates back more than 3,000 years to ancient India.

Most people associate the practice of branding with ranchers burning their mark onto their cattle and livestock to easily identify them. Over time, the marks on the cattle held a more significant meaning: they differentiated the quality or other characteristic of the cattle.

Branding took off in the late 1800s with the growth in the use of logos to help people recall consumer-packaged goods through image association. A long list of brands began using logos during this time. Heinz introduced a logo for its horseradish sauce in 1869, then adapted it for selling ketchup when it was launched in 1876. Levi Strauss & Co. was founded in 1837, but began featuring its logo with two horses on its denim products in 1886. Johnson & Johnson used its first logo in 1887. Coca-Cola's logo was trademarked in 1893. The use of these logos trained people connect a name, mark, or other brand identification with a product or service.

Today, brands place imagery or iconography that connote a subliminal or deeper meaning into their marks and visual identity to convey important messages or benefits about what the product or service delivers. For example, if you look at the FedEx logo, there is an arrow formed from the negative space in between the "E" and the "x" that connotes positive advancement. In the Amazon logo, the arrow expresses an abstract smile as well as telling you that the company delivers everything from "a" to "z." In the Wendy's logo, if you look carefully at the neckline of the dress, you'll see the word "MOM." In fact, every mark should make some type of statement about the brand.

A great deal of time and consideration is spent by marketing professionals, designers, and executive leadership to ascertain a business' values, the attributes that they want to people to feel about the brand, its personality, its differentiators, and much more. All those factors are distilled into a visual identity that includes a logo, color palette, typography, and guidelines on usage.

Businesses spend a lot of money, resources, and time to create their brand platform and accompanying visual identity, and frequently they incorporate deeper values-based imagery into the look and feel of their brand.

Definition of Branding

Ask 100 marketing professionals to define the term branding, and you'll receive 100 similar but different definitions. It's a little like asking someone to describe what it means to be in love. Part of the reason for all the different answers is that people experience the brand of an organization or person from their own unique perspective. Also, many marketers want to reinforce their own brand through their definition of branding. Myself included.

The American Marketing Association defines brand as ". . . a name, term, sign, symbol, or design, or a combination of them, intended to identify the goods or services of one seller or group of sellers and differentiate them from those of the competition." This is a good description, but it is not complete.

In his book "Branding for Dummies," author Bill Chiaravalle states "Brand refers to the set of characteristics that arise in a customer's mind when that person hears your name or sees your logo." Good, but branding extends beyond what a customer thinks. Branding affects how people feel.

In her book "Small Business Marketing for Dummies," Barbara Findlay Schenck provides this definition: "Branding simply involves developing and consistently communicating a group of positive characteristics that consumers can identify with and relate to your name." Yes, hopefully, a company communicates positive characteristics and they stick. But what happens if they don't?

Marketing visionary and leading author Seth Godin takes a slightly more scientific approach to the subject: "[Prediction of what to expect] x [emotional power of that expectation] = a brand." Interesting, but a little heady.

T. Scot Gross, author of "Micro Branding," offers this explanation: "Brands are defined by the customer. They exist as a feeling that extends beyond the product itself. The brand experience includes your marketing, customer service, even feelings shared customer to customer." If I were attempting to write a comprehensive, academic definition, it would be pretty close to this one. This is one of the best definitions that I found in my research, mostly because it hints at the other aspects of branding that people tend to overlook, especially the operational delivery of a product, service, vision or idea, or knowledge / data.

All these definitions and many, many others that are not listed here are fine explanations for branding. However, in my 25-plus years of experience in branding, I have developed my own, more straightforward definition:

Branding is the alignment of what you say about yourself with what you actually do, and how that shapes others' perception of you.

Let's unpack this statement, starting with "what you say about yourself." For people, what you say about yourself literally comes out of your mouth, how you appear (i.e., your attire, personal style, and body language), and how you comport yourself (i.e., how you behave and live your life). You can communicate about yourself through a wide range of personal marketing, such as social media posts, personal or professional websites, bylined articles or op/eds in media outlets, videos and podcasts, and much more. A key part of personal marketing involves networking and meeting people at industry events, trade shows, work-related events, philanthropic or charity events, etc. Through all these channels, a person affects his or her perception by others.

For celebrities, their ability to affect others' perceptions of them is exponentially strengthened through their platform, a term that refers to the combination of all the previously mentioned personal marketing channels with whatever medium makes them well-known (e.g., TV, sports, film, music, books, politics, art, food / cooking, etc.).

Time for a pop quiz: which of these celebrities has the largest social media followings on Instagram, according to *Brandwatch*?

- Miley Cyrus
- Nicki Minaj
- Virat Kohli
- Neymar
- Jennifer Lopez
- Taylor Swift
- Khloè Kardashian
- Kendall Jenner
- Justin Bieber
- Beyoncè
- Kim Kardashian
- Selena Gomez

- Ariana Grande
- Dwayne "The Rock" Johnson
- Lionel Messi
- Kylie Jenner
- Cristiano Ronaldo

There may be some names on this list you do not recognize, depending on how much you follow pop culture and the worlds of fashion, entertainment, and sports. But all of them have more social media followers by far than the *USA Today, New York Times, Wall Street Journal, Washington Post, Los Angeles Times,* and *Chicago Tribune* have readers *put together.* At least 8 of the celebrities on above list have more Instagram followers alone than the combined readership and social media followers across all channels (e.g., Facebook, Instagram, Twitter) for these top-six newspapers in the U.S. That's saying something when you consider that the *New York Times* has more than 54.6 million Twitter followers alone, as of November 2022.

All these celebrities have spent years cultivating, nourishing, and advancing in their careers to grow these massive followings. The effort on their part was deliberate and—due to the huge numbers of followers they have—they wield tremendous public influence that can be monetized (more on this later).

In spring 2018 after about 15 months of the President Trump administration, many celebrities who watched the Commander-In-Chief use his persona and brand awareness to gain popular support to win the election felt as though they may give the Oval Office a run in 2020. One of them was Dwayne "The Rock" Johnson, the wrestler-turned-megamovie star. Photos and videos of him standing at a podium with signage that read "The Rock" Johnson 2020 appeared across the Internet and social media. He and his managers floated the idea, both for branding and to gauge the receptivity of the idea with the general public. In appearances throughout 2018 and 2019, Johnson continued to stoke the rumors of a presidential run.

Now, be assured, some of that showmanship was to sell movies and TV shows. During this period, he had four tentpole movies hit the silver screen: *Rampage, Skyscraper, Fast & Furious Presents: Hobbs & Shaw,* and *Jumanji: The Next Level.* At the same time, he had two hit television shows on: *Ballers* and *WWE Smackdown!*

However, his continued flirtation with running had to be taken seriously. Why? Besides a natural charisma that makes him seemingly one of the most likeable people on the planet, and the fact that he's clearly an intelligent businessman who has nurtured his brand, he has built a gigantic follower base on his social media channels that can be mobilized for things like voter registration and turnout.

Going back to the list of celebrities with the largest Instagram followings, Johnson ranked third on the list with a whopping 172 million followers, according to a February 21, 2020 ranking in the outlet *Brandwatch*. Putting that follower base into perspective, it equates to two percent of the world population and more than half of the U.S. population. And that's only on one social media channel. Add another 58 million followers on Facebook and 15 million on Twitter (in 2020), and Johnson's follower base on just those three channels is more than 245 million. Even if you assume some percentage of that base follows him on all three channels, that's a lot of influence! If Johnson had run for President of the United States, and he surrounded himself with smart campaign managers who could advise him on policy, he would have no problem performing the necessary fundraising to make his candidacy a strong contender for the Oval in 2024 or 2028.

As of August 2022, Johnson's Instagram followers reached 334 million, which is larger than the 329.5 million population of the United States, according to the 2020 U.S. Census.

For the record, the above list is in reverse order of Instagram followers with soccer great Cristiano Ronaldo the highest, Kylie Jenner, soccer great Lionel Messi, then Johnson, and so on, ending with Miley Cyrus. Only three companies made the top-20 list of most Instagram followers: Instagram itself, which feels a little like cheating; National Geographic; and Nike.

What an organization says about itself involves standard marketing and communications across a wide range of channels, the most well-known ones being print (newspapers, magazines), broadcast (TV, radio), and online (website, social media).

However, there are other ways that an organization communicates with its target audiences that may not be as obvious, but nonetheless play an important part in how people perceive it. Product packaging or presentation can set the tone for how customers perceive a product or service. Drinking a bottle of Voss water just feels different than Dasani. It's the shape of the bottle, the material it's made of (glass versus plastic), and column-like design. More important, it's how you feel holding that sleek glass bottle in your hand, rather than the thin, crunchy plastic one. It's the same reason that Starbucks plasters a giant green mermaid logo on the sides of its cups. It's not just about Starbucks turning you into a walking billboard with its products. It's equally, if not more important, that you know that people see you carrying the Starbucks cup, versus McDonald's, Dunkin' or Peet's.

For a person "what you actually do" refers to your actions and inactions, speech, appearance, who and what you surround yourself with, and much more.

In July 2019, after losing to Simona Halep in the Wimbledon women's tennis championship, Serena Williams, arguably the greatest female athlete who's ever lived, was asked by a reporter a real "gotcha" question: "There have been a few comments made in the last couple of weeks from people like Billie Jean King that maybe you should stop being a celebrity for a year and stop fighting for equality and just focus on tennis. How do you respond to that?"

What made the question provocative were two facts: 1) Serena Williams had beaten Halep in the previous three times that the two had met in Grand Slam matches and 2) the loss was Williams' worst in her Wimbledon finals career. Winning only 4 games total in the match, she had never been defeated so convincingly in any prior Grand Slam final.

In the immediate face of defeat and being asked a stinging question, Williams' answer was bold, inspiring, and classy: "Well, the day I stop fighting for equality and for people that look like you and me will be the day I'm in my grave." Note what Williams didn't do. She didn't question the role of King, a renowned women's rights advocate. She didn't get upset and challenge the reporter with a "how dare you ask me that?" response of any kind. She answered the question the way she played tennis: head on, with dignity, taking personal responsibility, and making a point (pun intended).

Her response received universal praise across news cycles and social media platforms, including the attention of one of the top Democratic presidential candidates at the time and future U.S. Vice President, Sen. Kamala Harris, D.-Calif., who retweeted video of the question and answer, posting, "@serenawilliams is right. We must never stop fighting for equality."

The story doesn't end there, of course. Even people like me who have never met King and certainly don't know her recognized the framing of the question by the reporter did not add up to who and what King stood for (i.e., her brand). It seemed like a complete disconnect that King would suggest that Williams or anyone else would "stop fighting for equality." And indeed, that's not what King said. In an interview with the British website Metro, King made the comment that all of Williams' commitments—including her marriage, daughter, business, and fighting for gender equality—would make winning another Grand Slam title "much harder."

As soon as King heard about the confusion around her comments, she very quickly cleared things up on Twitter, setting the record straight: "I would never ask anyone to stop fighting for equality. In everything she does, Serena shines a light on what all of us must fight for in order to achieve equality for all." Her post put an end to the issue.

What's the branding lesson here? For both Williams and King, their "what you say about yourself" and "what you actually do" aligned, even in the face of confrontation where it would be easy to attack back and take a different brand path. Both women's response in the face of misinformation and indirect accusation further strengthened their respective iconic brands.

Conversely, celebrities like Pete Rose and Lance Armstrong show us what it's like when someone says one thing but does something completely different. After accepting a lifetime ban from Major League Baseball in 1989 for gambling on the Cincinnati Reds when he was the team's manager, Pete Rose *vehemently* denied betting on baseball for 15 years until—in 2004—he admitted that he bet on games in his autobiography. If you followed Rose's saga during the 1990s, his denials were so strong that many fans (myself included) gave him the benefit of the doubt or—at least—marginalized what he may or may not have done. That is, until the truth came out.

In 2005, Lance Armstrong did something that no one will likely ever do again: he won his 7th consecutive Tour de France bicycle race. It was one of the greatest individual accomplishments in the history of sports. The achievement was made even more stunning by the announcement in October 1996 that he was diagnosed with testicular cancer that had spread to his lungs, lymph nodes, abdomen and brain. He fought the cancer and was (and continued to be) a survivor. The following year, he founded the Lance Armstrong Foundation to benefit cancer research and cancer patients. Other than Tiger Woods, there wasn't a stronger brand in sports at the time.

Armstrong's brand was Teflon. Nothing stuck to it, including a 21-month investigation in 2002 into whether the US Postal Team used performance-enhancing drugs (PEDs) during the 2000 Tour de France. In 2004, Armstrong sued David Walsh, who co-authored a book that accused him of taking PEDs. In the same year, Armstrong filed for an emergency ruling in a Paris court trying to order the publishers of a book that suggested he was doping during races to insert a denial by him. In May 2010, Armstrong's former teammate Floyd Landis made doping allegations against him. In 2012, the U.S. Anti-Doping Agency filed doping charges against Armstrong, whose attorney called the charges "wrong" and "baseless."

For years, Armstrong attacked people who even hinted that he was doping, suing them and issuing strong denials in public forums. I remember seeing him do it on TV. Like Rose, his denials were vehement. Then, on January 13, 2013, during an interview with Oprah Winfrey, Armstrong admitted to using PEDs during his cycling career. His brand was Teflon, until it wasn't, and he lost all his sponsors and the foundation that was named after him.

"What you actually do" pertains to how an organization delivers its products or services to its target audiences. That delivery informs how people experience the brand, and it should match or exceed "what the organization says about itself."

When the delivery exceeds, it can be absolute magic.

Take Apple, for example. The Apple brand stands for innovation. Its products challenge the status quo, and they target consumers who "think different." That's what Apple says about itself. "Think different" was one of its first taglines, supported by a national advertising campaign that featured silhouetted dancers set against a bright color background, then the Mac-versus-PC ads with television actor Justin Long. Every aspect of their marketing screamed, "don't conform, be unique, stand apart."

What made Apple so successful is that its products and services matched this message, right down to the flowing white speaker wires on the original iPod that people could see 50 feet away; an iTunes online service that makes finding, buying, and organizing music and video content very easy; the sleek iMac that is a staple for college students across the U.S.; and iPhone 14 that offers the highest-quality camera in a smartphone. What's more? All the products work seamlessly together, where content can be shared across all of them.

The tricky part about branding is the last part of the definition: "how that (i.e., aligning what you say with what you do) shapes others' perception of you." The tricky part is that—while you can influence how others perceive your brand—you cannot control it. Sometimes, you can align what you say with what you do and remain consistent with your brand, but still not have the intended effect on how others perceive you.

Why Branding Is Important

Branding serves two primary purposes; one is proactive and the other reactive. On the proactive side, good branding will promote specific emotional and literal concepts about a person, thing, or organization to instill certain expectation(s) with its target audiences when they experience the brand.

To better understand the concept of branding, let's play a word-association game. What's the first word or concept that pops into your mind when I say: Volvo, the car manufacturer?

If you're like me, that word is "safety." Even the 20-something students at Chapman University, where I used to teach upper-level public relations courses, said the same thing.

Volvo spent millions and millions of dollars to ingrain the concept of safety in our minds whenever we think about or see one of its cars. Old television ads from the 70s and 80s showed Volvos driving off a bridge, smashing headlong into each other, and crashing into a wall to demonstrate how the crash dummies came out okay. That core brand concept of safety lingers to this day with Volvo. Interestingly, in recent years, other car manufacturers have seemingly lapped Volvo with the number of Insurance Institute for Highway Safety (IIHS) Top Safety Pick+ awards, most notably BMW, Genesis, Hyundai, Kia, Lexus, Mazda, Mercedes-Benz, Subaru, and Toyota. But, because Volvo capitalized on that credibility in the 1970s and 80s, we view it as the safety gold standard today.

How about your one word or concept for Coca-Cola?

Let me ask the question a different way: What is the first image that pops into your mind when you think of Coca-Cola? Consider it a moment...

For most people, it is the luscious brown liquid being poured into a water-beaded glass with fizz spraying up, accompanied by the crackling sound of carbonated bubbles bursting. Why do we think this? Because hundreds of millions of dollars have been spent by The Coca-Cola Company over decades to emblazon that image in your mind.

For what purpose? To drill the concept of refreshment so deep into your subconscious that—when you need to be refreshed—you instinctively think: I'll have a Coke. Actually, you probably don't even think about it in the literal sense. You simply choose the product when you walk into a convenience store after a workout or long day watching your kids on the soccer field.

Point being, it's less about the product and more about the concept of feeling refreshed and what comes with it: happiness. Coke may not necessarily be the best drink after a lot of physical exertion or a long walk in the hot sun. A better choice for rejuvenating yourself may be Gatorade, Powerade or some other "replenishment" drink. But we've been conditioned to grab a Coke product under these circumstances.

These examples demonstrate how a brand can be proactive. On the other side, brands must be reactive to withstand attacks against them. A wide and varied host of attacks can negatively affect a brand, including product recalls, government regulation, declining sales and/or profits, internal scandals (fraud, insider trading, etc.), poor life choices by executives, changing market dynamics, supply chain shortages, new competitors, product or service obsolescence, change in organizational leadership, globalization, natural disaster, large-scale accidents or catastrophes, environmental pressures, consumer backlash, lawsuits, and so on. This list is nearly endless.

If you have ever managed the social media presence for a multinational consumer brand, you know that the assaults on your brand through that medium are 24/7 nonstop. The interesting (and daunting) part is the amazing variety of the trolling attacks. Regardless of how harsh they may be, a brand must respond in a brand-consistent manner, which usually involves remaining polite and professional.

Social media is just one medium of communications for a brand. What happens when a negative story affects your brand for several days of national broadcast news cycles? How does your brand respond to that pressure, when you're a punchline on the late-night talk show circuit?

The following diagram gives a sense for how a brand must be both proactive and reactive at the same time:

What You Need to Know About Branding

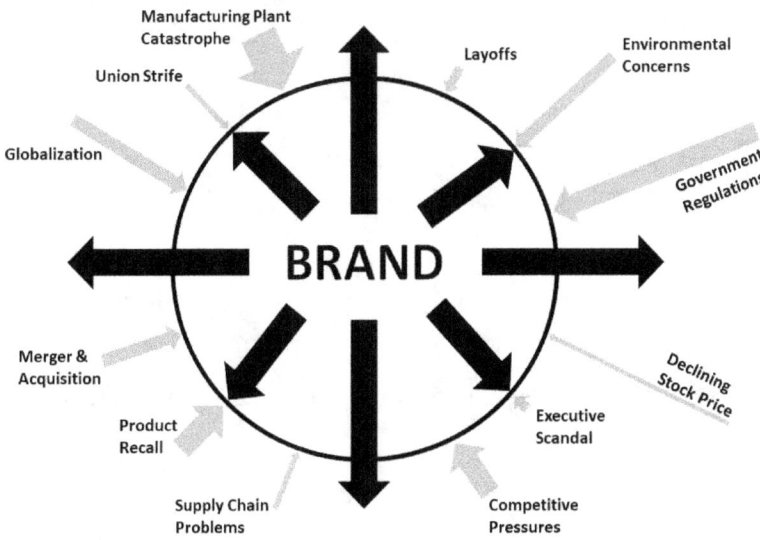

Note the different lengths of the arrows that are "attacking" the brand "bubble." Some have long lead times and enable some measure of preparation; some are very short or nearly real-time, especially when crisis strikes. The bigger concept with this diagram is that branding is always on. It's constant. Branding never sleeps. It never takes a day off.

This idea of always-on branding will be very important as we discuss what it means for your Godly brand.

Chapter 2

Everything Has a Brand, Even Dogs

THE FIRST THING TO understand about branding is that everything has a brand. Cities have brands, and—depending on the city's business goals and marketing efforts—they are clearly defined. I live near Huntington Beach, California, and a professional friend is the public information officer (PIO) for the city. Part of her role as head of communications for the city is to reinforce its brand as "Surf City, USA." To strengthen that brand, the city hosts all types of beach-related events, including professional surfing and beach volleyball contests. Much of the economic prosperity of Huntington Beach can be directly attributed to its brand.

More broadly, and to make the point, when we think of whether to vacation in Paris, London, Athens, Rome, or New York City, each of those cities conjures specific feelings and thoughts, whether you have visited all of them and experienced them for yourself.

Sports teams have brands (think: Los Angeles Lakers versus Boston Celtics). Movies certainly depend on branding. Would you rather watch a new Star Wars movie, new Harry Potter film, or new James Bond flick? Each of those series comes with its own expectations from moviegoers based largely on the branding of prior films or the marketing of the new film.

Government agencies have a brand, perhaps not so carefully nurtured. Right now, if I told you that you had to leave your current employment situation and work for either the Central Intelligence Agency (CIA), Environmental Protection Agency (EPA), or Internal Revenue Service

(IRS), which would you choose? If I added the National Aeronautics and Space Administration (NASA) or U.S. Department of Health and Human Services, would you choose either of them?

Dogs have brands. If you were in the market for a dog, which breed would you choose based on what you've heard or know about it? A lab? A beagle? A greyhound? A poodle? A Jack Russell terrier? A pitbull?

Everything has a brand. It's just a matter of how well-defined that brand is. Some are well-known; some are not.

Most important, people have a brand. And, of course, you have a brand, whether you realize it or not. Developing your Godly brand is the purpose of this book, and later chapters will guide you through exercises to define it.

Successful Brands

Branding is big business, with billions of dollars spent by well-known companies to nurture what is called "unprompted recall," that being your awareness and connection of a brand with a product, service, or feeling without having to be reminded of it. Those billions of dollars that are invested ultimately lead to sales of products and/or services, trade agreements, increased shareholder value, and much more.

Each year, several industry organizations and media outlets attempt to quantify the value of the world's leading brands by publishing best-of lists. Top publications in advertising (Adweek) and business (Forbes), along with powerhouse ad agencies (Millward Brown and Interbrand), all weigh in on which brands they believe are the most valuable.

Looking at these different lists, while the order of the rankings may vary, most of the leading players are consistent. Produced by Kantar, the 2022 BrandZ™ Top 100 Most Valuable Global Brands ranked Apple as the top worldwide brand with a value of US$947 billion, followed by Google with a $820 billion value. Amazon, Microsoft, and Tencent (Chinese internet and technology company) round out the top-five brands.

In *Forbes'* 2020 annual study of the world's most valuable brands, Apple is number one with US$241.2 billion in value, eclipsing second-place Google with $207.5 billion. Microsoft, Amazon, and Meta Platforms (Facebook and Instagram) represent third through fifth on the list.

Interbrand's 2021 list is Apple (US$408 billion), Amazon ($249 billion), Microsoft ($210 billion), Google ($196 billion), and Samsung ($74 billion). Two things to note between these three lists: 1) there's general agreement with the top brands, with four of the top five across all three lists; and 2) the value is calculated in the hundreds of billions.

How these list-makers associate dollar amounts to the value of these brands is a complicated, seemingly arbitrary mix of mathematics and—frankly—irrelevant to the discussion of Godly branding, except to say that brand awareness that leads to conversion (i.e., getting you to do something, like buy a product) is worth big-time money. In fact, these dollar values are so high, we might even call them priceless. And the concept of your Godly brand being priceless is something that we will explore in the coming chapters.

Corporate Brands

Beyond dollar value of brands, the more important thing to review from a Godly branding perspective is how these brands achieve and maintain their value. Many published articles and books have been written to identify what well-known corporate brands do to become and remain successful. While the terms and descriptions may differ depending on the source you read, all the articles and books boil down to these five things that strong brands do:

Know Their Target Audience

In a business context, your target audience(s) is the segment(s) of the population that you want to "convert" on your message, product, service, or brand proposition. Conversion is the process of getting your target audience to make a behavior change and take action, whether that is to buy, sell, vote, strike, write a letter to a Congress member, visit a website, take a pledge, or whatever you want them to do.

Each target audience has a distinct demographic, psychographic, socioeconomic profile that requires specific messaging, look and feel of pictures and graphics, tone of voice, and approach in any communications with them. Notice that I say, "with them" and not "to them." Ideally, brands know their targets audiences well enough to do and say things through their marketing and product/service delivery that enable awareness, then engagement, then conversion.

Why must brands know their target audiences really well? Because people don't "buy" the brand for the person or organization that it represents; they "convert" on the brand for *themselves*. A consumer's engagement is all about what that brand says about the person. To illustrate the point, answer this question: do you shop at Wal-Mart, Kmart, or Target? As a consumer, you may naturally gravitate to one of the three brands based on your own personality, life circumstances, income, etc. Brand managers at these three department store companies all have a clear picture of who their respective target audiences are and what appeals to them. The marketing from these brands reflects this clear picture and understanding.

Because all brands don't appeal to all people—and, even if they did, no brand has enough budget to market to *everyone*—they must appeal directly to their target audiences, and that begins with understanding all the details about them.

Offer Something Unique

Good brands must effectively differentiate themselves from both their direct competition and to their target audiences. To do that, they must offer something unique to the market that is deliberate, distinctive, and tailored to those audiences.

One of my favorite brands is the tee-shirt manufacturer, Crazy Shirts. I stumbled upon the company's retail outlets in Waikiki on my first trip to Hawaii in 2001. The tee-shirts have very stylized Hawaiian graphics with iconic imagery (e.g., Diamond Head, Napali Coast, honu). In other markets where the company has retail outlets, the graphics match the region (Golden Gate Bridge for San Francisco, Gila monsters in Las Vegas, pirates in Key West). All of them have the same, distinct graphic style. And that's one of the reasons that I buy the shirts.

Crazy Shirts does something unique in the manufacturing of their premium tee-shirts. The company dyes its shirts in an array of different substances to add a distinctive color and *smell* to the fabric. These exotic dyes include volcanic ash, blue curacao liqueur, kona coffee, chili, hemp, rum, wine, and even beer and money. More recently, the company has added hibiscus, key lime, rose, pineapple, and blackberry dyes. This blend of colors and odors is cool, and it's one of the reasons that I buy the shirts.

Crazy Shirts isn't the first tee-shirt manufacturer to dye their shirts in unique substances. In fact, the company isn't even the only Hawaiian tee-shirt provider that dyes its shirts in natural elements. Red Dirt Shirts operates a handful of retail outlets in Hawaii, Arizona, and Utah.

The number-one reason why I buy Crazy Shirts is its tees remind me of being on vacation, the relaxation of being on the Islands, the memories of spending quality time with my family, etc. Even the shirts that I have purchased at the San Francisco, San Diego, and Palm Springs stores evoke the same brand experience for their respective locations. Most of the time, if I travel to a location with a Crazy Shirts outlet, I will add a visit to that retail store to my itinerary as if it were one of the must-see landmarks.

This explains why the only time that I've ever stepped foot into the nearest Crazy Shirts retail store to my home in Orange County, California, was during the COVID pandemic when I couldn't travel. The outlet is in Laguna Beach, only 30 miles or so from my house and even closer to my work. I associate the brand with being on vacation in a "far away" place where I can unwind and get away from my busy life for a few days. That's my brand experience with the company. Others may have a different brand experience. For example, the company sells a whole line of clothing centered on a silly-looking cat. I have no interest in these shirts, but—I know from speaking to a few of the store managers when I visit— there is a rather large fan base for those tees.

Because the brand associates itself with "getting away," you're likely *never* to see Crazy Shirts outlets in New York, Chicago, Boston, or Washington, D.C. All these locations are vacation destinations. But they are not the "right" vacation destinations with a distinct connection to nature that fits the brand.

How do I know that this effect is what the brand attempts to create? The company's website used to say so: "Crazy Shirts heritage is deeply ingrained in the Hawaiian Culture. From our humble beginnings, it has always been the ambition to transport our fans on the endless adventure in ever day life. Whether you are sitting on a beach in Hawaii or skiing the slopes of Colorado, we have set out to capture fun and adventure where ever our fans find themselves." Later in the same About Us description, you'll find: ". . . we create or help people save memories."

You may be wondering, "Hey, branding the concept of 'getting away' isn't unique; other brands pray upon one's bloodlust to escape to a remote beach on a distant shore."

Caribbean Joe is an apparel company that squarely plays in this place. The company's brand philosophy is clearly articulated on the corporate website: "We believe in the island spirit of warmth and hospitality. And we believe that summer is way too short and that vacations are a state of mind."

So, Crazy Shirts and Caribbean Joe? Pretty close, right? Yes, both are apparel companies that drive home the concept of the "island" spirit. However, one clearly associates itself with the Caribbean Sea, while the other aligns with the Hawaiian Islands. Both want you to think about vacations in a tropical setting. One is clearly upscale. The other is not. One is relaxed. The other is crazy. Both offer clothing and accessories, but their brands operate in very distinctive ways, offering their customers a unique experience.

Crazy Shirts is the only tee-shirt company that focuses its brand on the appeal of the Hawaiian culture and adventure. If another company tried to move into this space and take marketshare from Crazy Shirts, it would have to differentiate itself based on cost, quality of product, style, service, etc.

Deliver with a Commitment to a Brand Experience

Good branding involves a clear understanding of the experience that you want to convey, followed by a commitment to delivering it with style, passion, a fine attention to detail, and a willingness to "set things right" within reason when the experience fails to deliver. One must be careful with the last point of rectifying mis-fired brand experiences, as there are—sadly—a lot of "trolls" in the world who are happy to take advantage of you, if you let them.

Every successful brand in the QSR (quick service restaurant) sector approaches the delivery of their product, service, and brand experience with laser-focused devotion. A former commercial real estate client of mine worked with Dunkin' to build new stores in a handful of Southern Californian coastal cities when the brand reintroduced itself into the market in 2014. In helping this client by writing a comprehensive marketing plan to promote the stores in their various communities, I reviewed the Dunkin' U.S. Brand Guidelines, a 98-page book that outlines every single detail about how a franchisee would implement the brand through messaging in multiple languages, signage (indoor and outdoor), menu options, customer service expectations, and so forth. Everything, and I do mean everything, that had to do with the in-store delivery of the brand was spelled out in detail, both what you could do and what you could not do.

In addition to this document, there was a full-featured website with many times more documents on things such as competitive blunting (i.e., keeping customers from going to other brands), employment forms, employee management tools for incentivizing team members, a wealth of sales tools for specific audience and time-of-day segments (e.g., how to drive afternoon coffee purchases), and a 23-page booklet on specifically how to market your Dunkin' storefront in your respective community. This is only a sample of the repository of documents that are made available to anyone who wants to operate a Dunkin' franchise.

While I have never seen the McDonald's, Starbucks, or Taco Bell versions of these documents or website, those brands offer similar tools to ensure the proper delivery of a brand experience to current and prospective customers.

Is all this documentation really necessary? Yes! Because delivering a strong brand experience means that you have carefully considered how you want consumers to think, feel, and behave with your brand, then stressed the details to ensure the highest probability that the outcomes you want will occur.

Remain Consistent in Delivering that Brand Experience

McDonald's does a really good job of maintaining a constant brand experience when you visit any of its restaurants. The food may taste a little different overseas. And there are different menu items in different parts of the U.S. and the rest of the world. But a Big Mac bought in Bethesda, Maryland, tastes the same as one purchased in Laie, Hawaii. (I speak from experience.)

With automobile brands, I prefer Toyota for its reliability. I'm not a "car guy." I just want to know with a measure of assuredness that my car will start when I turn it on and get me to where I want to go. I want maintenance costs kept to a minimum. I'm not very interested in how I look in that car, how it drives, etc.

My family has owned four-cylinder Toyotas since the late 1980s for this very reason. They are marvelously consistent. Not sexy, but consistent. You almost never have engine problems as long as you reasonably care for them.

When I bought a new 2004 Camry, I told my then-four-year-old daughter that she would eventually get the car when she was old enough to drive. She spent her entire adolescence with the understanding that she'd get that car. As she got closer to driving age, she began to chide me about washing and taking care of "her car." You know what happened when she turned 15 years old and began taking driving lessons? She did so in that Camry. Within days of her getting her license, I purchased a new Toyota for myself and officially turned over the keys to the Camry to her.

How did I know that my daughter would learn to drive on that Camry 11 years before it happened? My wife and I owned a 4-cylinder Celica that lasted from 1989 to the early 2000s, when we gave it to her parents. They drove it for another few years, then sold it. Before that, my wife learned to drive on a used Celica that she drove up to Los Angeles for school every day. My father-in-law drove a 1973 4-cyclinder Toyota truck when I moved to California in 1989 and kept it for another few years, until he sold it. Several years later, while on a business trip in Las Vegas, he saw the truck on the street, and it was still alive and well. I knew that my daughter would use the Camry to learn to drive because of the brand consistency of 4-cylinder Toyota engines.

Constantly Strive to Make the Brand Experience Better

If you have ever worked for a good marketing services firm (PR, advertising, social or digital), you have undoubtedly experienced the "what cool thing are we going to do next year" internal brainstorming session that occurs a few weeks before a client's budget cycle begins for the next year. A firm conducts that brainstorm with the understanding that whatever work was performed *this* year—whether good or really good—will not suffice for *next* year. The firm must propose something more, something better, something that evolves from the current work. Why? Three primary reasons.

First, in formulating a new "big idea," the firm demonstrates to its client that it cares enough to proactively come up with solutions to advance the client's business goals.

Second, a firm can increase its billings only if it can propose new, additional work that the client approves. If the firm continues with business as usual, it jeopardizes its capability to realize more in fees. In fact, in many cases, a client will become bored or take the firm for granted when new ideas are not flowing and *reduce* a budget.

Third, the exercise underscores a culture of proactive problemsolving and strong customer relationship management at the firm that keeps high-performing employees engaged and triggers them to always be thinking, "how can I make this better for my client." This latter mindset typically yields the added benefit of clients that become raving fans of the firm and actively tell their network of contacts, "You have to work with these guys; they're always thinking/working on my behalf."

The same concept works for non-service brands. They constantly need to evolve or grow the brand experience lest the fickle consumer move on and/or their capability to charge more money will shrink. Sometimes, new offerings can be in response to competitive pressures. Regardless, savvy brands live under the clichéd mantra: "If you ain't growing, you're dying."

Fast-food chains constantly add new menu items to lure current and prospective patrons. McDonald's added coffee drinks to their menu to primarily compete with Starbucks; the addition also delivers value to its customers who want a low-cost, convenient coffee alternative. Of course, Starbucks expanded its breakfast and food options to compete with McDonald's.

Automobile manufacturers will introduce new features in each new model year. While I'm still gawking over large-screen back-up cameras in my Toyota Highlander, self-driving cars will be the industry's next wave of innovation and offer consumers a better brand experience. Amusement parks add new rides. Fashion-designers choose exact shades of blue, orange or green that will be next season's "It" color. Industries and brands within them are constantly changing things up to make the consumer experience better.

Christian Brands

There are many well-known and successful corporate brands that are based on Christian principles that guide how they do business. Here is a short list of some of the more prominent ones:

- **Alaskan Air:** The international air carrier places Old Testament bible verses on the trays of its in-flight breakfasts and "reflect the beliefs of this country's founding."
- **Anschutz Entertainment Group (AEG):** A prominent Christian activist, founder Phil Anschutz owns conservative publications such as *The Washington Examiner* and *The Weekly Standard*, and financially supported family friendly and Christian films such as *The Chronicles of Narnia*.
- **Chick-fil-A:** With more than 1,500 restaurants in 39 states, Chick-fil-A was founded by a devout Southern Baptist Truett Cathy who believes that all employees "should have an opportunity to rest, spend time with family and friends, and worship if they choose to do so," which is why each location is closed on Sundays.
- **Curves:** The company's gyms create a men-free environment where women of all shapes and sizes can work out. Its founder Gary Heavin is a born-again Christian who is known for his conservative political views.
- **eHarmony:** Founded by Christian psychologist Dr. Neil Clark Warren in 2000, eHarmony is one of the most well-branded online dating and matchmaking services.
- **Forever 21:** The clothing retailer has sold tee-shirts with the messages "Jesus ♥ You" and "Holy." In addition, the store owners, the Chang Family, place the biblical reference "John 3:16" on the bottom of their store bags.
- **HE>i (HE is greater than i):** According its website, HE>i is a lifestyle company / clothing brand that is based off of the Bible verse John 3:30—"HE (Jesus) must increase, but I must decrease." In addition, the company's "purpose is to produce quality clothing and accessories to encourage, inspire, and share the good news of our savior, Jesus."
- **Hobby Lobby:** A national chain of roughly 500 arts-and-craft stores in 41 states, Hobby Lobby's first mission statement is "Honoring the Lord in all we do by operating the company in a manner consistent with biblical principles," adding the following, "We believe that it is by God's grace and provision that Hobby Lobby has endured. He has been faithful in the past, we trust Him for our future."

- **In-N-Out:** California-based burger chain known for its fresh ingredients, timeless menu, and personal customer service, In-N-Out prints Bible verses on its packaging, including—as an example—John 3:16 on the bottom of its soft drink cups.
- **Interstate Batteries:** The company sells more than 16,000 different types of batteries, and its mission is "to glorify God as we supply our customers worldwide with top quality, value-priced batteries, related electrical power-source products, and distribution services."
- **Mary Kay:** Founder of the giant cosmetics company, Mary Kay Ash promotes the following motto for her team: "God first, family second, career third." In her biography, she writes, "God has blessed us because our motivation is right. He knows I want women to be the beautiful creatures he created."
- **ServiceMaster:** The company better known for its sub-brands Merry Maids, Terminix, and American Home Shield operates under a "foundational commitment" to "Honor God in all we do."
- **Tyson Foods:** The company's core values state that it "strive(s) to honor God" and "be a faith friendly company," and the company employs approximately 120 office chaplains, who provide "compassionate pastoral care," according to the corporate website. The founder of world's largest chicken company, John Tyson, speaks openly about his Christian beliefs.

Other companies are based on Christian values and reflect them in their business practices, including insurance company Aflac; construction and farm machinery manufacturer John Deere; Texas-based grocery store H.E.B.; and retailer J.C. Penney.

What do these and other Christian brands have in common? Three things are apparent: 1) past and current leadership who are/were believers and imbued the brand with faith-based values; 2) openness about demonstrating their faith-based values to the public; and 3) ongoing adherence to those values in their operations. While these factors may seem straightforward, not every Christian-led business is open about its faith-based values or operationalizes them. Fact is, there is a fair amount of risk in a business openly embracing its faith-based values. For starters, openness about being Christian may cost a company some business opportunities from non-believers, affect its capability to recruit certain individuals who do not want to be associated with it, or bring a perceived higher level of scrutiny from community members who will watch closely how the company's leadership and employees reflect the love of God in their words and deeds.

Conversely, there are three important considerations to remember about how being open with one's faith can bring untold business opportunities. First, Jesus commands us to "be my witnesses . . . to the ends of the earth (Acts 1:8)," so we are meant to share our faith. God opens all kinds of doors that you cannot imagine when you trust Him. Second, a key aspect of branding is to appeal to specific target audiences. No brand, regardless of its seeming universality, is meant to appeal to *everyone*. McDonald's doesn't target vegans, for example. Presuming a Christian business understands to whom its products or services appeal, it can market strategically to those audiences, communicating tailored messaging and benefits that will resonate with them. Third and most interesting, God has given Christian businesses and brands a support infrastructure, and it extends way past the church.

Some businesses describe themselves as Christian, while others use terms such as *business as mission* (or BAM) or *kingdom businesses*. There are hundreds of professional Christian business associations across the U.S., including Christian Business & Marketplace Connection, Christian Business Fellowship Association, Christian Business Men's Connection, Christian Business Network, Christian Women Business Organization, Christian Women in Business, Christians in Business, Full Gospel Business Men's Fellowship International, and International Fellowship of Christian Businessmen.

Professional Christians have a community of fellow believers in business to which they can turn for guidance, leadership, and opportunity, and it does not take much online digging to find these organizations in your local area.

In *Section 3*, we will explore how Christian businesses can define their brand and values to better reflect their specific God-given mission in the world.

Chapter 3

Personal Branding Differs from Godly Branding

DURING THE LATE 1990s and early 2000s, personal branding was a very hot topic, with many print publications and online articles devoted to how to advance one's own brand. These articles commonly walked through the various steps to create a personal brand statement to center one's brand as well as different outreach methods to promote it (e.g., social media, speaking engagements, bylined articles). Perhaps not as hot a topic as 10–15 years ago, there remains a steady flow of written work about personal branding, this book included. To understand Godly branding, one must first understand personal branding.

What is Personal Branding?

There are a lot of definitions for the term "personal branding." In her book *Personal Branding For Dummies*, author Susan Chritton defines it as "a marketing strategy focused on your most important product: you."

In their book Be Your Own Brand, authors David McNally and Karl Speak define personal branding as "a perception or emotion, maintained by somebody other than you, that describes the total experience of having a relationship with you."

For the purposes of this book, personal branding is the practice of marketing and communicating yourself, your career, your business or product line (especially if your name is attached to it), your expertise or opinions, or any other facet of yourself. It can involve the use of your name, likeness, or other representation of yourself in the promotion of a product, service or intellectual property (IP). Again, it is the alignment of what you say about yourself with what you actually do, and how that shapes people's perceptions of you.

There is a lengthy list of top global brands named after the individuals who founded them, including Disney, Louis Vuitton, Walmart, Ford, J.P. Morgan, Deloitte, Chase, Cartier, Colgate, Goldman Sachs, Dell, John Deere, Kellogg's, and Nordstrom. In addition to corporations, there are very successful product-oriented personal brands, such as Kylie Cosmetics, Air Jordan shoes, and Newman's Own.

Big brands will market personal brands to sell products. This occurs in entertainment and sports every time a celebrity endorses a brand in a commercial, advertisement, event appearance, etc. Actors, musicians, and artists hire publicists to perpetuate their brand and market their work, their lifestyle, the products or services they endorse, their movies or TV shows, their charity involvement, and even their whereabouts in an attempt to expand awareness about themselves. Think someone like Miley Cyrus, Lindsey Lohan, or the Kardashians, who seem as though they are endlessly pursuing tabloid and blogger coverage.

In general, greater personal-brand awareness equals a greater ability to sell. Because personal branding emphasizes certain characteristics of an individual, it acts very much like traditional branding of products and companies.

Kim Kardashian West, for example, will sell a single tweet on her @KimKardashian Twitter feed of story on Twitter for tens of thousands of dollars. How can she command that type of money for a single post? As of August 2022, her Twitter following numbers more than 73.3 million people. She built that following over nearly 12 years, having joined Twitter in March 2009.

If a brand like Apple, The Coca-Cola Company, or Toyota wanted to advertise in Cosmopolitan, Newsweek, USA Today, or any other high-circulation consumer outlet, it would pay tens of thousands of dollars for the placement. The circulation for Cosmopolitan, Newsweek, and USA Today each ranges in the low millions of subscribers.

The math is simple: one Twitter post from Kim Kardashian reaches 73.3-million-plus loyal fans, more than 7 times the combined circulation of all three of those outlets. And that 7x multiplier is a conservative estimate. The 73.3 million is probably more like 10 times the combined circulation.

Personal branding has taken on a whole new meaning in today's digital and social media-driven world where a personality can cultivate an online presence with many millions of followers, then monetize that following by selling their influence. It's not just the well-known brands like the celebrities mentioned above.

Have you heard the name StampyLongHead? If you have a child who's into the video game Minecraft, there is no way you missed Stampy, whose real name is Joseph Garrett. He is an English YouTuber who posts volumes of videos about his adventures in the game. When my now college-age son was a preteen and played the game religiously, he constantly watched Stampy videos. Viewers like my son made StampyLongHead one of the ten most watched YouTube channels in the world in 2014. That viewership made Garrett a multi-millionaire.

Christian Celebrities and Their Brands

Quickly, without doing a Google search, name the top 5 *living* Christian celebrities that the general public would know is Christian. Sorry, well-known singers to most Christians like Chris Tomlin, Lauren Daigle, Jeremy Camp, or Kari Jobe will not be recognizable to mainstream America. Big-time Christian authors like Joyce Meyer, Max Lucado, Lee Strobel or Rick Warren may have a better chance, although I'd argue that only Pastor Warren would have a shot due his *The Purpose Driven Life* book and selection by then President-elect Barack Obama to deliver the invocation at his inauguration after the 2008 election.

How about religious leaders? Pope Francis tops the list, right? There's one. Lakewood Church pastor and noted author Joel Osteen is number two. What other leaders would the general public know?

Let's move onto entertainers, TV and movie stars, and sports figures. Former NFL quarterback and author, Tim Tebow immediately comes to mind. That's number three. Because of his former stardom, Kirk Cameron may be another, although he's been away from the limelight for years. After that, there are a host of sports stars that I've heard profess thanks to God after winning a championship or achieving a professional milestone, led by Stephen Curry and Kevin Durant, two professional basketball players. My youngest son is a huge Curry fan and wears a Curry-branded bracelet that has "I can do all things through Christ who strengthens me" (Philippians 4:13) inscribed on it.

If you start researching Christian celebrities, you'll find there are a lot of them. If you read Christian publications and blogs yourself, you may know many of them because they are covered in those outlets.

American actor Chris Pratt received a lot of attention in the media when he posted on Instagram in December 2018 regarding his then-fiancé, now wife Katherine Schwarzenegger: "Thrilled God put you in my life." A few weeks later, he posted: "Proud to live boldly in faith with you." The picture of her on the post features an image of Jesus next to the verse 1 Tim 1:14. These posts came after a September 2018 Associated Press interview where he referred to himself as "Pro-Jesus, Pro-Christian."

Singer and songwriter Faith Hill was raised in a devout Baptist family and got her start as teenager singing in churches. She has stated that "Having a backbone of spirituality makes me a little stronger. I pray a lot, and when I first moved to Nashville, that's what kept me alive." Her husband country singer and songwriter Tim McGraw is also Christian.

Producer, director, and actor Tyler Perry created the Medea movie character that he plays himself. The character is not Christian, but is funny and enables people to reflect on their personal lives and the decisions that they have made. The role helped him become a major star and producer in Hollywood. In an interview on Beliefnet, when asked about the role of faith in his life, he commented: "It is extremely important. I am a Christian, I am a believer, and I know had I not been a person of faith, I couldn't be here in this place, and I wouldn't be walking the path that I'm on now. And I think the greater good of the path I'm on now is to teach people to learn to forgive and move on, in a way that's done through the healing power of humor." For those who do not know, Perry is a powerhouse Christian who has spoken in tongues, publicly anointed pastors of churches, donated millions to Christian charities, and regularly speaks about the impact that his faith has on his life.

In an interview with *GQ* magazine, American actor Denzel Washington shared, "I read from the Bible every day, and I read my Daily Word." He related an experience at the West Angeles Church of God in Christ where he felt the impact of the Holy Spirit, which he described as a "tremendous physical and spiritual experience."

The Jonas Brothers (Joe, Kevin, and Nick) were known to pray before each of their concerts, and they wore purity rings to symbolize their pledge not to have sex until marriage.

In August 2020, pop superstar Justin Bieber and his wife Hailey got baptized together at Lake Coeur d'Alene in Idaho. In posts on his Instagram channel to his 143 million followers, he wrote, "This was one of [the] most special moments of my life. Confessing our love and trust in Jesus publicly with our friends and family."

As if the Biebers' highly public declaration for Christ wasn't huge enough, the last two years saw the emergence of another potentially gigantic Christian brand: American rapper and music mogul Kanye West. He's one of the best-selling music artists with more than 140 million records sold worldwide and one of the most-awarded artists of all time with 21 total Grammy Awards. In October 2019, he released *Jesus Is King*, a Christian hip hop album, which became the first ever to top the U.S. *Billboard* 200, Top R&B/Hip-Hop Albums, Top Rap Albums, Top Christian Albums and Top Gospel Albums at the same time. In November 2019, Joel Osteen hosted West and his Sunday Service Choir at Lakewood Church in Houston. On Christmas Day 2019, West and Sunday Service released another album *Jesus Is Born*.

Fans of West's music likely know of his religious comments. But if you do not follow his music, you probably didn't know about his ties to Christianity prior to the press surrounding *Jesus Is King*. His public professions of faith date back to his 2004 album *The College Dropout* that included the song "Jesus Walks," which has overt declarations about prayer and trust in God. The chorus goes like this:

> (Jesus walk)
> God show me the way because the Devil's tryna break me down
> (Jesus walk with me)
> The only thing that I pray is that my feet don't fail me now
> (Jesus walk)
> And I don't think there's nothin' I can do now to right my wrongs
> (Jesus walk with me)
> I wanna talk to God but I'm afraid 'cause we ain't spoke in so long
> (Jesus walk)

In the last verse of the song, West directly addressed some of the blowback that he had already received before the album's release from record executives who never thought the song would be played on the radio because of its heavy religious lyrics:

> The way Kathie Lee needed Regis, that's the way I need Jesus
> So here go my single, dawg, radio needs this

> They say you can rap about anything except for Jesus
> That means guns, sex, lies, videotape
> But if I talk about God my record won't get played, huh?

Of course, God had other plans, and "Jesus Walks" became a widely played success, and *The College Dropout* went triple platinum in the U.S., raked in 10 Grammy nominations including Album of the Year and Best Rap Album, which it won. When asked about his beliefs by reporters, West said, "I have accepted Jesus as my Savior. And I will say that I fall short every day."

In January 2019, West affirmed his Christian beliefs via his Twitter channel. In October 2019, while publicizing *Jesus is King*, West told late night talk show host Jimmy Kimmel "I'm just a Christian everything" when asked if he considered himself a Christian music artist.

In addition to being one of the greatest music artists of this generation, West has struggled with mental health, having been committed to the UCLA Medical Center with hallucinations and paranoia in 2016, and admitting to David Letterman that he has bipolar disorder during a 2019 interview.

West's mental health and his actions shape his Godly brand. In an Instagram post on July 22, 2020, his wife, Kim Kardashian West, referred to him as "a brilliant but complicated person who on top of the pressures of being an artist and a black man, who experienced the painful loss of his mother, and has to deal with the pressure and isolation that is heightened by his bi-polar disorder." This post came after a wave of news coverage when West took to Twitter to accuse her of infidelity and trying to have him committed as well as what one tabloid called a "rambling and chaotic speech at his first presidential rally at North Charleston's Exquis Event Center in South Carolina." Ultimately, West was a non-factor in the presidential election. But, when the 2021 Grammys nominations were announced, *Jesus is King* was up for best contemporary Christian music album.

The list of living Christian celebrities includes a wide range of entertainment personalities that you'll recognize:

- **Garth Brooks:** The American singer and songwriter, and one of the best-selling music artists of all time, includes a dedication or thank-you tribute to God, Jesus, or both in all of his album covers.
- **Kristin Chenoweth:** The actress and singer who was raised Baptist once told the *National Catholic Reporter*: "I'm an actress and a singer and I'm also a Christian. I just want to be like Jesus, forgiving

and loving and nonjudgmental, accepting of everyone even if they don't agree."

- **Stephen Colbert:** The former *Colbert Report* star and *Late Show* host is a devout Catholic who once told *GQ* Magazine: "I am here to know God, love God, serve God . . ."

- **Alice Cooper:** The rock-n-roll legend known for shock antics during his performances converted to Christianity. His book *Golf Monster* includes references to how he became a Christian.

- **Mel Gibson:** The actor, writer, director and producer who was the creative force behind the production and distribution of *The Passion of the Christ* in 2004, which remains to this day the highest-grossing Christian film of all time.

- **Kathie Lee Gifford:** The American talk show host and author refers to herself as an "Imperfect follower of Jesus and really imperfect mother to two amazing human beings," on her Twitter feed and has spoken about the profound impact that evangelist Billy Graham had on her life.

- **M.C. Hammer:** The former rapper best known his hit songs "U Can't Touch This," "2 Legit 2 Quit," and "Pray" is an ordained minister in the Church of God in Christ. Now, the "M.C." stands for "Man of Christ."

- **Patricia Heaton:** The American actress best known for her role on *Everybody Loves Raymond* stated during an interview with *The Blaze*: "You try to be a model of kindness and love and forgiveness to all those around you, because you have received kindness and love and forgiveness from God through Christ. That's what Christianity is."

- **Reba McEntire:** The American country singer, songwriter, actress, and record producer related during an interview with *Guidepost Magazine* about her childhood: "[Grandma] told me about David, Moses and Daniel, and the special gifts that God had given them, like courage and leadership and prophecy."

- **Mr. T:** The American actor best known for his role on A-Team frequently appears on the TBN Christian television network and—during an interview with Larry King—declared that he's Christian.

- **Carrie Underwood:** The former American Idol winner and best-selling author posts Bible verses in her social media feeds and refers to herself as "Blessed and grateful!" on her Twitter feed.
- **Elijah Wood:** The actor best known for playing Frodo Baggins in the *Lord of the Rings* trilogy said during an interview with *Time Out Magazine*: "I was raised a Christian. I believe in the Bible and that's a good thing—I believe more in a personal relationship with God..."

There are a lot of other names of entertainers, actors, and other celebrities who have shared their faith publicly, including but not limited to Angela Bassett, Lacey Chabert, Charlie Daniels, Robert Duvall, Vince Gill, Jeff Gordon, Jeff Foxworthy, Evander Holyfield, Toby Keith, Dikembe Mutombo, Brad Paisley, Deion Sanders, Martin Sheen, Emmitt Smith, John Tesh, and Kurt Warner.

Each of these individuals have made public proclamations of faith through speeches; interviews; music, songs and lyrics; television and movie roles; performance on a playing field, basketball court, or boxing ring; and other areas of his or her personal life. In short, they glorify God through their actions, and they do it sufficiently to be recognized in the media for it. As we look at Godly branding, this public demonstration of faith is the starting point.

What Is Godly Branding and How It Differs from Personal Branding

As its name implies, *personal branding focuses on the person or self*. It is the promotion of self to sell, influence or gain something. Also, as the name implies, *Godly branding does not center on self, but rather God*. This focus glorifies God through one's actions, words, and soul.

Some of the world's most successful brands were started as personal brands: Ford Motor Company, Harkins Theatres, Nordstrom, Newman's Own, and Walmart, just to name a few. These brands have contributed immensely to local and national economies. Well-established entertainers, sports figures, authors, and entrepreneurs all have their personal brands to advance their individual business interests. And God has blessed all of them with varying levels of financial success. But few are demonstrably Godly brands.

Why? Because, if lived out properly, Godly branding adds a foundational layer of brand delivery based on the behaviors, actions, and beliefs of Jesus and God followers who are chronicled in the Bible.

What I realized through the Lord's guidance as I dove deeply into researching the lives of 30 or so of the most well-known figures in the Scriptures was that they all had qualities in common. From Moses to James the Apostle or Hannah to Mary, the mother of Jesus, there are recurring qualities to their brands that felt like a distillation of all the lessons, laws, and God-inspired guidance that we see throughout the Scriptures.

There are literally thousands of verses throughout the Scriptures that instruct us how we should live. Here is just a small sampling:

- Deut 5–6
- John 13:34–35
- Rom 12
- Eph 4:17–32
- 1 Cor 13
- Gal 5:13–26
- 1 Pet 1:1–25
- 1 Pet 2:11–25

How does one reconcile these passages and many others in the Scriptures into his or her personal makeup? As the Holy Spirit-inspired Word of God, we—as His followers—must obey all of His laws and decrees. That said, there are a lot of qualities to live by that are crammed into these chapters and verses that include the 10 Commandments, the love chapter from 1 Corinthians, Jesus' commission to His disciples, multiple references from the Apostle Paul in his various epistles, and much more.

Most Christians hear or read these passages, get the gist, and attempt to live their lives accordingly. Certain verses stick with us, though. John 13:34–35 comes to mind: "A new command I give you: Love one another. As I have loved you, so you must love one another. By this everyone will know that you are my disciples, if you love one another." Josh 24:15 is another: ". . . as for me and my household, we will serve the LORD." First Corinthians 13:2 is yet another: ". . . if I have a faith that can move mountains, but do not have love, I am nothing." And there are many, many others.

But how do these God-instructed behaviors translate into how you act and your overall Godly brand?

First, we must look at the life of Jesus. He modeled the perfect brand that God the Father calls us to live by. He obeyed His Father in all He did, and thus glorified the Father with a perfectly sinless life. The challenge for many believers may be that Jesus' model is an unsustainable, unachievable standard due to His being the Living Son of God. Intellectually, we get it. We strive to live by Jesus' example knowing that we'll fall short; however, the pursuit of the model is worthy.

In our hearts though, we want to succeed and, when we fail, it can be discouraging, guilt-inducing, saddening, or depressing. We pray for forgiveness and seek repentance, as we should. At a certain point though, either consciously or subconsciously, we sort of give up the pursuit of Jesus' model and simply try our best, knowing that our sin keeps us from attaining this perfect standard.

Sometimes, it's easier to look at the examples of others who are closer to us in standing, maybe even perceivably worse. In comparison to a murderer, an egregious adulterer, or persecutor of the church, we can more easily relate to the sinful nature of these people, and even see ourselves and our sin in a different light. That's one of the many reasons that the Bible simply isn't just the story of Jesus; it involves many others who sinned, repented, and were saved, like Moses, David, and Paul. In those frail, human, sinful examples, we see ourselves.

Besides looking at the life of Jesus, we can look at the lives of God followers throughout the recorded history in the Scriptures. We can evaluate the models of how they lived and draw conclusions for how we should live today.

As it turns out, when you look at the lives of the 30 or so most commonly known figures in the Bible, certain brand attributes begin to emerge across all of them. In fact, there are eight attributes that they have in common. You could call these eight attributes a repeated model for how they lived their lives and how others perceived them. Of course, this model maps right back to Jesus and His life on earth. The big difference is the encumbrance of sin in the lives of the various biblical figures. These eight attributes include the following:

1. loves others
2. shows patience
3. demonstrates a servant mindset

4. trusts and obeys God's commands
5. forgives
6. glorifies God through thankfulness
7. is a member of God's church/community
8. is an agent of change for God's kingdom.

If God called His followers in the Scriptures to live out these eight brand attributes, He calls us to do the same. Living out a Godly branded life comes with certain expectations. The chapters in *Section 2* cover how Jesus and other biblical figures reflected these eight brand attributes in everything they do. These concepts apply to all God followers, whether you're wildly well-known as Moses was in his day to the entire nation of Israel or David was as king of Judea and later Israel, or not well-known, like Joseph sitting in an Egyptian prison or Mary, the mother of Jesus, resting in a Bethlehem manger. All Godly brands are very well-known in heaven.

Methodology

God led me to determine these eight attributes through lots of research, being in the Word, listening to and reading scriptural observations from others, and employing the same methodology for brand development that I use professionally (more on that later). Most important though, the Holy Spirit spoke to me constantly, offering insights to help me see the pattern of these attributes.

Once I saw the pattern of a few of the attributes, such as "loves others," "shows patience," and "obeys God's commands," I started looking for others. This process went on for a few years, until I eventually landed on eight brand attributes. To track these attributes and match them to the top biblical figures, I created tables that correlated the figure with a scripture passage where he or she demonstrated the attribute.

To show you the methodology, here is an example of one of the tables for "Is an Agent of Change" for God's kingdom:

Figures	Context	Verses
Abraham (Abram)	God promises "all peoples on earth will be blessed through you."	Gen 12:3
Daniel	After Daniel survived the lion's den, King Darius "issued a decree that in every part of my kingdom people must fear and reverence the God of Daniel."	Dan 6:19–28
David	David becomes king over Israel after conquering Jerusalem and reigns for 40 years.	2 Sam 5
Elijah	Elijah defeats the prophets of Baal, has them seized and slaughtered, then brings rain after severe drought.	1 Kgs 18:16–46
Elisha	Elisha performs many miracles and anoints Jehu the new king of Israel.	2 Kgs 9:1–13
Esther	Esther saves the Jews from King Xerxes' decree.	Esth 8
Isaac	Isaac was the second of the patriarchs of Israel, and the father of Esau and Jacob.	Gen 25
Isaiah	God commissions Isaiah to prophesy to the people of Israel.	Isa 6
Jacob	Ten of Jacob's children became the founders of tribes of Israel, along with Manasseh and Ephraim.	Gen 29–33
Jeremiah	Jeremiah was called to prophecy by God to proclaim Jerusalem's coming destruction by invaders from the north.	Jer 1:14–16
John (disciple)	John, together with the Apostle Peter, took a prominent part in the founding and guidance of the church.	Acts 3:11–26
Joseph	Joseph saved his family and the surrounding nations from severe famine.	Gen 47
Joshua	Appointed by Moses, Joshua led the people of Israel into the Promised Land.	Deut 34:9
Mary	Mary bore Jesus, the Son of God, and raised Him.	Luke 2
Nehemiah	Nehemiah oversaw the rebuilding of Jerusalem.	Neh 1–4
Moses	Moses was the greatest of all prophets in Israel, leading God's people from Egypt to the Promised Land.	Deut 34:10–12
Noah	Noah built an ark to safe his family and preserve the human race from the Great Flood.	Gen 6–8
Paul	Paul became the great evangelist for the church of God, other than Christ Himself.	Acts 13
Peter	Peter is the rock upon which the Church of Christ is built.	Matthew 16:18

Figures	Context	Verses
Ruth	Ruth is one of the few women who is mentioned in the lineage of Christ.	Ruth 1–4
Samuel	Samuel helps transition leadership of the people of Israel from biblical judges to a kingdom under Saul, then from Saul to David.	1 Samuel 8–16
Sarah (Sarai)	God promised Abraham that she would be "a mother of nations" and that she would conceive and bear a son.	Gen 17:16
Solomon	Solomon was the wisest person to ever live other than Jesus and built the temple for the Name of the Lord.	1 Kgs 1–6
Timothy	Timothy traveled with Paul; he was the first Christian bishop of the church in Ephesus.	2 Tim 4:1–5

These biblical figures demonstrated one more quality that is not among the eight attributes: acknowledgement of God's sovereignty in their lives. That quality exists across all eight attributes and will be explored further in the next chapter.

Why Your Godly Brand Makes a Difference

Two natural questions arise early in the consideration of Godly branding: 1) where in the Bible does it talk about branding and 2) where in the Scriptures does it talk about the effects of bad branding. Both questions roll up to the larger question of "why should I care about my Godly brand?"

Let's start with the first question. No, there are no instances of the words brand or branding in the Scriptures. However, there are more than a dozen occurrences of the concept of "setting an example" in both the Old and New Testaments. Implicit in the concept of branding is the idea of being an example to others of how you live, believe, and act. It starts with John 13:15 and Jesus, who said: "I have set you an example that you should do as I have done for you." He said this after washing their feet in an act of complete servitude.

Jesus is not alone, though. Paul and Peter repeatedly mention following their examples in their respective epistles. Paul implores the followers in Ephesus to "Follow God's example, therefore, as dearly loved children and walk in the way of love, just as Christ loved us and gave himself up for us as a fragrant offering and sacrifice to God." (Eph 5:1–2)

In 1 Cor 11:1, Paul tells the followers in Corinth to "Follow my example, as I follow the example of Christ." Paul also tells his protégé Timothy who is new to leading a flock of followers: "Don't let anyone look down on you because you are young, but set an example for the believers in speech, in conduct, in love, in faith and in purity." (1 Tim 4:12)

Paul wrote in his first letter to Timothy: "But if you suffer for doing good and you endure it, this is commendable before God. To this you were called, because Christ suffered for you, leaving you an example, that you should follow in his steps. He committed no sin, and no deceit was found in his mouth.'" Verse 22 cites a reference from Isa 53:9, which means that even the prophets understood the blamelessness of Jesus' brand many hundreds of years before He was born.

These verses and others like them all point to the idea that Jesus, the prophets, and the apostles all set examples for us to follow and reflect to others today. As for the second question about the effects of bad Godly branding. You may be tempted to wonder the following: "Does my brand really make a difference?" The answer is an emphatic YES!

The clearest depiction of this need to be vigilant about your Godly brand comes from chapters 2–3 from Paul's letter to the Romans. In the early chapters, Paul lets loose on the followers in Rome for their derision, sinful behavior, and poor example (2:17–24):

> Now you, if you call yourself a Jew; if you rely on the law and boast in God; if you know his will and approve of what is superior because you are instructed by the law; if you are convinced that you are a guide for the blind, a light for those who are in the dark, an instructor of the foolish, a teacher of little children, because you have in the law the embodiment of knowledge and truth—you, then, who teach others, do you not teach yourself? You who preach against stealing, do you steal? You who say that people should not commit adultery, do you commit adultery? You who abhor idols, do you rob temples? You who boast in the law, do you dishonor God by breaking the law? As it is written: "God's name is blasphemed among the Gentiles because of you."

The church's Jewish members were using their heritage and knowledge of the law to stand apart and above the Gentiles. They abused their role as being members of God's chosen people and "light to the world." Even worse, their focus on the law shone a bright light on their breaking it. Verse 21 basically says, "you aren't practicing what you preach," referring to the law. Then, Paul charges them with stealing, committing adultery, getting mixed up with idols, and generally breaking the law. Not good. What's worse? The Jewish members' blasphemed God's name with their poor example before the Gentiles. This isn't just a reputation problem. The Gentiles saw this sinful behavior and spoke of it among themselves, and it all dishonored God and gave the Evil One a foothold to turn some number of them away from the Word of God.

When your poor Godly brand threatens to turn people away from the body of the Lord, you have a *really big* problem. As the Apostle James wrote: The Judge is standing at the door! (James 5:9). That Judge, of course, is God. He will act to preserve souls whom He has called as His own. And, if it gets bad at your church, organization, city, or country, the consequences will be destruction:

> In a similar way, Sodom and Gomorrah and the surrounding towns gave themselves up to sexual immorality and perversion. They serve as an example of those who suffer the punishment of eternal fire. (Jude 1:7)

Point being, your Godly brand does matter, both in the keeping of it for yourself and as an example to others.

Identifying Your Godly Brand Comes Before Determining Your God-Given Purpose

In 2002, Pastor Rick Warren's global best-seller, *The Purpose Driven Life*, began its journey to becoming the best-selling non-fiction hardback book in history (according to *Publishers Weekly*) and—along the way—helping hundreds of millions of people across the planet better understand and answer the question: "What on earth am I here for?" The book delves into the five purposes for which God followers exist: planned for God's pleasure; formed for God's family; created to become like Christ; shaped for serving God; and made for a mission.

Purpose is another concept about which much has been written. For the sake of simplifying purpose for our discussion on branding, let's define it as a *God-driven mandate to serve Him in a specific ministry at a given time for His glory*. This mandate is something that you come to understand through thoughtful prayer, listening to the Holy Spirit for guidance, and counsel with God followers in your life, and it should direct your focus in life and consequential actions. Or, you may have fallen into your purpose by God's grace and direction, and are just now thinking about it.

Philippians 2:13 tells us "for it is God who works in you to will and to act in order to fulfill His good purpose." Stated differently, God will do in you whatever He asks you to do. He will equip you, inspire you, and help you achieve it.

God wants you to understand and deliver on your purpose in fulfilling His divine will. He wants you to act in a way that glories Him and serves His plan for this world. However, before you get to purpose, you must consider your brand. Reason being, *your brand defines how you will approach your purpose*. It is the underlying foundation for everything you do in life: how you think, feel, and act; what you do and don't do; and ultimately how people both perceive and relate to you. If your brand and purpose are not aligned, you will find life challenging and likely unsettling. Conversely, once you identify your brand, your purpose stands to become far clearer as will the path to achieving it.

In a business setting, the need to define your brand before purpose is usually clear, as it spells out how you sell your product or service. Will you be a value (i.e., lower cost) versus premium (i.e., higher cost) provider? Is your business focused on a high-quality product / service or more concerned with offering outstanding customer support? Is your business innovative? Striving to be the market leader or well-regarded niche player? And the list of questions goes on . . .

If you look up the definition of the word purpose in the dictionary, you'll see: "the reason for which something is done or created or for which something exists." That's the expression of purpose as a noun. You'll also see purpose expressed as a verb: "have as one's intention or objective." The problem with the verb form of purpose is that it introduces another word that needs to be defined, that being "intention." What is meant by intention? Again, back to the dictionary: "a thing intended; an aim or plan."

The reason for comparing the noun and verb forms is that—all too often when thinking of their purpose—people go right to "God placed me on this earth to do [fill in the blank]." Once believers feel that they understand their purpose, they will start telling others about what they perceive that purpose to be, then doing things to support it. And this approach to serving God works, unless or until one of these conditions occur:

- God doesn't fully bless that purpose-ministry that you undertake, making it difficult to achieve, or you outright fail
- You embark on fulfilling your perceived purpose, but something inside you doesn't feel right, as if you and your gifts are not aligned with it
- Your purpose interferes with your faith-walk with and worship of God
- You haven't yet figured out your purpose

Referring back to Pastor Rick Warren's *The Purpose Driven Life* the book's website describes the book as "a manifesto for Christian living in the 21st century . . . a lifestyle based on eternal purposes, not cultural values." Using biblical stories and letting the Bible speak for itself, Warren clearly explains God's five purposes for each of us:

- We were planned for God's pleasure so your first purpose is to *offer real worship*.
- We were formed for God's family so your second purpose is to *enjoy real fellowship*.
- We were created to become like Christ, so your third purpose is to *learn real discipleship*.
- We were shaped for serving God so your fourth purpose is to *practice real ministry*.
- We were made for a mission so your fifth purpose is to *live out real evangelism*."

All five of these purposes are truisms, and I highly encourage you to read the book, which covers the topic of purpose across 42 daily devotionals that comprise the book. Looking at these five truisms though, they're all based on verbs or actions: offer, enjoy, learn, practice, and live out. They address the *why* and *what* of leading a Godly branded life. But further exploration is required to help each of us understand the *how* we will lead a Godly branded life.

Frankly, it's hard to be additive on this topic of purpose given Pastor Warren and others' books. The four humble comments that I'll add to the dialogue pertain to how Godly branding and God-given purpose relate to each other:

Personal Branding Differs from Godly Branding

1. *Understanding your Godly brand helps you fulfill your purpose*

Neither you nor your business will understand whether you are having an impact / making a difference with your target audiences (God, community, church body, customers, etc.) unless you define what you stand for, then see it realized or not. This isn't about how well you communicate your messages. People can receive your talking points, marketing calls-to-action, or messages on packaging, but how they perceive and eventually connect with you, your product, service, cause, or campaign will be based on your brand.

Case in point, I love fresh-squeezed orange juice, and for many years I would occasionally pick up a carton of Tropicana pure premium orange juice with lots of pulp. The packaging was unmistakable. It featured a straw stuck into a vivacious, plump orange. A key attribute of the brand implied by the image was that you were literally sucking the freshest juice right out the orange. The word "fresh" didn't appear anywhere on the packaging. That's because the concept of being fresh, like being trustworthy or acting with integrity, is something that must be experienced by your target audiences, not told to them. The image carries that freshness attribute for the brand.

Then PepsiCo, which owns the Tropicana brand, decided to rebrand it. The rebrand resulted in hideous packaging. Instead of showing us a fresh orange, there was a message across the top that says, "squeezed from fresh oranges," which is a direct violation of the show-don't-tell tenant of branding. The fresh orange with a straw was replaced with a generic glass that looked like it came straight out of a hotel ballroom business meeting. Not only did PepsiCo eliminate a core brand attribute, it reinforced a generic, work-related concept that flatly did not resonate with target audiences. The purpose of the redesign was to help increase sales. However, after losing $130 million in sales, PepsiCo went back to the original packaging.

If PepsiCo and its marketing arm took the time to look at the core brand attributes for Tropicana, which they have, and seen that freshness was at the top of the list, they likely would not have redesigned the packaging. During the review of the packaging designs for the misfire carton, someone should've asked the question, "does this really connote the concept of freshness?" Either they didn't ask the question, or they convinced themselves that the tall glass and message at the top did the job. They were wrong.

You need that list of your brand attributes to guide all of your decision-making, and—if you have it—you will understand which messaging and actions will align with them and which will not. Your brand attributes are meant as a touchstone for you to always ask when presented with a life or business opportunity: does it align with and help advance my Godly brand? If it does, consider proceeding with the opportunity. If it doesn't, don't do it.

2. *God gave us different abilities to realize our brand and purpose*

Regardless of what you determine your Godly brand and/or purpose to be, you are here on earth to carry out God's will. God made each of us differently to carry out His will, and some of us were given what society and humankind may perceive to be better abilities and gifts than others. From Rom 9:21, "Does not the potter have the right to make out of the same lump of clay some pottery for special purposes and some for common use?" In the context of the verse, the Apostle Paul uses "potter" to refer to God. The concept of God as the potter and each of us as the clay that He molds to His liking is mentioned numerous times in the Scriptures, including Isa 29:16; 64:8; Jer 18:6; and 2 Tim 2:20.

This Roman 9 verse adds a special nuance, though. It makes clear that some are created for a "special purpose" and some for "common use." Unpacking this concept with an example, God meant for Billy Graham to be the most important evangelist for His church in the 20th Century. He equipped Graham with the skills, drive, and endurance to accomplish His work. God also provided opportunities and blessings to actualize his rise to prominence. Graham literally impacted the lives of hundreds of millions of God's followers across this planet. Probably, billions.

In contrast, if this book positively affects one person toward living a Godly branded life, I'll consider it a great blessing from the Lord. God had different plans for me. I didn't fully realize my purpose until I reached my 40s. That's all part of His grand design and plan.

Completing this book may be all that God has in store for my life. Or, He may enable me to write additional books that I believe He has inspired me to consider, speak to audiences about the importance of living a Godly branded life, or find other ways to spread His Word in this world to help the Holy Spirit work in the hearts of others. With God's help, I have identified this purpose for my life.

What is your purpose? What is that one thing that you know you are burning to do for God?

If you don't know, or you've never thought about it, now is the time. The only way you will come to understand your purpose is through defining your Godly brand, deep introspection and prayer, and calling out to God to help you understand. Be prepared though, it may take some time before you understand your purpose. It took decades for Abraham, Jacob, Joseph, and Moses to realize and fulfill their respective purposes.

But I promise you that—if you do ask God to help you understand your purpose—He will reveal it to you.

3. *Everyone has a purpose in God's plan, even "bad guys"*

If you accept as a God follower and believe that God is omniscient, all-knowing, and all-powerful (you should!), then likely you realize that there are many, many ways in which God moves and carries out His plans on earth that are quite simply beyond our human abilities to comprehend. We can't see God's entire plan; even Jesus did not know the timing of His return (see Mark 13:32). Because we cannot understand all of His plans, there are certain things in our walk of faith that we must accept by faith. I try to remember this aspect of faith when I see tragic things happen in the world and in my personal life. It helps me rationalize to some extent the awful things that we can see in our fallen world when we read or watch the news. It also helps me cope when—for example—I hear of friends with a two-year-old son who just had surgery for brain cancer. All of these things are part of God's perfect plan, whether we like them or not.

One question that I continue to ponder is: does God use bad people to carry out His plan? The answer is yes. The Scriptures are filled with examples of bad people, some of them downright villains, who play a role in God's plan on Earth. Few villains in the Bible were worse than King Herod. In Matthew 2, when he realized that the Magi had outwitted him, "he gave orders to kill all the boys in Bethlehem and its vicinity who were two years old and under, in accordance with the time he had learned from the Magi." He wanted to preserve his power and, to do that, he committed genocide. He also helped fulfill multiple Old Testament prophecies having to do with the mourning of the people in Ramah (Jer 31:15), the Son of God coming out of Egypt (Hos 11:1), and Jesus being called a Nazarene, when Joseph—hearing that Herod's son Archelaus was the ruler—took the family to Nazareth. These fulfilled prophecies all point to Jesus as our Messiah.

In Exod 9:16, God used Pharaoh to show His "power and that my name might be proclaimed in all the earth." Following in the footsteps of his forefathers, Pharaoh subjugated the Israelites into forced hard labor. When Moses and Aaron arrived to set them free, Pharaoh rejected them. With a hardened heart, Pharaoh refused to free the Israelites through nine plagues that ravaged the whole of Egypt. Not until the 10th plague and the death of every firstborn person (and livestock) did the stubborn leader finally relent (12:31–32). Even then, Pharaoh and his armies pursued the Israelites into the wilderness until they were wiped out in the Red Sea (14:26–28).

Through all of Pharaoh's actions, God's plan for His people was realized. Several significant outcomes occurred as a result of Pharaoh's hardened heart and his harsh treatment of the Israelites:

- **Passover:** Four days before the Exodus, the Israelites were instructed by Moses to set aside a lamb (12:3). During the day on the 14th day of month (i.e., Nisan), they were to slaughter the animal and use its blood to mark their lintels and door posts. Before midnight on the 15th day, they were commanded to eat the lamb. The holiday remains practiced by people of Jewish faith to this day.

- **Festival of Unleavened Bread:** Immediately after Passover, the Israelites were to eat unleavened bread for seven days. "On the first day hold a sacred assembly, and another one on the seventh day. Do no work at all on these days, except to prepare food for everyone to eat; that is all you may do. Celebrate the Festival of Unleavened Bread, because it was on this very day that I brought your divisions out of Egypt. Celebrate this day as a lasting ordinance for the generations to come." (12:15b–17)

- **Consecration of the Firstborn:** Moses commanded his people, "For seven days [in the month of Aviv] eat bread made without yeast and on the seventh day hold a festival to the Lord. On that day tell your son, 'I do this because of what the Lord did for me when I came out of Egypt.' This observance will be for you like a sign on your hand and a reminder on your forehead that this law of the Lord is to be on your lips. For the Lord brought you out of Egypt with his mighty hand. You must keep this ordinance at the appointed time year after year." (13:6, 8–10)

- **Fear of God and Moses:** After the Egyptian army was destroyed by the waters of the Red Sea, "when the Israelites saw the mighty hand of the Lord displayed against the Egyptians, the people feared the Lord and put their trust in him and in Moses his servant." (14:31)

None of these ordinances or outcomes, as well as the Israelites' journey to and entry into the Promised Land, would have occurred without God working through Pharaoh.

4. *Know your limitations*

A critical part of fulfilling your God-given purpose is knowing your limits, that being your strengths, areas of development, and those things that don't come easily to you, you can't stand doing, or you flat-out can't do. You need to be self-aware about your personality and abilities.

Moses knew his limitations when he pleaded with the Lord to relieve him from the responsibility of having to go to Egypt to rescue his people. From Exod 4:10, "Pardon your servant, Lord. I have never been eloquent, neither in the past nor since you have spoken to your servant. I am slow of speech and tongue." Despite the Lord telling him, "Now go; I will help you speak and will teach you what to say," Moses still refused, "Pardon your servant, Lord. Please send someone else." Verses 14–15 tell us that "the Lord's anger burned against Moses and he said, 'What about your brother, Aaron the Levite? I know he can speak well. He is already on his way to meet you, and he will be glad to see you. You shall speak to him and put words in his mouth; I will help both of you speak and will teach you what to do.'"

Moses eventually overcame his lack of confidence in public speaking, but—at that point—he knew he needed help. And the Lord gave it to him.

The Apostle Paul tells us that there are different kinds of gifts of the Spirit: "To one there is given through the Spirit a message of wisdom, to another a message of knowledge by means of the same Spirit, to another faith by the same Spirit, to another gifts of healing by that one Spirit, to another miraculous powers, to another prophecy, to another distinguishing between spirits, to another speaking in different kinds of tongues, and to still another the interpretation of tongues. All these are the work of one and the same Spirit, and he distributes them to each one, just as he determines." (1 Cor 12:8–11)

If you've been given the gift of faith, for example, you may not be as strong in other gifts. Therefore, those others may be areas where you are limited in your abilities to perform them.

Knowing your Godly brand is vital to reflecting God's love and power in your life, and better understanding your purpose in His great plan. It is also critically important in directing how you lead your life and the actions you perform, which is the subject of the next section.

Section 2

What Is Godly Branding

A deep dive into the eight brand attributes that make up your Godly brand and how they were demonstrated throughout Scriptures by the most prominent figures in the Bible.

Chapter 4

Your Body is a Temple (for Branding)

"Do you not know that your bodies are temples of the Holy Spirit, who is in you, whom you have received from God? You are not your own; you were bought at a price. Therefore honor God with your bodies."

—1 COR 6:19–20

OVER THE YEARS, I'VE tried to think of visual ways to relate what a brand is and how it is constructed. If constructed properly and nurtured, a brand should stand the test of time. There are well-known brands today in the U.S. that were founded more than 300 years ago. When one thinks of standing the test of time, what comes to mind? In my case, I think of ancient architecture, specifically, one of my bucket-list places to visit: the Parthenon, a former temple on the Athenian Acropolis in Greece.

Construction of the temple began in 447 BC and completed in 438 BC, with further adornments made to the building until 432 BC. When built, the Parthenon was dedicated to the goddess Athena. Later, in the sixth century AD, it was converted to a Christian church dedicated to the Virgin Mary. In the 1460s, it became a mosque. Then, of all things, it was a munitions dump when—in 1687—a bomb set off a massive explosion that severely damaged the building and its sculptures. Despite all of these varied uses of the Parthenon and several events that caused it extreme damage, the edifice still stands to this day more than two-and-a-half millennia later.

If you haven't had the pleasure of visiting the Parthenon, there is another great example of a structure that is based on classical Greek architecture. It's the Lincoln Memorial in my hometown of Washington, D.C.

The Parthenon's classical architecture lends itself to a graphical depiction of branding, beginning with its foundation, or euthynteria. The entire superstructure of the building—columns, walls, and frieze (part of the entablature) and pediment—were set on the euthynteria. Next comes the columns that support the frieze and pediment, a horizontal structural element that supports the roof. The frieze and pediment encircle the entire building and include the major decorative elements of the Parthenon that depict famous events, battles, and happenings, all things of historical importance.

Beyond a quick snapshot of ancient Greek architecture, these elements correlate to various elements that construct your Godly brand.

A foundation supports your core brand attributes (columns), which supports the ornate roof that depicts the purpose and actions of your life (frieze). While it may seem weird to use the image of a pagan temple to relate the structure of your Godly brand, the classical architecture that it represents and how such a structure can withstand the test of time are the more important points. But before we get to building the structure of our Godly temple, we must build the foundation on the proper surface.

Building a Firm Foundation on the Rock: Jesus

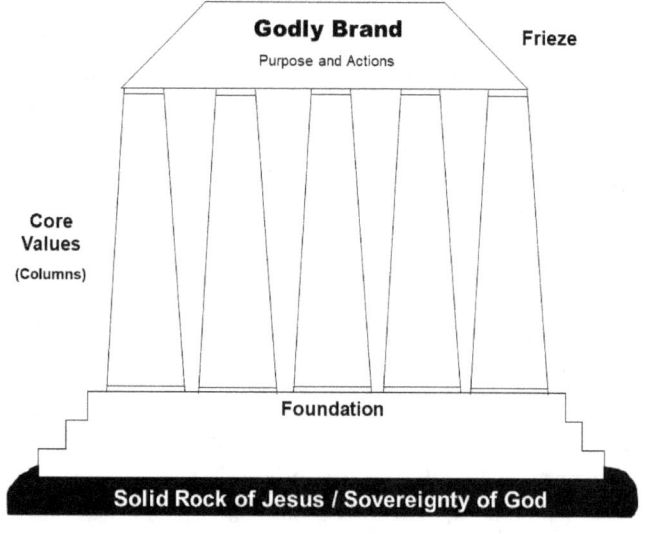

There was no greater example for how we should live than Jesus, our Risen Savior and the Rock upon which we build our Godly temple. He showed us how we should love, be patient, lead, evangelize, and much more through His every action and every word. Mostly, He taught us obedience to the His Father. That being said, it can be difficult though to reconcile the fact that Jesus was without sin and one with the Father in heaven with being human, being like us. Stated differently, one may be tempted to look at Jesus and think: "He was perfect in every way. How can I live up to that standard? I can't." And you would be right. You cannot live up to the blameless standard of Jesus because we are sinful creatures. Thank the Lord that He died on the Cross to redeem us from our sin and guilt!

However, Jesus' perfection and blamelessness doesn't mean that He wasn't human and experienced the same emotions as we do. One of my favorite stories in the Bible comes from Matthew 8:5–13 and involves the faith of a Roman centurion:

> When Jesus had entered Capernaum, a centurion came to him, asking for help. "Lord," he said, "my servant lies at home paralyzed, suffering terribly."
>
> Jesus said to him, "Shall I come and heal him?"
>
> The centurion replied, "Lord, I do not deserve to have you come under my roof. But just say the word, and my servant will be healed. For I myself am a man under authority, with soldiers under me. I tell this one, 'Go,' and he goes; and that one, 'Come,' and he comes. I say to my servant, 'Do this,' and he does it."
>
> When Jesus heard this, he was amazed and said to those following him, "Truly I tell you, I have not found anyone in Israel with such great faith. I say to you that many will come from the east and the west, and will take their places at the feast with Abraham, Isaac and Jacob in the kingdom of heaven. But the subjects of the kingdom will be thrown outside, into the darkness, where there will be weeping and gnashing of teeth."
>
> Then Jesus said to the centurion, "Go! Let it be done just as you believed it would." And his servant was healed at that moment.

I love this passage for two reasons: 1) the humility and faith demonstrated by the centurion, who simply knows that Jesus will handle his request; and 2) Jesus' reaction to this faith. In the NIV translation, Jesus was "amazed" and stated emphatically "Truly I tell you, I have not found anyone in Israel with such great faith." Other translations use the word "astonished" to describe Jesus' reaction.

In this passage, we see Jesus—a member of the triune God, all powerful, all knowing—react with genuine surprise to the faith of a Gentile. This passage really hits home that Jesus simply didn't live out a rote human life, going through the motions until His purpose from the Father to suffer and die on the Cross was fulfilled. He experienced life to its fullest. And that's deeply comforting to know.

This passage is one where we really see the personality of Jesus. At some level, despite His and the Father's profound love for us, it must have been deeply trying for Jesus to walk this earth, preaching and healing and giving all of Himself, and still have to deal with the non-believers, skeptics, ego-driven leaders, vindictive religious figures, and the vast number of people who "just didn't get it." Thank the Lord that He loved us so much to persevere with us!

Here though, with the centurion, Jesus came across a living example of the type of follower that He's looking for, and he was a Gentile. A person who accepted Jesus' authority in his life, was humble, and believed. It must have been such a pleasant surprise to Jesus that—even though He knew the centurion would cross His path that day—He still greeted the encounter with relief, delight, and amazement. It's as if Jesus said: "Finally! Someone who gets Me!"

Jesus' anger over His father's temple being turned into a market offers another demonstration of His humanity. That story is found in John 2, and it follows Jesus' first miracle in Cana when he turned water into wine. Verse 13 tells us that Jesus then went up to Jerusalem for the Jewish Passover. From verses 14–17:

> In the temple courts he found people selling cattle, sheep and doves, and others sitting at tables exchanging money. So he made a whip out of cords, and drove all from the temple courts, both sheep and cattle; he scattered the coins of the money changers and overturned their tables. To those who sold doves he said, "Get these out of here! Stop turning my Father's house into a market!" His disciples remembered that it is written: "Zeal for your house will consume me."

The part that always strikes me is that Jesus was angry enough to stop, consider how he was going to force everyone out, and made a "whip out of cords." That process took at least a few minutes, which means that Jesus got upset, stayed riled up as he wove together the cords, possibly even muttering under his breath, then took action. How many of us have had instances in our lives very much like this one, where we held onto our anger as we prepared to act? I dare say: all of us.

What do these two stories mean for us? Jesus was and is relatable. He is not some distant, perfect being "up in the clouds" that we cannot relate to. He is present and personal with us. Ps 30:2 states: "Lord my God, I called to you for help, and you healed me." Deut 31:6 tells us to "be strong and courageous. Do not be afraid or terrified because of them, for the Lord your God goes with you; he will never leave you nor forsake you." Jesus will always be there for us, to help us in whatever we need. Here's the fun part. While we cannot attain his utter and complete blamelessness, we can look at other aspects of His walk on this earth and learn from it, and not dismiss His example as "well, I can't do that, so skip it."

During His life on earth, Jesus exhibited a wide range of different human attributes. However, the absolute driver for everything He did was the recognition of and submission to His Father's sovereignty over this world and His life. This singular element of His brand and yours is vitally important because—without submitting to God's sovereignty—none of what is outlined in this book will work. *Everything* in this book is predicated on your submission to God's leadership and control in your life.

Not submitting to God's sovereignty means that you refuse every tenant in the Bible, for everything there is built on the recognition that God is sovereign over all things and—because of this—all honor and glory are due His name. It means that you do not trust God with your life or how He works through you to carry out His kingdom-building plans. As Rom 8:28 tells us: "And we know that in all things God works for the good of those who love him, who have been called according to his purpose." Trusting Him is a key component of loving Him.

With Jesus and the other 20+ figures, everything they did in life was born from the underlying, undeniable truth that they recognized God's ultimate authority in their lives. All of them relied and trusted God to direct their words and actions. Whether it was Jesus constantly recognizing the Father's presence in His life and on the path to the Cross, or Daniel telling King Darius that no man can interpret his dreams but only God (Dan 2), or Joseph saying the same thing to Pharaoh about his dreams (Gen 41), all of them acknowledged God's sovereignty in their lives and their complete dependency on God to carry out their respective work.

For anyone who calls him- or herself a follower of God, the recognition of His leadership in your life is where it all starts. That means turning your life over to God to guide you and constantly turning to Him in prayer to do so are NOT optional. Otherwise, you will—as Jesus put it—"be like a foolish man who built his house on sand" (Matthew 7:26), and it is easily washed away. Stated another way, failure to place your life in God's hands will result in ongoing anxiety, anger, fear, depression, and pervasive hopelessness throughout your life. How do I know that? Because I've lived it during periods of my life and so did most of the 20 biblical figures mentioned earlier at some point in their lives.

When have you experienced anxiety, anger, fear, depression, and hopelessness in your life? When these emotions linger, that's the sign that you may not be walking with God and trusting Him to lead the way.

There's a great example in Daniel 3 that demonstrates what wholeheartedly trusting God looks like. When King Nebuchadnezzar confronts Shadrach, Meshach and Abednego about why they did not fall down and worship the image of gold that he had set up, they replied, "King Nebuchadnezzar, we do not need to defend ourselves before you in this matter. If we are thrown into the blazing furnace, the God we serve is able to deliver us from it, and he will deliver us from Your Majesty's hand. But even if he does not, we want you to know, Your Majesty, that we will not serve your gods or worship the image of gold you have set up." This response reflects complete trust in God, regardless of the outcome of their lives.

While you can certainly keep reading this book and derive some insights from it, true change for your Godly brand will only occur when you acknowledge God's sovereignty in your life, trust His leadership, and turn to Him in regular prayer to guide you. It worked for Jesus. It worked for the 20 or more biblical figures. It will work for you!

God's Sovereignty

Being blunt: our God is a jealous God (Exod 34:14) and takes the worship of other gods *very seriously*. While sin is sin, and one type of sin is not greater than another, the worship of another god ahead of our God garners decisive and comprehensive correction from God (see Isa 1:4, Jer 3:13). God deals harshly with His followers who fail to recognize His sovereign power and acknowledge another god in their life, whether that be a literal other religion or placing something else above Him (e.g., work, pursuit of money or fame, human relationships, etc.). And the consequences can be dire.

For God followers, recognizing another god in their life seems like the "worse of all sins" to God because it is the most personal to Him. It is an overt rejection of Him, after He chose you to be a member of His holy family. Imagine that—for all time—God has known that you would be a member of His holy kingdom, and He even made the ultimate sacrifice for you in sending His only son to die on the Cross to save you through His grace. Then, knowing all of that, you still prioritize something else—another god—ahead of Him. Try to conceive of the worst, most humiliating rejection you have ever personally experienced in your life, then you can begin to get a sense of why God takes this issue very seriously.

The Old Testament is filled with passages of God's burning anger over the Israelites' following of fake, hand-made idols. The making of the golden calf in Exod 32 is a well-known story to us. God's reaction when He saw the Israelites commit this great sin was to tell Moses, "I have seen these people, and they are a stiff-necked people. Now leave me alone so that my anger may burn against them and that I may destroy them." Only Moses' intervention prevented their destruction.

The Book of Judges tells one story after another of how the Israelites turned away from God, who would then turn them over to their enemies. Under the oppressive rule of those enemies, the Israelites would cry out to Him, and He would send a judge to save them. That judge would die, then the Israelites would return to their evil worship of other gods. This yo-yo act with the Israelites went on for 380 years until the rule of King Saul.

After King Saul came King David, then King Solomon. After him, Israel and Judea had 39 kings before their exile to Babylon. Only five to seven of them followed God's ways, according to various biblical scholars. With that kind of track record, God fulfilled what Moses stated would be the penalty if the Israelites did not keep His ways and commandments. From Deut 4:25–27, Moses states, "After you have had children and grandchildren and have lived in the land a long time—if you then become corrupt and make any kind of idol, doing evil in the eyes of the LORD your God and arousing his anger, I call the heavens and the earth as witnesses against you this day that you will quickly perish from the land that you are crossing the Jordan to possess. You will not live there long but will certainly be destroyed. The LORD will scatter you among the peoples, and only a few of you will survive among the nations to which the LORD will drive you."

Moses' assurance to the Israelites eventually came true in their exile to Babylon, a corrective act by God to reconcile His people to Himself because His love for His people always endures. The Israelites serve as a lesson to us to honor God and—as Ps 32:5 tells us—acknowledge our sin and confess our transgressions to the Lord.

Foundation

> For no one can lay any foundation other than the
> one already laid, which is Jesus Christ.
>
> —1 COR 3:11

Indeed, Christ is our firm foundation, the Rock, upon which we should build our lives. His life provides the perfect example for how we should lead our lives. As covered in the next chapter, Jesus exhibited a great many brand attributes during His time on earth. The ones that directly pertain to how we should demonstrate our Godly brand include the following:

1. loves others
2. shows patience
3. demonstrates a servant mindset
4. trusts and obeys God's commands
5. forgives
6. glorifies God through thankfulness
7. is a member of God's community / church
8. is an agent of change.

If Jesus is the firm foundation and He lived a life that exhibited these eight brand attributes, it only makes sense that the foundation of our lives should be based on the same core values. This concept will be the easiest to understand and the hardest to carry out in our day-to-day lives. Why? Because our focus as sinful creatures—and we must accept that we are sinful creatures—is on ourselves, on whatever foundation we have created for ourselves.

In a Godly brand structure, all followers of Christ should have a foundation that looks like this:

Foundation

| Loves Others | Forgives | Shows Patience | Obeys God's Commands |
| Demonstrates a Servant Mindset | Glorifies God through Thankfulness | Is a Member of God's Community / Church | Is a Change Agent |

Columns

In the temple branding model, the columns represent those 3–5 attributes that make up your individual, personal brand. *Section 3* of this book will walk through exercises to help you ascertain your Core Values.

Core Values (Columns)

These Core Values are not characteristics (e.g., always on time or late, saves or spends money, etc.) or personality traits.

Core Values are what you believe and stand for. They answer the question: If I ask my close family and friends to describe me, what do I want them to say? Further, if I ask people who are acquaintances or business colleagues, what would they say?

Individuals and businesses need to carefully consider how they want others to perceive them, codify it, then promote it. *Section 3* will offer exercises to handle the considering and codifying of Core Values.

For individuals and businesses, promoting or positioning a brand happens all the time, especially with new companies. Most emerging brands claim to be something before they actually become that thing as a means of carving out a market position for themselves and to differentiate themselves from their competition. In these cases, their 3–5 values must have at least one unique element versus the other players in the market. With a former client of mine, an on-demand grocery delivery service, the company wanted to lean heavily on customer service as a market differentiator against the big, impersonal brands in the space. One of the Core Values in its brand platform was "neighborly." This company demonstrated this neighborly value by hiring super-friendly delivery drivers; dressing them in clean, casual uniforms; and empowering them to reduce a customer's bill in the field if something was wrong with the order (e.g., missing product, bruised fruit). Because these drivers had standard routes, they got to know frequent customers, like a neighbor. The owner knew what processes and operations he wanted to put in place to make this concept of being neighborly pervasive in everything the company did.

You, too, can identify and promote Core Values for yourself, your business, or your church that may not be literally true, and that's okay. It's not being deceptive, per se, unless you literally claim to be something you are not. The Core Values must be defensible and reflected in what you do (i.e., your actions). Also, they should glorify God and His purpose for your life, business, or church.

Frieze

If branding is the alignment of what you say about yourself with what you actually do, and how it shapes the perceptions of others, the frieze reflects what you do; it's the outcomes of your actions that people and God can see and hear.

In my experience, people and businesses simply don't give enough thought to their actions and, more precisely, their inactions. You've probably heard these clichés. "Eighty percent of success is just showing up," attributed to film director Woody Allen. "You miss 100 percent of the shots you don't take," from hockey great Wayne Gretsky. "Actions speak louder than words." "Don't just tell me. Show me." "You are what you do, not what you say you'll do." These sayings are emblazoned in our minds because somewhere along the line someone admonished us for not following through on what we said we'd do. Or, the opposite occurred. We were praised for doing something when others typically wouldn't. Regardless, the lesson here is "actions count." The bigger point is that people frame their perceptions of you based on your actions, and those opinions about you and your conduct form your reputation.

In public relations and communications, there is a whole discipline for how to shift others' perceptions of you called reputation management. Businesses must consider their reputations all of the time, especially retail companies that can be affected by negative reviews on the Yelps and Tripadvisors of the world. For individuals, given the growth of social media and other online forums that can affect your reputation, an entire crop of businesses has sprung up to help you manage your online reputation and—if necessary—defend it against attackers.

In service-based businesses (accounting, law, public relations, etc.), it's a cliché, but it's true: your reputation is everything. A good or bad reputation has a direct bearing on your new business prospects. The same can be said about your reputation as it relates to your ability to do God's work. Prov 22:1 tells us, "A good name is more desirable than great riches; to be esteemed is better than silver or gold." Verse 3 takes the concept one step further, "The prudent see danger and take refuge, but the simple keep going and pay the penalty."

There are two concepts here to unpack. First, your reputation is more important than any riches you may amass. The world will tell you that's crazy thinking. The world says, "If you have lots of money, who cares what people think. If you have money, you don't need to worry about your name because—well—you have lots of money. Money solves everything." Here's the problem: it's earthly thinking. People who think about money in this way are missing the heavenly reward aspect of salvation. This reward is literally priceless. Stated a different way, who cares how much money you amass in this world if you miss out on your place in heaven. As the ole saying goes, "you can't take it with you," and make no mistake, your name is on a list in heaven. Or, it's not. Trust me, you want to be on that list.

Second, people who do not consider their name or reputation will pay a penalty. To start, if you're not careful, that penalty may be not inheriting your place in the kingdom of God when you pass from this earth. Penalties in *this* world may involve disgrace, dishonor, distrust, removal of privileges, loss of family and friends, and so much more. Think about some of the greatest celebrity falls from grace: Bill Cosby, O.J. Simpson,

Matt Lauer, Tiger Woods, Lance Armstrong, Michael Jackson, or Harvey Weinstein. These collapses were spectacular and played out in the full public eye. Tiger Woods and Mel Gibson have returned to their professions, but the others have either been blackballed from their respective industries or landed in jail. Political leaders such as Richard Nixon, John Edwards, and Anthony Weiner experienced falls that cost them their careers in public service.

In a religious context, two recent falls from grace occurred with former Liberty University president Jerry Falwell Jr. and his wife Becki as well as former Hillsong NYC pastor Carl Lentz. Both parties were caught up in highly publicized scandals that ended their ministries. It doesn't take much research into these Godly-branding catastrophes to recognize that—in both cases—the individuals involved became more enamored with their personal status and gain than protecting their work for God.

Fortunately, there are a lot of figures in the Bible whose actions spoke well of their Godly brand.

Biblical Example: Ruth

The story of Ruth gives us an example of marvelously consistent character and strength. She offers one of the more straightforward examples of branding in the Bible. Other than references to being in the lineage of Jesus, virtually every reference to her is included in the Book of Ruth. Throughout the four short chapters of the book, there are several clear references to her character and actions that help inform her brand.

Defining Brand Moment (i.e., First Thing We Think About)

In the first chapter of Ruth, Elimelek and his wife Naomi moved from Bethlehem to Moab because of a famine in the land. While there, their sons married Moabite women, Ruth and Orpah.

After 10 years, Elimelek and the two sons died. Naomi decided to move back to Bethlehem, and her daughters-in-law went with her. On the road, Naomi implored her two daughters-in-law to return home. Orpah headed back, but Ruth begged "Don't urge me to leave you or to turn back from you. May the LORD deal with me, be it ever so severely, if even death separates you and me." Naomi relented, and Ruth went with her to a foreign land, leaving behind everything she knows.

This decision is huge, given how women—especially widows—were treated at that time. Without protection from their husbands, both Naomi and Ruth were vulnerable to exploitation and societal abuse. As a Moabite woman going to Israel, Ruth stood to face even greater hardships. Despite this, Ruth demonstrated her loyalty and devotion to Naomi by staying with her as they headed back to Bethlehem.

Ruth's Core Values

What do we know about Ruth? She was important enough in the lineage of Christ to merit having her own book in the Bible. Despite the few references to her throughout the rest of Scriptures, we can identify several key attributes or characteristics about Ruth:

- Foreigner / Moabite woman (Ruth 1:4, Ruth 2:6, Ruth 2:10)
- Wife of Mahlon or Kilion (Ruth 1:4–5)
- Loyal / devoted to Naomi (Ruth 1:6–10, 2:11–12, 3:10, 4:15)
- Kind (Ruth 1:8, 3:10)
- Determined (Ruth 1:18)
- Resourceful (Ruth 2:2)
- Willing to work / hard worker (Ruth 2:7, 2:17–18, 2:23)
- Gracious / thankful (Ruth 2:10)
- Blessed (Ruth 2:12, Ruth 4:14))
- Humble (Ruth 2:13)
- Trusting (Ruth 3:5)
- Noble / Virtuous (Ruth 3:11)
- Boaz' wife (Ruth 4:13)
- Mother (Ruth 4:13)
- In the lineage of David (Ruth 4:18–22, Matthew 1:5)

Of these characteristics, if I were writing a brand platform for her, the five that most represent her Core Values are the following: 1) foreigner; 2) loyal / devoted; 3) hard worker; 4) resourceful; and 5) mother.

Ruth identified herself as a foreigner to Boaz in Ruth 2:10. Being a foreigner, especially a Moabite, in Jerusalem was a big deal. Remember, the Moabites tried to have Balaam curse the traveling Israelites in Num 23. In Deut 23:3, Moabites and their descendants were forbidden from entering the assembly of the Lord to the tenth generation. In Judg 3:14, we read that the Israelites were subject to Eglon king of Moab for eighteen years. Eventually, Moab was made subject to Israel. Her being a Moabite woman was part of her brand identity.

Ruth's loyalty was unquestionable. Where Orpah went home, Ruth remained with Naomi on the trip back to Jerusalem, brought her food, and eventually gave her a grandson. Her hard work is what got her noticed by the overseer of Boaz' fields, and he gave a strong accounting of her when Boaz asked who she was (Ruth 2:7). She was resourceful, both carrying out all the instructions that Naomi gave her regarding Boaz that occurred in Ruth 3 and knowing when to judiciously speak to him about being a guardian-redeemer for her family, which Naomi did not tell her to do. Lastly, bearing a son who she named Obed saved her, demonstrated her love to Naomi (Ruth 4:15), and placed her as one of only five women mentioned in the lineage of Christ in Matthew 1.

If we were creating a brand temple for Ruth, it may look something like this:

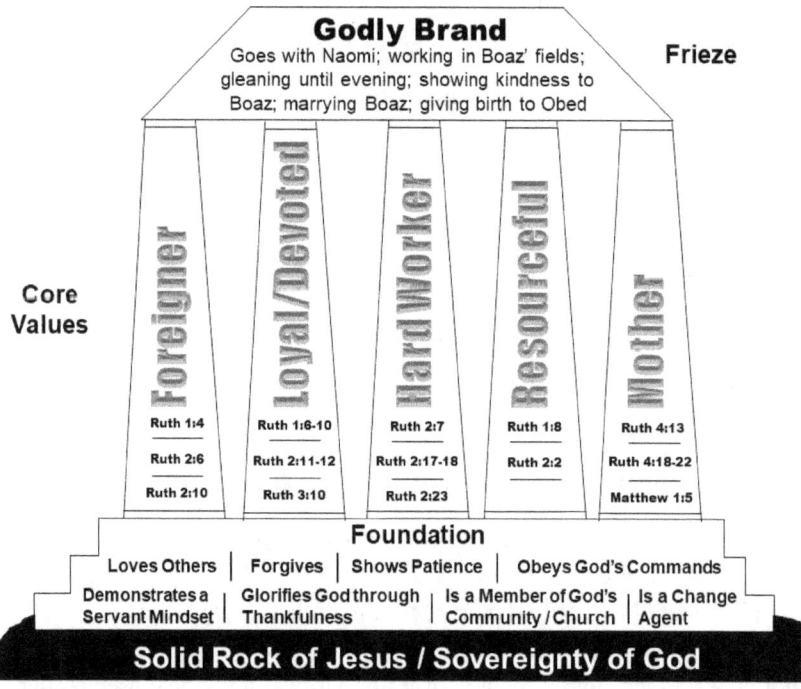

This type of brand audit can be done for every significant biblical figure. Some figures like Moses, David, and Paul who we follow in Scriptures for decades of their lives may have two or three brand temples as they evolve their brand during the course of their lives. We will discuss evolving your brand in chapter 19 on Aspirational Branding.

When looking at Ruth and other significant figures in the Bible, one starts to notice certain patterns in Core Values and behaviors, and that is the subject of the next section.

The Firm Foundation: Eight Brand Attributes for God's Followers

Being completely dependent upon God in your life is an amazing choice to make in one's life. It can take some people years and years to arrive at the decision. For others, it can happen in seconds. That's the beauty of the Holy Spirit working in our lives. Regardless of how, where, and when you make the decision to utterly rely on God to direct your life and make you His instrument on earth. Once you do, there are brand attributes that you should reflect as a natural byproduct of that choice.

To revisit, a brand attribute is an idea that you want people to think when they hear, see or consider your brand. For example, the following concepts may pop into your head when you think of Billy Graham (evangelical), Michael Jordan (competitive), Abraham Lincoln (honest), Oprah Winfrey (trustworthy), and so on. Two things to note here: 1) these attributes are abstract, not concrete descriptions (e.g., Michael Jordan [championship basketball player]) and 2) brand attributes are not behaviors, although your behavior is most certainly affected by your brand attributes.

In *Section 3*, exercises will help you define your individual brand attributes. Here though, the brand attributes pertain to being a God follower. When you hear someone say "Christian" or "God follower," what brand attributes immediately come to mind?

There are eight brand attributes that should be universally applicable to all believers. Stated differently and more absolutely, if you call yourself a Christian, you must reflect these eight attributes. The major figures in the Bible exhibited them in one form or another. This section will explore these eight brand attributes and how you can reflect them in your life.

The eight brand values are 1) loves others, 2) shows patience, 3) demonstrates a servant mindset, 4) obeys God's commands; 5) forgives; 6) glorifies God through thankfulness; 7) is a member of God's community / church; and 8) is an agent of change. These attributes are framed as verbs because they demonstrate who you are by what you do, and that action shapes the perception of others. Each of these attributes should be part of *someone else's* answer when he or she is asked to describe *you*.

Let's say that I join the board of trustees at church and someone who doesn't know me asks someone who does, "hey, who's that Rhodes guy?" Based on how I conduct myself, the person who knows me would likely say something like, "Yeah, he's been going to the church for a few years. He's a marketing guy. He helped rebrand the church a couple years ago. He's got a great servant heart for the Lord." In just four brief sentences, four of the attributes were covered: 3) demonstrates a servant mindset, 4) trusts and obeys God's commands; 7) is a member of God's church; and 8) is an agent of change. I served by doing the re-brand, was obedient in following the Lord's plan, was and is an active member, and made a difference by changing something in God's kingdom. In this case, it was helping with a name and logo change for my church and its satellite. That's how you pragmatically demonstrate these attributes.

To some extent, these eight brand attributes cross-over with each other. For example, a love for others can lead to a willingness to serve. Also, different people will exhibit these attributes in various ways. People may find some of them easier to adopt in their lives than other ones. And, of course, no one but Jesus was able to model all of them all of the time and perfectly. These eight attributes are the foundation upon which to build your Godly brand.

In the next chapter, we start with arguably the most important attribute of the eight: loves others.

Chapter 5

Brand Attribute—Loves Others

"Teacher, which is the greatest commandment in the Law?" Jesus replied:
"'Love the Lord your God with all your heart and with all your soul
and with all your mind.' This is the first and greatest commandment.
And the second is like it: 'Love your neighbor as yourself.'"

—MATTHEW 22:36-38

IT IS TOUGH TO imagine reflecting a Godly brand without feeling and demonstrating love for others, as that is the "second greatest commandment." In Matthew 22, the Sadducees followed by the Pharisees both tried to trap Jesus in intellectual snares with various law-based questions, such as "Teacher, which is the greatest commandment in the Law?" That's in verse 36 of the chapter. Jesus replies with the first and greatest commandment, "Love the Lord your God with all your heart and with all your soul and with all your mind," which comes from Deut 6:5 and Moses' speech to the Israelites before they crossed into the Promised Land. Right on the heels of that comment in verse 39, Jesus adds "And the second is like it: Love your neighbor as yourself," referring to Lev 19:18.

In issuing the call to follow the second greatest commandment, Jesus harkens back to the law. The "Love your neighbor as yourself" reference hits the Pharisees on their own turf: the law. More important, it demonstrates that God's will for how we should live and interact with others goes back to the beginning of the law as handed down by Moses.

As Jesus approached the end of his days on earth, in intimate privacy of the Last Supper, He extended the "Love your neighbor as yourself" command to "As I have loved you, so you must love one another." In John 14:34-35, Jesus issues a new command: "A new command I give you: Love one another. As I have loved you, so you must love one another. By this everyone will know that you are my disciples, if you love one another." Jesus understood how challenging His departure from this world would be on the disciples. He knew that they would need a full measure of love and support from each other to carry out the Father's will for their lives. Two key phrases from these verses jump out:

- "As I have loved you"—Jesus sets the standard by which the disciples should love each other, and that standard is Himself. What is that standard? From John 10:11: "I am the good shepherd. The good shepherd lays down his life for the sheep." And from John 15:13: "Greater love has no one than this: to lay down one's life for one's friends." Jesus laid down His life for His disciples and everyone else on the Cross. That level of sacrifice of your life is what Jesus called them and us to do. Pretty high standard, right?

- "By this everyone will know that you are my disciples"—By reflecting a Jesus-level love of one another, the disciples would demonstrate to the world that they are indeed His followers. This short phrase is a direct call-to-action to live a Godly branded life. That includes love of others.

Speaking to the value of love in one's life, the Apostle Paul wrote a mike-drop passage on this issue from 1 Cor 13:1-3: "If I speak in the tongues of men or of angels, but do not have love, I am only a resounding gong or a clanging cymbal. If I have the gift of prophecy and can fathom all mysteries and all knowledge, and if I have a faith that can move mountains, but do not have love, I am nothing. If I give all I possess to the poor and give over my body to hardship that I may boast, but do not have love, I gain nothing."

Paul continues with the definitive explanation of what love is and how it is demonstrated. It's a passage most believers know well: "Love is patient, love is kind. It does not envy, it does not boast, it is not proud. It does not dishonor others, it is not self-seeking, it is not easily angered, it keeps no record of wrongs. Love does not delight in evil but rejoices with the truth. It always protects, always trusts, always hopes, always perseveres. Love never fails."

So, you may be thinking . . . in a chapter that covers the first of the eight brand attributes on loving others, and it has 16 "sub-attributes" (e.g., patient, kind, does not envy), you may be getting worried about *all the things* you'll need to do to live a Godly branded life.

Loving others means demonstrating all these sub-attributes, yes. But being compassionate to others is where it all starts. What's telling about Jesus' parable of the Good Samaritan is not that Jews and Samaritans didn't get along; it's the example of sacrificial help that a total stranger gave to another person who culturally he shouldn't care about. We regularly see stories of people helping strangers in emergency situations in the news. To me, the demonstration of loving came when the Samaritan took ownership of the problem by paying for the wounded man's care with the innkeeper, then—despite having his own personal agenda derailed by taking the time to help a stranger—making the commitment to come back and pay for any additional costs the innkeeper may incur. That compassionate ownership of someone else's problem is rare indeed.

Doing Things for Others With No Expectation of Receiving Anything Back

Whenever I'm on one of the online news aggregators like Yahoo, MSN, or CNN, I frequently see clickbait articles like "7 Keys to a Lasting Relationship." I rarely click on them because I know they'll be missing the most important key: find a partner with whom you can share your faith. One thing that I hope these articles recommend (but likely don't) is to demonstrate sacrificial love for your partner. Anyone who has been in a healthy long-term relationship will—at some point—do something for their partner with no expectation of reciprocation. Small examples include day-to-day chores around the house. My wife hates doing the laundry; she admits it. And for the first 25 years of our marriage until my eldest son got old enough to take it on, I largely did the laundry. Even when my wife did the laundry, she never sorted socks. She loathed trying to match them up. So, that task entirely fell to me.

One key to a lasting relationship is to perform these types of small sacrifices, or moderate ones like taking responsibility or blame for something that wasn't your fault. If a relationship survives that first argument between partners where one blames the other for something that was his or her own fault, and the other accepts that blame as a means to positively move on despite knowing the truth, that relationship just took a very strong step toward lasting a long time. In this case, the other person sacrifices the point of being right for the needs or health of the partner, without the expectation that the blaming partner will say "I'm sorry" or "You're right; I'm wrong." One hopes the blaming partner admits this. But it doesn't always happen.

Scriptures are filled with these types of sacrificial love. Jesus performed them throughout His adult ministry, healing the blind, lame, demon-possessed, leprous or spiritually distraught without any expectation of anything in return. His actions were purely sacrificial love, including the greatest act: dying on the Cross to redeem us.

As Jesus' disciples picked up His ministry, and 72 of them were dispatched by Him to go out into surrounding lands to spread the Gospel (Luke 10), they continued to demonstrate these acts of sacrificial love without any expectation of anything in return.

From the Old Testament, there are three examples of this sacrificial love with no expectation of receiving anything back. First, one of the reasons I just love the story of Ruth is the love that Boaz shows her, because he has heard what she did for his relative Naomi. In Ruth 2:11–12, he goes so far as to bless Ruth, a complete stranger to him, for her actions: "I've been told all about what you have done for your mother-in-law since the death of your husband—how you left your father and mother and your homeland and came to live with a people you did not know before. May the LORD repay you for what you have done. May you be richly rewarded by the LORD, the God of Israel, under whose wings you have come to take refuge." He offers her some food, which she desperately needed, then instructed his harvesters to let her glean the barley fields and not bother her. Finally, that night, he let her take an ephah of barley back to Naomi.

There was nothing that Ruth could give Boaz in return for this kindness. She acknowledged as much, "You have put me at ease by speaking kindly to your servant—though I do not have the standing of one of your servants." (2:13)

In 1 Sam 18, Jonathan, son of King Saul, shows sacrificial love toward David after he killed Goliath. Scriptures tell us in verses 1–4 that "Jonathan became one in spirit with David, and he loved him as himself. From that day Saul kept David with him and did not let him return home to his family. And Jonathan made a covenant with David because he loved him as himself. Jonathan took off the robe he was wearing and gave it to David, along with his tunic, and even his sword, his bow and his belt." You've heard the old expression, "give him the shirt off your back?" Jonathan gave David his robe and tunic, his belt, and his weapons. He gave David everything of significance to his person.

David had saved Israel through the killing of Goliath and his faith in God. But Jonathan's gifts were more than simple gratitude for that act. Jonathan repeatedly helped David throughout their lives together, aiding and abetting the former shepherd when King Saul wanted to kill him (see 1 Sam chapters 19-20). What could David give Jonathan in return? Not much, other than his love. Jonathan's sacrificial love toward David felt like a knowing that David was "God's chosen one" to be the next king, not him. And Jonathan was fine with that.

Arguably the greatest example of doing something for another with no expectation of receiving anything back is the story of Hosea and Gomer. An allegory of God's uncompromising love for His people Israel despite their prostitution with other gods, God calls Hosea to marry the prostitute Gomer. She bears him three children.

Gomer left Hosea, just as the people of Israel left the Lord. She was a "promiscuous woman" and was "loved by another man." The first verse of chapter 3 acknowledges that she is "an adulteress." Nevertheless, God instructed Hosea to "Go, show your love to your wife again . . . Love her as the LORD loves the Israelites." Hosea bought her for fifteen shekels of silver and about a homer and a lethek of barley (3:2). Then he told her, "You are to live with me many days; you must not be a prostitute or be intimate with any man, and I will behave the same way toward you." Despite her abandonment and adultery, Hosea rescued her with only the hope that they could live as a married couple.

The question for you is simple: how can you show acts of sacrificial love to your partner, family members, friends, co-workers, or others, knowing that you will not receive anything in return?

If You Have a Hard Time Loving Others

Let's face it, some people don't like being around other people. They find people trying at best and—at worst—untrustworthy, manipulative, or simply not worth their time. If you're a person who really doesn't like other people for whatever reason, I will humbly submit to you that you pray for openness to the will of God to change your heart in this area. We are not meant to be loners in the faith. We are meant to share our faith with others, thereby enabling the Holy Spirit to have the opportunity to multiply our faithful interactions.

Think about the parable of the bags of gold found in Matthew 25:14–30. Jesus tells of a master who gives three servants varying amounts of gold. To one, he gave five bags. To the second, he gave two bags. To the third, he gave one bag. The first two servants doubled their money upon the master's return. The third hid his money for fear of losing it and the master's reaction. When learning that the lazy servant had not done anything with the opportunity afforded him, the master's response is telling: "So you knew that I harvest where I have not sown and gather where I have not scattered seed?" The master's expectation is that his servants do something with the blessings that he gave them. The first two fulfilled this promise. The third did not and was thrown out into the darkness.

If you do not like people for whatever reason, understand that God harvests where He has not sown and gathers where He has not scattered seed, meaning that—by minimizing how much you interact with others—you minimize your part in carrying out His perfect plan through your life. Because God's work will advance with or without you, by not serving Him, you are the one who will be diminished. My humble advice is to find something small, like a prayer group or leading coffee break, and get involved in a ministry somewhere. Begin the process of interacting with people, and God will bless you for it. Guaranteed!

Chapter 6

Brand Attribute—Shows Patience

> Be still before the Lord and wait patiently for him; do not fret when people succeed in their ways, when they carry out their wicked schemes.
>
> —PS 37:7

LET'S BE HONEST. WHEN you saw the cover of this book and you thought about which eight attributes make up your Godly brand, the idea of *showing patience* didn't come to mind. Loving others, forgiving others, or being thankful . . . those attributes are more obvious. But showing patience? Yet, as you will read in this chapter, the Scriptures are filled, and I mean filled, with God followers having to be patient for God's will and plan to be fulfilled.

So that we're all on the same page, the definition of patience from the dictionary is "the capacity to accept or tolerate delay, trouble, or suffering without getting angry or upset." We're going to look at three dimensions of being patient: 1) patience with others, 2) patience with yourself and your interactions in the world, and 3) patience with God and His plans. Interestingly, a person can be extremely patient with others, yet have no patience with him- or herself, or vice-versa.

Jesus showed profound patience through His human life. In fact, next to His fathomless love for us, perhaps His constant patience was the next most amazing attribute that He demonstrated during His ministry on earth. Remember, He was God incarnate, meaning He knew all things, including how sinful people were and how slow to understand His followers would be.

Dealing with us humans is no small matter. We are inferior to Him in every way, including our mental abilities or lack thereof. He had to impart His mission on earth as well as the wondrous concepts of heaven and eternal life to people who lived 2,000 years ago. For this reason, He resorted to parables among other things to attempt to simplify these things.

If you've been a churchgoer, you have undoubtedly heard the concept of Jesus speaking to humans equated with humans speaking to animals. The most common analogy is the farmer trying to talk the goose into coming into his barn on a bitterly cold night, and the goose refusing to do so. The farmer thinks to himself, "if only I were a goose, I could lead this goose to safety."

Throughout the Scriptures, there are examples where Jesus expresses his unending patience, and some of them are very telling. In John 14, Jesus comforts His disciples, telling them: "Do not let your hearts be troubled. You believe in God; believe also in me. My Father's house has many rooms; if that were not so, would I have told you that I am going there to prepare a place for you? And if I go and prepare a place for you, I will come back and take you to be with me that you also may be where I am. You know the way to the place where I am going."

To which, Thomas says "Lord, we don't know where you are going, so how can we know the way?" This comment sets up one of the most recognized verses in the Bible, when Jesus answers: "I am the way and the truth and the life. No one comes to the Father except through me. If you really know me, you will know my Father as well. From now on, you do know him and have seen him."

Now, here comes the sad part. Philip still responds, "Lord, show us the Father and that will be enough for us." After everything, Philip asks for more proof of Jesus' relationship with His Father and His power.

If this scene played out like a mafia movie, the head of the crime family would slap the questioning lieutenant across the side of the head, then admonish him for asking such a dumb question. I dare say, many of us may snap back with a "Seriously?!" Or, we may just walk away, dumbfounded. But, this is Jesus. He simply asks Philip, empathetically: "Don't you know me, Philip, even after I have been among you such a long time?"

Reading this passage, it feels as though Jesus is genuinely hurt by His friend's question. Despite this hurt, Jesus continues, because he must ensure that all the disciples understand: "Anyone who has seen me has seen the Father. How can you say, 'Show us the Father'? Don't you believe that I am in the Father, and that the Father is in me? The words I say to you I do not speak on my own authority. Rather, it is the Father, living in me, who is doing his work."

I often wonder how the disciples could see everything that they did—all the miracles, the healings, the walking on water, the controlling of the weather—and still ask questions like this. It just seems as though the disciples weren't paying attention. Or, as fishermen and the like, perhaps they simply could not comprehend Jesus' awesome power and relationship to the Father.

Jesus pushes past His disappointment and turns it into a teachable moment. It's one thing is to express patience in a moment of disappointment with a friend or loved one. Another is to show it when someone wrongs you, especially harms you physically. Another example of Jesus' patience that boggles the mind comes in the aftermath of His arrest in the Garden of Gethsemane. Jesus was bound and brought before the high priest Annas. From John 18, verses 19–23:

> Meanwhile, the high priest questioned Jesus about his disciples and his teaching.
> "I have spoken openly to the world," Jesus replied. "I always taught in synagogues or at the temple, where all the Jews come together. I said nothing in secret. Why question me? Ask those who heard me. Surely they know what I said."
> When Jesus said this, one of the officials nearby slapped him in the face. "Is this the way you answer the high priest?" he demanded.
> "If I said something wrong," Jesus replied, "testify as to what is wrong. But if I spoke the truth, why did you strike me?"
> Then Annas sent him bound to Caiaphas the high priest.

Here, Jesus attempts to politely explain His ministry to Annas, much like a defendant before a judge who knows he or she is "in the right." Yet, one of the officials slaps Him for a perceived lack of respect for the high priest, insubordination, or just to be cruel, likely all three reasons. Now, Jesus had at His immediate disposal the entirety of the heavenly armies. Frankly, He didn't even need the heavenly hosts. He could have thought about a punishment for that official in an instant, and it would have happened. There are few moments in Jesus' life and ministry that more clearly capture his holiness than this moment where—if we were in His shoes with His power at our beck and call—we would have handled it in a completely different manner.

Jesus did and does have that kind of power. When provoked in a manner that I dare say most of us would have whipped back with blasting the guy across the room, He remained patient and unprovoked. Perhaps, that official struck Jesus to test Him or incite a sinful response. One argument in favor of the official trying to provoke Jesus as his motivation was the fact that immediately after Jesus did not give into a sinful or desperate response, Annas sent him to his son-in-law Caiaphas for further questioning. Annas tested Jesus' resolve and, upon His holy response to physical abuse, sent Him away.

Tolerance / Forbearance with Others

Eph 4:2 tells us to "Be completely humble and gentle; be patient, bearing with one another in love." Unless you're a very special person, tolerance and its close relative forbearance toward others are hard to live out. The use of the term tolerance here refers to being open-minded, accepting, or perhaps lenient with someone or something. Forbearance pertains to showing self-control or restraint. Both terms involve a reaction of patience to a given situation: one describes more of a mental approach (tolerance) whereas the other may be regarded as more physical (forbearance).

The more I read the Bible, the more impressed I am with Moses as a leader. Because he goes through seasons in his life where his Godly brand evolves, and he starts out as a reluctant leader (see Exod 3–4). But he gets stronger as he ages and leads the Israelites while wandering in the desert. In Exod 32, Moses saves them from God's burning anger in the wake of the golden calf worship. In Exod 34, he implores the Lord to continue journeying with the Israelites when He threatens to leave them, due to their stiff-necked behavior. In Num 11, Moses prays to the Lord to stop the fire that He has rained down on the outskirts of the Israelite camp, because of their complaining. In Num 12, Moses' own brother and sister, Aaron and Miriam, rebel against him. When God strikes Miriam with leprosy, Moses pleads with Him not to kill her. In Num 14, the people revolt at the prospect of going into the Promised Land when 10 of the 12 scouts return with bad reports of Canaan. They threaten to stone Moses and Aaron, and the Lord appears at the tent of meeting, ready to unleash His anger. Once again, Moses pleads with Him for mercy. In Num 16, Korah, Dathan, and Abiram challenge Moses' leadership, and Moses falls face down, calling out the Lord to settle the matter, which He does.

Repeatedly, Moses was under siege from the Israelites, and even his closest family. Yet, despite all of the challenges, he remained faithful to God and did not rise up in anger to ask the Lord to strike down his aggressors, which the Lord would have done if Moses had asked.

However, even the most patient person reaches a point where he or she lashes out after years of testing his or her patience. It happened to Moses. And it cost him dearly. In Exod 20, the Israelites reached the Desert of Zin and—because there was no water for the community—"the people gathered in opposition to Moses and Aaron. They quarreled with Moses and said, 'If only we had died when our brothers fell dead before the Lord!'"

Moses and Aaron went to the entrance to the tent of meeting, and the Lord told them what to do: "Take the staff, and you and your brother Aaron gather the assembly together. Speak to that rock before their eyes and it will pour out its water." Note the phrase, "speak to that rock." In verse 10, "[Moses] and Aaron gathered the assembly together in front of the rock and Moses said to them, 'Listen, you rebels, must we bring you water out of this rock?' Then Moses raised his arm and struck the rock twice with his staff. Water gushed out, and the community and their livestock drank."

Because Moses struck the rock and didn't just speak to it, the Lord told him that he would not enter the Promised Land. For me, the telling part of the passage was Moses' name-calling the Israelites "you rebels." Clearly, years of frustration bubbled up at that point, causing Moses to simply lose it.

The Book of Deuteronomy includes long passages of Moses getting decades of frustration, all the wrongs that he patiently internalized, off his chest. Included in his pain was the fact that he would not get to cross the Jordan into the Promised Land, due to his disobedience with striking the rock. He pleaded with the Lord to let him enter Canaan, until the Lord flatly told him: "That is enough. Do not speak to me anymore about this matter." (Deut 3:26)

Moses held the Israelites responsible for his not being able to cross the Jordan, too. In Deut 4:21, he tells his people: "The Lord was angry with me because of you, and he solemnly swore that I would not cross the

Jordan and enter the good land the LORD your God is giving you as your inheritance." After this though, Moses turned to the instruction that he knew his people will need after he was gone. He resumed his leadership role one last time, giving them the greatest commandment: "Love the LORD your God with all your heart and with all your soul and with all your strength." (Deut 6:5)

Moses' greatness is summed up in Deut 34:10: "Since then, no prophet has risen in Israel like Moses, whom the LORD knew face to face, who did all those signs and wonders the LORD sent him to do in Egypt..."

Tolerance / Forbearance with Yourself

Nothing tests your patience like sin. The temptation that comes with our sinful nature is constant and innate within us. Because sin is hardwired into our makeup, we struggle with it every moment of our lives. And that's a lot of pressure.

When considering what that pressure is like, the first analogy that comes to mind is interrogation. At the movies and in books, or sadly in the news, we see and hear how tactics such as waterboarding and torture are used to get a person to comply. Master interrogators know that it's just a matter of time before they break down even the most stalwart subject. Our sinful nature is the ultimate master interrogator. It knows just the right questions to ask; it knows what we care about; it knows who we love and who we don't; and it is acutely aware of every single weakness we have and how to apply pressure to each one to make us eventually break. It will break us down, and it will do so often. Since you can't resist your sinful nature, the questions are how often and how deeply do you let it "break you."

The Apostle Paul struggled with this very issue as he wrote the Book of Romans, from chapter 7:15-20: "I do not understand what I do. For what I want to do I do not do, but what I hate I do. And if I do what I do not want to do, I agree that the law is good. As it is, it is no longer I myself who do it, but it is sin living in me. For I know that good itself does not dwell in me, that is, in my sinful nature. For I have the desire to do what is good, but I cannot carry it out. For I do not do the good I want to do, but the evil I do not want to do—this I keep on doing. Now if I do what I do not want to do, it is no longer I who do it, but it is sin living in me that does it."

If you struggle with specific chronic sinful behavior, please do not let repeated lapses and recurrences of them discourage you to the point where you don't think you are worthy of salvation. There is no expiration date on repentance, except your own death. Have patience with yourself. Recognize and accept that you are a sinful creature. At the same time, also accept that God sent His Son to die on the Cross to remove those sins, if you have faith. Turn over your pain and frustration to the Lord. Find patience and strength through prayer.

Tolerance / Forbearance with God and His Plans

Speaking of the patience of Job, you can't write a chapter about being patient without covering him. In the first chapter of the Book of Job, he learns of the theft of all of his oxen and donkeys by the Sabeans, who executed all but one of his servants. Then, fire from God fell from the heavens and burned up all his sheep and accompanying servants. Then, the Chaldeans raided his lands and stole all his camels, putting his servants to the sword. Lastly, he learned that a mighty wind caused the house where all his sons and daughters were feasting to collapse, killing all of them. In seven short verses, Job literally loses all his earthly possessions and his children. Job 1:22 tells us that "In all this, Job did not sin by charging God with wrongdoing."

In chapter 2, Satan goes "next level" with causing Job trouble and suffering by afflicting him "with painful sores from the soles of his feet to the crown of his head." The pain was so bad that Job took a piece of broken pottery and scraped himself with it as he sat among the ashes. To add yet another insult to injury, in a tremendous show of loving support, Job's wife told him to "Curse God and die!" rather than maintain his integrity with God.

But that wasn't the end of Job's suffering. Three friends joined him as a show of unity in his pain, but, before long, they challenged that very integrity. For more than 35 chapters, the four men go back and forth over the cause of Job's suffering. Job acknowledges that God is against him: "The arrows of the Almighty are in me, my spirit drinks in their poison; God's terrors are marshaled against me." (6:4) Soon though, his friends are against him, questioning what Job must have done to garner God's condemnation. As you can imagine, that kind of "support" becomes hurtful to Job. At one point, he calls them "miserable comforters" in chapter 16:2.

As the friends make their arguments against him, Job makes one defense after another, until he cries out to the Lord for a fair trial of his worthiness. In chapters 31 and 32, Job recounts all the ways that he would present his arguments to the Lord, if He would listen. Job's patience is on full display during these heated discussions. First and foremost, he never curses the Lord, despite the provocation by the three friends that could've easily caused him to do so. Second, although greatly aggrieved by those friends, he doesn't curse them either. He simply endures the verbal and physical suffering. Finally, as the arguments among the four men crescendo, the Lord appears in chapter 38. His first statement is "Who is this that obscures my plans with words without knowledge?" Indeed, how could Job understand the Lord's all-powerful plans? And in his humble response to that question in 42:3, Job admits "Surely I spoke of things I did not understand, things too wonderful for me to know." Then three verses later, he humbles himself before the Lord: "Therefore I despise myself and repent in dust and ashes."

Job's reward for patiently speaking the truth about God? From 42:12, "The LORD blessed the latter part of Job's life more than the former part." Then 42:16–17, "Job lived a hundred and forty years; he saw his children and their children to the fourth generation. And so Job died, an old man and full of years."

In light of the story of Job, when have you questioned what God was doing in your life? How did you respond? Reflecting on that time, how might you respond today?

Chapter 7

Brand Attribute—Demonstrates a Servant Mindset

> Each of you should use whatever gift you have received to serve others, as faithful stewards of God's grace in its various forms.
>
> —1 PET 4:10

DEMONSTRATING A SERVANT MINDSET may be the most difficult of the eight attributes simply because many of us are conditioned to excel, be a leader, win, and generally get ahead in a manner that would seem to preclude being a servant. That me-focused approach to life affects us all. Most of us generally do not humble ourselves before God and others, but rather think about how we'll be praised (or at least recognized) for what we do. Most of us certainly do not approach life with a thought of how we can serve others *ahead* of ourselves.

It's easy to speak in broad brush strokes on this issue because we are all sinners and inherently self-centered. Even the most giving individuals who work in social service or a godly ministry and spend their lives helping others will have bouts with sin and selfishness. No one is perfect. On the other end of the spectrum, business or government leaders who have attained status may read this passage and wonder, "Servant? In my position, how exactly does that work?" It can be difficult to reconcile the demands of leadership, constantly making decisions that affect people, dealing with the demands on your time, or coping with people who constantly want things from you (especially profitability). There are Godly leaders who humbly offer a path to find the right balance. Here's an example.

Chris Wing is CEO of SCAN, a Southern California-based not-for-profit organization committed to keeping seniors healthy and independent. If you read his bio on the scanhealthplan.com website, you'll see that he "works directly with SCAN's board of directors, leadership team and employees to develop innovative ways to advance the company's mission on an individual and community level. This includes being a leading voice on the national stage as he advocates on behalf of seniors, ensuring their needs are heard as America's healthcare landscape continues to evolve."

What you'll also see if you keep reading is "He is a founding board member of Resplendent Hope, a faith-based organization that is committed to bringing layperson trauma counseling training to third-world countries. For years, he served as the chair of Africa New Day, a faith-based organization committed to transforming lives in the Democratic Republic of Congo through leadership development, education and spiritual development."

I worked with Chris for two years on Africa New Day (AND), helping the organization with its branding, marketing and development. What always impressed me about Chris as I watched him preside over the AND board of directors was the selflessness with which he was open to the ideas of others (even when he was not in alignment with them); the focus on doing the Lord's work, not his own agenda; and the general humility that he brought to his role. Chris runs a multi-million-dollar business with hundreds of employees, and he regularly interacts with local, state, and federal government contacts to enact his company's healthcare agenda. He is an important businessman. Yet, he's the type of leader who will apologize to you if he's running a few minutes late to a teleconference.

You'd never know it from his involvement with AND, where his focus is on helping men, women and children in the Democratic Republic of Congo half a world away. His ties to the country and the cause of bringing the love of Christ to that desperate part of the world are his wife Aimee, whose family served as missionaries in the region, and his relationship with the organization's founders, Camille and Esther Ntoto. But the reason that he was so effective as AND's chair is that he had and continues to have a heart for people and serving them. It goes beyond simply caring about people. It's faith in action. He leads efforts to help others. And because God is the center of his life, he does so in humility.

Chris represents a model of the servant mindset in executive leadership in business. But there was no greater model for this mindset than Jesus. The Apostle Paul highlights Christ's humility and servitude in Phil 2:1-8 when he writes, "he [Jesus] made himself nothing by taking the very nature of a servant."

In John 13, Jesus—the all-powerful Son of God—humbled himself as a servant to His disciples through the washing their feet. He did this act to demonstrate the selflessness and servant mindset that they would need to advance His ministry on earth (versus 12-17):

> When he had finished washing their feet, he put on his clothes and returned to his place. "Do you understand what I have done for you?" he asked them. "You call me 'Teacher' and 'Lord,' and rightly so, for that is what I am. Now that I, your Lord and Teacher, have washed your feet, you also should wash one another's feet. I have set you an example that you should do as I have done for you. Very truly I tell you, no servant is greater than his master, nor is a messenger greater than the one who sent him. Now that you know these things, you will be blessed if you do them."

Jesus set an example of how the disciples should act once He was no longer with them. And they were going to need that example because guiding the formation of the early church would require compromise, sacrifice, and tolerance, which are all aspects of adopting a servant mindset. Just think about the tectonic-plate shifts of God opening the church body to the Gentiles and commissioning the former persecutor Paul as an apostle to them. Jesus knew that the disciples needed this guidance toward servitude from His interactions with them.

In Mark 10:35-44, we see James and John, the sons of Zebedee, ask Jesus to have the places of honor next to Him in His glorious kingdom, and—more important—the indignant response from the other 10 disciples to this request.

The other 10 were upset, and not because James and John were not reflecting the proper humility that was fit for a disciple of Jesus. No, the other 10 were upset over the notion of deservedness for the honor, as if to say "Why do they think they should be seated next to Jesus? Who do they think they are?" I dare say, given the same situation, virtually all of us would react the same way. Our tendency as sinners in such situations is to think about our place, fairness for ourselves, and our deservedness for things. But that's not the way Jesus wants us to think and feel. His response:

> Jesus called them together and said, "You know that those who are regarded as rulers of the Gentiles lord it over them, and their high officials exercise authority over them. Not so with you. Instead, whoever wants to become great among you must be your servant, and whoever wants to be first must be slave of all. For even the Son of Man did not come to be served, but to serve, and to give his life as a ransom for many."

Now, here's the tough part. Not only are we called to be servants of God and for others, but we are instructed to amplify or multiply the effect of that servitude to advance God's kingdom, using the spiritual gifts that He has given us. Here again, Jesus' parable of the bags of gold informs us how—as good and faithful servants—we are to be faithful to God and multiply what He has entrusted to us.

Perhaps the greatest example of the type of servant mindset that God wants us to demonstrate comes from Mary, the mother of Jesus. When told by the angel Gabriel that she would conceive the "Son of the Most High," news that threatened to upend her engagement to Joseph and standing in the Jewish community, she replied "I am the Lord's servant. May your word to me be fulfilled." (Luke 1:38) She acknowledged and accepted her role of service to the Lord. In fact, a few verses later, she celebrated her blessing with a song that begins, "My soul glorifies the Lord and my spirit rejoices in God my Savior, for he has been mindful of the humble state of his servant." How many of us would respond with such fervent thanks to God if an angel told us that everything that we planned for our lives would change?

Living a life of humility

Remember the Mac Davis song from the early 80s: *It's Hard to Be Humble*? The refrain goes something like this:

> Oh Lord it's hard to be humble
> When you're perfect in every way
> I can't wait to look in the mirror
> Cause I get better looking each day
> To know me is to love me
> I must be a hell of a man

> Oh Lord It's hard to be humble,
> But I'm doing the best that I can

It's a fun song. Sadly though, it captures the sentiment that many people across the world feel about themselves. "When you're perfect in every way" may get switched with any number of alternatives, including "When you're as important as I am," "When you're as successful as I am," "When you're as busy as I am," or "When you're as great as I am." That last one was Muhammad Ali's famous quote. But each of us can use one or more of these excuses to avoid living a life of humility.

Problem is, Jesus was quite clear on this topic. From John 15:5, "I am the vine; you are the branches. If you remain in me and I in you, you will bear much fruit; apart from me you can do nothing." Living a life of humility begins with acknowledging the undeniable truth that you literally cannot accomplish anything without the divine providence of God. Everything comes from God. Everything.

In Old Testament times, a conquering king would enter the city on a warhorse, leading a parade. He rode "above the people" due to the height on the horse, and the procession was meant to bring him glory. In contrast, riding a donkey in a celebratory parade sent an entirely different message: one of humility. On a donkey, a king rides at the level of the people, making easy eye contact with them.

In Jesus' case, He entered Jerusalem among the people, not elevated above them like a conqueror. He was sending a very clear message about the type of king that He was, which was very important given the crowd's chanting in John 12: "Blessed is the king of Israel!" The people wanted a king who would conquer the oppressive Romans and lead their nation to greatness. Make no mistake, Jesus could have given them that outcome. But that wasn't why He was there.

Jesus lived the ultimate life of humility, because He had the power to literally do anything in the world He wanted and didn't use it, despite being tempted to do so many times. Given our "get even" culture today, I wonder how many of us would refrain from exacting payback on the various political and religious leaders, soldiers, and onlookers with whom he came in contact on his way to the Cross.

Serving Others

Ever notice how often people in the Old Testament refer to themselves as a servant? Take Abraham, for example, in Gen 18 when the three visitors appear by his tent. He bowed low to the ground and said, "If I have found favor in your eyes, my lord, do not pass your servant by." Once more in the chapter, Abraham refers to himself as a servant to the three visitors. At the beginning of the next chapter, when the two angels arrived at the gateway to Sodom, Lot bowed down with his face to the ground and said, "My lords, please turn aside to your servant's house. You can wash your feet and spend the night and then go on your way early in the morning."

There are hundreds of servant references throughout Scriptures, including more than 40 times for Moses and more than 50 times for David. Others are included, too: Abraham (Gen 26:24), Jacob (Gen 32:4), Joshua (Josh 24:29), Ruth (Ruth 3:9), Hannah (1 Sam 1:11), Samuel (1 Sam 3:9), Jesse (1 Sam 17:58), Isaiah (Isa 20:3), Daniel (Dan 9:17), and so forth. In these cases, these figures are servants of other people and/or servants of God.

In the Old Testament, the Hebrew word for servant is `ebed, which has the dual connotations of action (i.e., doing the work of being a servant) and obedience. For all the above-mentioned names, they performed acts of work on behalf of others, often in important leadership roles, and were obedient to their people, king, and/or God. Every prophet sent by God served these roles, calling Israel and its people to repentance and a re-commitment to their covenant with God. In fact, the Book of Isaiah includes four songs that describe the accomplishments and suffering of servants sent by God (42:1–7; 49:1–6; 50:4–11; 52:13—53:12).

The most prominent figures in the Bible including Christ—adopted and demonstrated a servant mindset for the benefit of others and did so in service to God, fulfilling His plan in this world. The natural question for us is: in following their earthly example, what have you done as a follower of God in service to others? And, do you constantly lead your life looking through the lens of how you can help others?

There can be a lot of motivations as to why someone may serve another: fear, obligation, lack of freedom, self-glorification, a hope for reciprocation, and so on. But the kind of service that Jesus demonstrated, and the kind we are called to perform is based on obedience, harkening back to `ebed.

In Rom 12, the Apostle Paul talks about this kind of humble service and how we are to use them for the sake of our church body:

> Do not think of yourself more highly than you ought, but rather think of yourself with sober judgment, in accordance with the faith God has distributed to each of you.
> We have different gifts, according to the grace given to each of us. If your gift is prophesying, then prophesy in accordance with your faith; if it is serving, then serve; if it is teaching, then teach; if it is to encourage, then give encouragement; if it is giving, then give generously; if it is to lead, do it diligently; if it is to show mercy, do it cheerfully.

How are you serving others in God's name? If you are unclear on your answer or it's been a long time since you've been involved in a kingdom-building ministry, take this moment to consider where and how you can get involved in serving others. If you're pressed for time right now in your life, choose something small like greeting during a Sunday morning service, handling refreshments in between services, visiting someone who is alone and could use your support, providing food to a person or family that needs it, or simply finding someone you can pray for.

Serving Your Community

God very explicitly tells us to serve the communities in which we live, work, and play, and gives us an extreme example in Scriptures to make the point. In 2 Kgs 24, we read how "the Lord sent Babylonian, Aramean, Moabite and Ammonite raiders against [Jehoiakim] to destroy Judah, in accordance with the word of the Lord proclaimed by his servants the prophets." Nebuchadnezzar, king of Babylon, invaded the land and installed Jehoiakim as his vassal for three years until he died. Verses 8–17 tell the story of the brief reign of Jehoiachin, who followed him and did evil in the eyes of the Lord.

The officers of Nebuchadnezzar advanced on Jerusalem and laid siege to it, and the king himself came up to the city while they were besieging it. Jehoiachin had no choice but to surrender, and Nebuchadnezzar "carried all Jerusalem into exile: all the officers and fighting men, and all the skilled workers and artisans—a total of ten thousand. Only the poorest people of the land were left."

As verses 3–4 tells us, "Surely these things happened to Judah according to the Lord's command, in order to remove them from his presence because of the sins of Manasseh and all he had done, including the shedding of innocent blood. For he had filled Jerusalem with innocent blood, and the Lord was not willing to forgive."

The Israelites had been exiled to Babylon. The prophet Jeremiah writes to the "surviving elders among the exiles and to the priests, the prophets and all the other people Nebuchadnezzar had carried into exile from Jerusalem to Babylon." That letter is found in Jer 29. In the letter, the prophet tells the people to settle down and make Babylon their home, issuing a command from God that begins in verse 5:

> "Build houses and settle down; plant gardens and eat what they produce. Marry and have sons and daughters; find wives for your sons and give your daughters in marriage, so that they too may have sons and daughters. Increase in number there; do not decrease. Also, seek the peace and prosperity of the city to which I have carried you into exile. Pray to the Lord for it, because if it prospers, you too will prosper."

In short, Jeremiah tells them to prayerfully seek the wellbeing of the city they are now in and love their neighbors, despite it being a foreign city. Why would God instruct them to be this way? One answer is for their own peace. However, God had bigger plans for His people. Verses 10–12 and 14b include a promise from Him to bring back His people to Jerusalem:

> This is what the Lord says: "When seventy years are completed for Babylon, I will come to you and fulfill my good promise to bring you back to this place. For I know the plans I have for you," declares the Lord, "plans to prosper you and not to harm you, plans to give you hope and a future. . . . I will gather you from all the nations and places where I have banished you," declares the Lord, "and will bring you back to the place from which I carried you into exile."

By promising the exiles a future back in Jerusalem, God gave them hope and removed their fear. By instructing them to be good neighbors and help their city prosper, God's plan ultimately would accomplish two important things: 1) enable His people to be a shining example of His love to a foreign people, thereby glorifying His name; and 2) set the stage for a latter king (Cyrus) to show mercy to Jerusalem and let the exiles return.

What does all of this mean to us today? Scriptures tell us in Jesus' own words, "You have heard that it was said, 'Love your neighbor and hate your enemy.' But I tell you, love your enemies and pray for those who persecute you, that you may be children of your Father in heaven." (Matthew 5:43-45a) We are to serve our communities, even when they are hostile toward us. Like the exiled Israelites in Babylon in 600 BC, we can reflect God's perfect love to our neighbors, pray for them, and serve them. What is one act of kindness that you can bring to someone or some group of people in your community that reinforces your Godly brand and glorifies Him?

Chapter 8

Brand Attribute—Demonstrates Trust and Obedience in God

> Trust in the LORD with all your heart and lean not on your own understanding; in all your ways submit to him, and he will make your paths straight.
>
> —PROV 3:5–6

WHEN WRITING THIS BOOK, I thought and prayed about separating trusting God and obeying Him into two separate chapters. They're both critically important to one's faith walk and deserving of separate chapters. But the Lord led me to the simple truth that the two are inextricably linked. If you trust God, you obey Him as much as possible. If you obey God, it's because you trust in His outcomes for your life.

When thinking about this brand attribute, it's pretty obvious; everyone should trust and obey, right? Yet, trusting and obeying God proves to be a stumbling block for everyone, going all the way back to the forefathers like Abraham, Isaac, Jacob, David and so on.

In Gen 15, when Abram tells God, "You have given me no children; so a servant in my household will be my heir," His response was "This man will not be your heir, but a son who is your own flesh and blood will be your heir." Verse 6 tells us: Abram believed the LORD, and he credited

Brand Attribute—Demonstrates Trust and Obedience in God

it to him as righteousness. The rest of chapter 15 is God making a sacred covenant with Abram to codify His holy promise.

Yet, at the start of the very next chapter, Abram agrees to his wife Sarai's plan to sleep with Hagar, her Egyptian slave, because they'd been waiting about 10 years since God made that promise for offspring. On one hand, Abram and Sarai actions are understandable. Most of us would be loathed to wait 10 months to conceive a child after such a promise, let alone 10 years. On the other hand, their actions reflect a fundamental lack of trust and obedience to God's promise.

Abram, later Abraham, makes up for it though with his willingness to sacrifice of his only son Isaac. In Gen 22, Abraham was instructed by God to go to a mountain that He leads him to. There, Abraham built an altar and arranged wood on it, knowing what God has asked him to do. Then, he bound his own son and laid him on the altar. Even though Abraham's faith was credited to him as righteousness by God, and people of faith for thousands of years have rightfully recognized Abraham's belief that God had the power to bring Isaac back to life, think about how truly difficult this action must've been for him. Yet, he trusted that "God himself will provide the lamb for the burnt offering." And that's the point where we should focus. It's easy to look at the examples of failure and say, "See there, that forefather should've trusted in God to deliver." Scriptures are replete with those missteps. But the Bible is filled with deep, sometimes astounding examples of trust in God.

And I'm not talking about blind faith and trust where a person refuses to accept the reality of a situation and naively, presumptively, or in a state of denial believes that the Lord simply will take care of it or God will provide. Depending on the situation, that can actually be putting the Lord to the test, which we are instructed not to do by Christ Himself.

In Luke 1, Gabriel tells Zechariah that Elizabeth "will bear you a son, and you are to call him John." His response, "How can I be sure of this? I am an old man and my wife is well along in years." Trying to give Zechariah the benefit of the doubt that he was speaking to an angel, and that was likely a completely new experience to him, he nonetheless made a mess of the situation. He was a learned, mature man of the law. Yet, he didn't grasp what was happening. His response was mired in self-focus, disbelief, and doubt. That response cost him the ability to speak for 8–9 months until his son was born.

The Apostle Paul introduces a concept of being a "living sacrifice" when talking about obedience, one that includes personal and physical sacrifice, even suffering. In Rom 12:1-2, the Apostle Paul encourages us "to offer your bodies as a living sacrifice, holy and pleasing to God—this is your true and proper worship."

Let's be clear that no service or amount of good works will earn our way into heaven. As it says in Rom 3:20, "Therefore no one will be declared righteous in God's sight by the works of the law; rather, through the law we become conscious of our sin." Restated, following the law implicitly—as some of the Jewish leaders in Jesus' day claimed to do—will not get it done. The law only shows us how far we're off. Then, in verses 22b-23 of the same chapter, "There is no difference between Jew and Gentile, for all have sinned and fall short of the glory of God." By ourselves, we can't do anything ourselves to earn God's grace, righteousness, or justification. Period.

Fortunately for us, there is great news is verse 24: "all are justified freely by his grace through the redemption that came by Christ Jesus." How? "This righteousness is given through faith in Jesus Christ to all who believe (verse 22a)." Note the need to believe. Also note, the word "freely," which means you don't need to try to earn salvation. You receive it through God's boundless grace.

If we can't earn salvation, what should we do? You've been given literally the greatest gift in your life. How should you respond? Fulfill our reasonable service to God by offering our bodies as a living sacrifice. That's what we can humbly do for God, not as a means of salvation, but rather a reflection of His grace in our lives. What exactly does being a living sacrifice mean?

It's safe to say that—while there have been many prophets and martyrs for God over the millennia—few of them have suffered physically the way Paul did. In 2 Corinthians, Paul writes to the church in Corinth that—in his absence—has embraced "super apostles" who are not only leading the followers there astray with false teachings, but also downtalking Paul and his apostleship. The first nine chapters of the book are a set-up to chapters 10-12 where Paul presents his argument against these naysayers, recounting his sufferings for Christ's sake (11: 23-27):

> I have worked much harder [than the super apostles], been in prison more frequently, been flogged more severely, and been exposed to death again and again. Five times I received from the Jews the forty lashes minus one. Three times I was beaten with rods, once I was pelted with stones, three times I was shipwrecked, I spent a night and a day in the open sea, I have been

constantly on the move. I have been in danger from rivers, in danger from bandits, in danger from my fellow Jews, in danger from Gentiles; in danger in the city, in danger in the country, in danger at sea; and in danger from false believers. I have labored and toiled and have often gone without sleep; I have known hunger and thirst and have often gone without food; I have been cold and naked.

Let's take inventory: 5 lashings, 3 rod beatings, 1 stoning, 3 times shipwrecked, 1 time adrift overnight in the open sea, constantly chased and endangered by the Jews, and a host of times being hungry, thirsty, sleep-deprived, cold, and naked. Let's remember that Paul's stoning in Acts 14 was so bad that the attackers "dragged him outside the city, thinking he was dead" (verse 19). And, of course, Paul himself was eventually martyred in Rome at the hands of Emperor Nero.

Biblical scholars who have traced Paul's three missionary trips and his final journey to Rome have determined that he traveled more than 10,000 miles during those trips. In the heat, the cold, the wind, the rain ... traveling on foot in those days took an extreme toll on the body. If all Paul did was the traveling, it'd be a tremendous physical sacrifice. Add the beatings that he took, and Paul truly offered all of his body for Christ.

In Isa 20, to reinforce a prophecy, God told the prophet Isaiah to "take off the sackcloth from your body and the sandals from your feet" to demonstrate exactly how the king of Assyria would lead away the Egyptian captives and Cush exiles: stripped and barefoot. This was a clear indication of the shame that Egypt would experience, and Isaiah carried on his life *for three years* this way.

God may not call us to suffer in the ways of Paul, Isaiah, or others in the Scriptures, but—for His sake—we will endure our own pain. It's an unfortunate and inevitable aspect of living in a fallen world. There are places in the world today where God followers are martyred for their faith. Again, we may not be asked to make that kind of physical sacrifice. But here's the real question: *would you be willing to do so, if God asked?*

What physical offering of our bodies are we willing to make for God? Start with the most obvious one: getting up on Sunday morning to go to church. Sleep is important, I know. You may be a night owl and like to stay up late on Saturday night. But consider making that small sacrifice.

Another bodily sacrifice may be volunteerism at church or other ministry. I am currently a teaching leader (TL) for Bible Study Fellowship

(BSF), and our weekly leadership meetings are 5:00am on Friday mornings. For 30 weeks each year, I get up and go to that 5:00am meeting. I'm an early riser, but by mid-afternoon on Friday, I'm hanging. This early rising is a blessing compared to the sacrifice that Christians around the world who are persecuted live with every day. But it is one small start to "offering your body" for Christ.

Lots of churches or religious schools have fundraisers that involve walking, jogging or running. Every church I've ever attended has some sort of "fix up a home in a low-income neighborhood" volunteer program. We're all busy people, prone to getting tired after long days of work or other errands. Any giving of your time in these circumstances can be an offering of your body for God.

In church stewardship and giving of tithes or offering, one thing that I've heard pastors say to encourage people to give is to remind them that "your stuff is not your stuff." It's a healthy reminder that everything given to us is from God, and we should cheerfully give back to Him some of the blessings that He has bestowed on us. It's a good message. Well, an extension of that mindset is "your life is not your life."

When you view your life through the prism of "it's all for God," it can be liberating. It's demonstrating a trust and reliance in Him that He will care for us or that His plan will suffice.

Chapter 9

Brand Attribute—Forgives

> But if you do not forgive others their sins, your
> Father will not forgive your sins.
>
> —MATTHEW 6:15

SHOWING FORGIVENESS IS ONE of the most important and easiest to understand of the eight attributes. But let's face it, forgiving is perhaps the hardest one to do. In fact, the worse a transgression committed against you is, the harder it is to forgive. Look no further than the inherent contradiction between these two adages: "You need to forgive and forget" and "Forgive, but never forget." Which is it? It's easier to forgive a sibling who thwacks you in the head while horsing around than it is a boss who passes you up for that promotion that you deserve, a significant other who you discover has been cheating on you, or a drunk driver who kills your child. Yet, in all circumstances, God calls us to forgive.

But some circumstances are brutally hard to forgive. Imagine you're a father of five, and your wife of 20-plus years is driving three of your children around the city on errands. During their travels, as they head down a 4-lane road, a sedan approaches from the opposite direction. Swerving around a car, the sedan loses control, crosses the center line, and plows head-on into your family's car at 78 miles per hour. Your three children are injured, but none with life-threatening injuries. But your wife isn't as fortunate. She's rushed to the hospital and dies the next day.

As details of the crash emerge, you come to discover that the other driver, who died in the crash, had "a substantial amount of methamphetamine" in her system and was cradling a dog on her lap (also killed in the accident) at the time of impact. The randomness of it all is sobering. Now, you're a widower and single father of five kids, including two who are under 10 years old. In the days that follow, local TV reporters conduct live remotes from the scene of the accident, retelling the facts of the crash over and over again, showing burn marks on the asphalt and debris lying on the side of the road. Because you're a prominent figure in your city, this coverage lasts far longer than usual. How would you feel toward the other driver who was responsible for the death of your wife, a pillar in the community? How would you feel toward God?

That's the story of NBA (National Basketball Association) coach Monty Williams, his late wife Ingrid Williams, and their kids. At the time of the accident in February 2016, Williams was an assistant coach with the Oklahoma City Thunder. At Ingrid's memorial service and in the time since her death, Williams has been nothing short of a paragon of strength and faith. His eulogy for the woman he loved reflects his deep, profound faithfulness. In it, he quotes Ps 133:1, Ps 73:1, and 1 John 4:16 within the first 65 seconds of his remarks. He follows those verses with, "We can't lose sight of the fact that God loves us." He proclaims the life-saving grace of Christ: "He loved me so much that He sent His Son to die for my sins." Then, he quoted Rom 8:28, saying "All of this will work out. As hard as this is for me and my family and for you, this will work out." He related the story of what appeared to be the end of his basketball-playing career at the age of 18 when he had a heart ailment, and how his then-girlfriend Ingrid told him that "God will heal your heart." And He did. Williams went on to play in the NBA. He repeatedly said, "This will work out." He reinforced our dependency on God, "What we need is the Lord."

Then, Williams did what I dare say few of us could do. He implored those watching to pray not just for his family but for the family of the driver of the sedan. "We hold no ill will toward the [other driver's] family," he boldly stated. "God loves us. God is love. . . . What Christ did on the Cross is important. Let's keep what's important at the forefront." His 7-minute eulogy is as powerful a witness for the Lord as you'll ever see, and I encourage you to Google "Monty Williams eulogy," and watch it.

News of the Williams family tragedy was covered on national news networks, including ESPN where I first saw his remarks. I remember being struck by Williams' strength and ability to forgive, even in that time so close to his wife's death.

There is no mistaking that Monty Williams is a man of God. And God has honored him for his faith. At the 2017 NBA Awards, Williams was presented with the inaugural Sager Strong Award, after retiring to take care of his family. In the video montage that accompanied William's acceptance of the award, NBA superstar coaches (Gregg Popavich, Doc Rivers, Billy Donovan) and players (Kevin Durant, Tim Duncan) commented on his faith. As he donned the brightly colored jacket for the award, he jumped right into glorifying God, recognizing Him in front of the entire NBA family.

Williams is now remarried. And he got back to coaching in March 2019. As he took the head-coaching reigns of the Phoenix Suns team, he again spoke of his faith helping him to move forward after the tragedy: "The Lord has given me a level of strength that I didn't have and still don't. Lamentations 3:22–23 says, 'His mercies are new every morning. Great is his faithfulness.' He's been faithful to me putting good people around me, having an unbelievable support system." Williams is a God-given model of forgiveness for all of us to follow. And he's not alone.

In my Bible Study Fellowship (BSF) class, cycling is a big thing. Easily 10 or so of our 35 group leaders are avid cyclists. In March 2019, one of them, Tom Sovilla was biking down Pacific Coast Highway one afternoon when he was struck from behind by a truck. People who saw the accident said the driver was looking down at his phone. Frankly, Tom is blessed to be alive. If I recounted his lengthy list of injuries, you'd wonder aloud how he lived, too. But God had plans for him. How do I know that? The two cyclists behind him when the accident occurred were doctors, who treated him on the scene.

God took Tom under His merciful wing, enabling him to slowly but surely recover. During his months in the hospital, Tom's faith was evident. When Tom was sufficiently recovered, the hospital approached him about doing news interviews about the incident and his forgiving the driver who hit him. He agreed.

In the interviews, Tom's story was told, and it included his faith and—as important—forgiveness of the driver who almost killed him. Not only did Tom forgive him, but he befriended him. If you Google "Tom Sovilla bike accident," you'll see a lengthy list of print, online, and local and national broadcast news stories that feature his testimony. Two completely unrelated people I know both saw coverage of Tom's story and commented on how strong an example of God he was. Out of Tom's pain and suffering, God's work was done. In a fallen world, he showed how one can turn from thoughts of entitlement, self-pity, anger and bitterness, or even revenge, and reflect the love of God, who has empowered Tom to get back on his bike and ride about 18 months after his accident. Simply awesome.

How would you handle the death of a spouse like Monty Williams or the near-fatal accident of Tom Sovilla? Would you respond with same depth of faith that both of them did?

In Scriptures, two stories of forgiveness are my favorites, one that most people recognize and another that's well-known but may be a little less obvious. Let's start with that one.

Esau wasn't the most pleasant guy in the Bible. In fact, he was a brut who traded his birthright for a bowl of stew and did things like marry two women who made life bitter for his parents (Gen 26:34–35). But the conniving that occurred between Rebekah, his mother, and Jacob, his brother, to deceive Isaac on his deathbed and take Esau's blessing was flat out harsh, even if it was part of God's plan. The story can be found in Gen 27. Rebekah conspires with Jacob to disguise him as Esau, wearing the skins of young goats to match Esau's hairy body. Mom and brother make some of Isaac's favorite food, and Jacob receives his father's blessing.

Esau returns from hunting wild game as his father requested to find out what happened. Isaac told him that "Your brother (Jacob) came deceitfully, and he has taken away your blessing." Furthermore, Isaac told him, "Behold, I have made him lord over you . . ." Verse 41 says that Esau hated Jacob because of the blessing with which his father had blessed him, and Esau said to himself, "The days of mourning for my father are approaching; then I will kill my brother Jacob." Rebekah heard about Esau's plans and sent Jacob to live with her brother Laban.

Flash-forward a couple of decades, Jacob has two wives, a dozen children, male and female servants, and lots of livestock. He is a wealthy man. He has broken away from his uncle Laban and is headed back to his land in Canaan. Fearful of Esau, he sent messengers to his brother, hoping to appease him with gifts. Esau responds by collecting four hundred men to meet Jacob. When his messengers reported this news to Jacob, he "was greatly afraid and distressed." He prayed to God, "Please deliver me from the hand of my brother, from the hand of Esau, for I fear him, that he may come and attack me, the mothers with the children. But you said,

'I will surely do you good, and make your offspring as the sand of the sea, which cannot be numbered for multitude.'"

Despite promises from God that he and his lineage would thrive, Jacob still feared Esau, who he had wronged many years earlier. He separated his servants and large numbers of his livestock, and sent them ahead as a present for Esau.

When Esau and his four hundred men arrived, what did the elder brother do? Curse Jacob? Tell him off with a long-rehearsed monologue? No! According to Gen 33:4, "Esau ran to meet him (Jacob) and embraced him and fell on his neck and kissed him, and they wept." It was an act of forgiveness and reconciliation. I've always wondered whether Esau felt guilty about driving his brother away with his threats so many years earlier. Regardless, God had blessed him, too, with plenty of livestock and wealth. All the things in the past were in the past, and Esau now valued having his brother back. It's a redemption story of sorts for Esau, based entirely on his ability to forgive his brother.

A more recognizable story about brotherly forgiveness is that of Joseph and his brothers. In Gen 37, 17-year-old Joseph tells his brothers and Jacob about two dreams that indicate that they will be subservient to him. Along with a special robe that Jacob gave him, the dreams made Joseph's brothers jealous.

The brothers took their flocks of sheep to pasture, and Jacob sent Joseph to check on them. When he approached the brothers, they seized him, tossed him into an empty cistern, and contemplated killing him. God delivered a caravan of Midianite merchants at just the right time, and Judah suggested that they sell him for 20 shekels of silver. The Midianites took Joseph to Egypt and sold him to Potiphar, one of Pharaoh's officials, the captain of the guard. Joseph then spent 13 years—his entire 20s—as a slave or in prison, all at the hands of his brothers.

Finally, after interpreting Pharaoh's dreams, he was set free from prison and made the ruler's second-in-command over all the land. Flash-forward after seven years of abundance and some portion of seven years of famine, Jacob sends 10 of his sons to Egypt to buy food. When they arrived, they met Joseph, but didn't realize it. From Gen 42: "As soon as Joseph saw his brothers, he recognized them, but he pretended to be a stranger and spoke harshly to them."

> "It is just as I told you: You are spies! And this is how you will be tested: As surely as Pharaoh lives, you will not leave this place unless your youngest brother comes here. Send one of

your number to get your brother; the rest of you will be kept in prison, so that your words may be tested to see if you are telling the truth. If you are not, then as surely as Pharaoh lives, you are spies!" And he put them all in custody for three days.

The next part of the story is among the most heartbreaking passages in all of Scriptures as the brothers sense that they're being punished for their past sins:

> They said to one another, "Surely we are being punished because of our brother. We saw how distressed he was when he pleaded with us for his life, but we would not listen; that's why this distress has come on us." Reuben replied, "Didn't I tell you not to sin against the boy? But you wouldn't listen! Now we must give an accounting for his blood."

Nine of the brothers went home to convince Jacob to let them bring Benjamin to Egypt to free Simeon, who was imprisoned by Joseph. But Jacob said, "My son will not go down there with you; his brother is dead and he is the only one left. If harm comes to him on the journey you are taking, you will bring my gray head down to the grave in sorrow." Eventually, when they ran out of food again, they were compelled to return to Egypt and took Benjamin with them. When they appeared before Joseph, there was another heartbreaking moment:

> As [Joseph] looked about and saw his brother Benjamin, his own mother's son, he asked, "Is this your youngest brother, the one you told me about?" And he said, "God be gracious to you, my son." Deeply moved at the sight of his brother, Joseph hurried out and looked for a place to weep. He went into his private room and wept there.

Eventually, Joseph revealed himself to his brothers in chapter 45. Verse 2 tells us that "he wept so loudly that the Egyptians heard him, and Pharaoh's household heard about it." And Joseph's brothers? They were "terrified at his presence" (v3). Why? The brothers, except Benjamin, spent decades living in guilt about what they had done. Now, the cold, stark reality of their past is standing right in front of them.

If you've ever seen someone cry hard like Joseph did without really understanding why he or she is wailing so loudly, it can be a dumbfounding experience. What the brothers didn't realize was Joseph's reaction was the relief of forgiveness after harboring pent-up feelings for many years. The betrayal when they sold him, all the years as a slave and the years spent in prison all came flooding back. It's really the rawest demonstration of emotion in the Bible with the possible exception of Jesus anticipating His death on the Cross in the Garden of Gethsemane.

No matter how much Joseph had grown in his walk with God, stricken with one setback then another until God enabled him to interpret Pharaoh's dream, he still had one test left. It's a little like Yoda telling Luke Skywalker that his final step before becoming a Jedi knight is facing his nemesis, Darth Vader. "Vader, you must face Vader," Yoda tells Luke. Joseph had to face the people who hurt him worse than anyone during his life in Egypt: his brothers. That's part of the reason he toys with them when they first appear in Egypt to buy food. He also tested their character to see if they were the same ole crummy brothers. The guilt they expressed along with Judah's leadership convinced him that they had grown to be better human beings.

Interestingly, the brothers didn't appear to forgive themselves. Seventeen years later, after Jacob comes down to Egypt, he dies. Gen 50:15 tells us:

> "When Joseph's brothers saw that their father was dead, they said, "What if Joseph holds a grudge against us and pays us back for all the wrongs we did to him?" So they sent word to Joseph, saying, "Your father left these instructions before he died: 'This is what you are to say to Joseph: I ask you to forgive your brothers the sins and the wrongs they committed in treating you so badly.' Now please forgive the sins of the servants of the God of your father."

When Joseph received their message, he wept. He realized that his brothers still feared him and his possible retaliation now that Jacob was gone. It saddened him that they still didn't realize that he had forgiven them. He was over it, so to speak. But they weren't. So, he reassured them in one of the great verses in Scriptures from verse 20: "You intended to harm me, but God intended it for good to accomplish what is now being done." Finally, the Scriptures tell us in verse 21 that "he comforted them."

Is there someone in your life that you need to forgive? Is there deep-seeded anger or resentment toward someone or something that you've pushed down so far you don't even realize it's affecting you? Confront it. Give it over to God in prayer. And, if that person you need to forgive is yourself, let's take a deeper look at that.

Forgiving Yourself

It is important to remember that forgiving extends to yourself as much as it does to others. A host of spirit-destroying outcomes result from not forgiving yourself for a mistake or transgression against oneself or another, including guilt and shame; depression, despair, and heartbreak; low self-esteem; close-mindedness and close-heartedness; and so much more. The temptation is to hold onto these negative outcomes as a form of self-inflicted punishment, and the cycle becomes a self-perpetuating one whereby guilt or shame drives deeper low self-esteem and self-worth.

Lack of forgiving oneself most certainly leads to death, likely a premature one, because all of the above-listed negative outcomes take a physiological toll on your life.

More critically, these negative outcomes can draw you away from God and put at risk your eternal life as a God follower. Why? Because you are deliberately making the decision to hold onto your sin and not forgive yourself when God asks you to turn to Him in prayer, confess, repent, and receive His grace. His boundless grace is right there, ready for you to receive. But you must decide to trust Him with your pain. You must be willing to let Him begin the healing process in your heart and spirit.

If you are a God follower, He placed you on this planet to carry out His will according to His plan. What has occurred in your life is not by accident and is meant to help fulfill His purpose. You must allow Him to work through your pain, no matter how deep.

Lest you think that living with guilt or shame, or possibly depression, is not reflected in the Bible, think again. The Scriptures are filled with examples starting with the very beginning with Adam and Eve. They ate from the Tree of Knowledge, and the Bible tells us that immediately they felt shame and clothed themselves (Gen 3:7).

As discussed in the last section, the 10 brothers of Israel clearly felt guilt and shame for decades based on their selling of Joseph into slavery.

David felt shame when Nathan confronted him about Bathsheba and the killing of Uriah in 2 Sam 12. From verse 13, "I have sinned against the LORD." David continues to express his guilt in Ps 51, which is titled "A psalm of David. When the prophet Nathan came to him after David had committed adultery with Bathsheba." From verses 3–6:

> For I know my transgressions, and my sin is always before me.
>
> Against you, you only, have I sinned and done what is evil in your sight; so you are right in your verdict and justified when you judge.
>
> Surely I was sinful at birth, sinful from the time my mother conceived me.
>
> Yet you desired faithfulness even in the womb; you taught me wisdom in that secret place.

These individuals did something heinous, held onto their guilt and shame for a period of time, then gave it up to God. And He delivered them. What is causing you guilt and shame? Cheating on your significant other? Turning to porn as a crutch? Steeling from someone? Has addiction caused you to hurt someone you love? Whatever it is, know that you can turn it over to God. Also, know that there will be consequences to your actions. But live with the full understanding that God will be with you every step of the way, and *He will deliver you.*

If you still need help or are dealing with guilt or shame over something, seek help from a pastor or mental health professional.

Chapter 10

Brand Attribute—Glorifies God Through Thankfulness

> So then, just as you received Christ Jesus as Lord, continue to live your lives in him, rooted and built up in him, strengthened in the faith as you were taught, and overflowing with thankfulness.
>
> —COL 2:6–7

YOU COULD ARGUE THAT we should glorify God through everything that we do, not just being thankful, and you would be correct. However, being thankful about the literally countless number of ways that God blesses each of us every single day and demonstrating that gratitude are the most obvious ways to glorify Him.

Being thankful should be the easiest of the eight brand attributes to live out, yet it seems to be the most overlooked. Most people simply do not take the time to pause to thank God for everything He has given them. Sadly, too often, we are like the nine men with leprosy whom Jesus healed but did not return to thank and praise Him (see Luke 17:11–19).

Stop for a moment as you read this book. Lift your spirit up from the page and consider for 30 seconds all the things that He has provided for you in this exact moment. Your life. Your health. Your wellbeing. A job. A beautiful planet to live on. Your country. Your neighborhood. Your church. A home. A car or bike or feet to walk. Your significant other. Your family. Your kids. Your grandkids. Friends. Support groups. Fellow believers. A sense of hope in your life. A discerning heart. Peace. A sharp mind. A chair to sit in. Your phone. Perhaps, the coffee you're drinking. Clean air to breathe. Time to read. All these things and many, many more are blessings from God in your life at this very moment. Now, consider the multiplicative—actually exponential—amount of blessings for every second of your life. The number of blessings that God has given you to this very instant in your life is limitless. If you stop to consider it, the thought of His blessings in your life is awesome and mind-blowing. It's literally infinite.

Even the little things count, too. If I'm driving and in a hurry, and I make a greenlight at an especially long-wait intersection—I'll say a little "popcorn" prayer of thanks to God. Anything that helps you in the moment, gives you hope, helps you avoid a problem or injury, puts you at ease or gives you rest are all good reasons to offer up a quick little prayer of thanks to God. It's like James 1:17 tells us, "Every good gift and every perfect gift is from above . . ." Acknowledging this truth is the level of recognition of His blessings that God wants for us to demonstrate.

When we give thanks, it takes the focus off us and places it onto God. It takes the attention off the negativity in our lives. This is vitally important because, according to an article in Psychology Today called "Negative Thinking: A Dangerous Addiction," 80 percent of our thoughts are negative, and 95 percent of them are repetitive, meaning we keep rehashing the negativity in our minds over and over. This leads to what's called negativity bias, defined as "our tending not to only to register negative stimuli more readily, but also dwell on these events." And boy, it is easy to dwell on the bad things in the world and our lives if we let our sinful thoughts take hold of us. In response to negativity bias, try thanking God for everything He has given you. When you do, I guarantee that you'll complain less. You'll be more pleasant to be around. Thanking God regularly will literally change your attitude and outlook.

Jesus thanked His father constantly for listening to Him and granting His requests. I always think of Jesus thanking the Father at the rising of Lazarus in John 11, when He says "Father, I thank you that you have heard me. I knew that you always hear me, but I said this on account of the people standing around, that they may believe that you sent me."

David frequently thanked God in his writings, including Pss 7:17; 9:1, 34:1, 44:8, 69:30, 86:12, 95:1–2, 100:4, 106:7, 107:8–9, 118:29, 136:1,

138:1–2, among others. Hannah gave thanks after the Lord blessed her with a son, who she named Samuel and dedicated to His service. Mary, the mother of Jesus, thanked God for allowing her to be His servant.

As you thank God for everything He has given you, a natural and expected outcome of that thankfulness is praise. Of course, praise can take different forms. You can privately praise God for the many blessings that He has bestowed on you. You can share praise in an intimate way with friends. At some point though, you need to express that praise publicly and—at least somewhat—boldly, depending on your personality. As the psalmist says in Pss 103:1–5, we are highly encouraged to bless His holy name:

> Bless the Lord, O my soul, and all that is within me, bless his holy name! Bless the Lord, O my soul, and forget not all his benefits, who forgives all your iniquity, who heals all your diseases, who redeems your life from the pit, who crowns you with steadfast love and mercy, who satisfies you with good so that your youth is renewed like the eagle's.

There are four primary reasons for this public pronouncement. First, note the last phrase of the passage: *who satisfies you with good so that your youth is renewed like the eagle's*. Giving Him praise is the proper response to His many blessings, not just because you are grateful (more on this in the next section), but it also renews your spirit and grants you satisfaction, which ultimately provides peace. If you are troubled in spirit, try praising Him for what He *has* given you. While it may seem counterintuitive when you're down, try it. You may be surprised at how well things turn around.

> Give thanks in all circumstances; for this is the will of God in Christ Jesus for you.
>
> —1 THESS 5:18

Second, you are part of God's master plan, and how His blessings affect your life and the lives of others are part of what He wants you to share as a member of His ministry on earth. From the "this little light of mine; I'm gonna let it shine" school of thought, God wants you to overtly connect the dots for others with how He has made an impact in your life and you can see Him working through you. God communicates His love through other people, and that could be you for someone else. That is done through praising Him.

I always love it when I ask someone, even a perfect stranger, "how's your day going?" and he or she says "Blessed." That's the mark of a God follower! Your day isn't just "good" or "fine." It's blessed. This response is a small way that you can praise God to others. God followers will likely understand the response and hopefully reply in kind to you. Don't worry about how non-believers will respond. They'll either register that your response is godly and move on or it'll simply go right over their heads until the Holy Spirit works in their heart.

Third, your praise helps others learn to praise. Beyond informing others how God has blessed you, the very act of praising Him encourages newer God followers to do the same and reinforces more mature ones in their faith walk. With newer God followers, praising Him can be and usually is a new and foreign concept. They need to be trained by those who are more seasoned.

Having managed people for years in a business setting, I frequently hear fellow managers and peers bemoan the fact that a team member just "doesn't get it," or doesn't seem able to handle a role or set of tasks. The first question I always ask is, "what kind of training has that person received." The overwhelming majority of the time, that question is met with a blank stare or a "Hmmm, um, we haven't trained him/her." Then, depending on the person with whom I'm speaking, I gently remind that manager, "how can you expect the person to do what you want without training them?"

In the same way, the all-knowing God understands that each of His followers needs both individual mentors as well as a community of followers to show new-to-the-faith believers the way. Your example of praise—either as a mentor or part of the church body—is key to that spiritual training.

> Amen! Praise and glory and wisdom and thanks and honor and power and strength be to our God for ever and ever. Amen!
>
> —REV 7:12

Fourth, what do you think you're going to be doing in heaven for the rest of eternity? Praising Him! Just as God wants us to help train newer believers in how to praise Him, He is training His followers on what being in heaven will be like.

Be Grateful

I'll be frank, it amazes me how ungrateful people generally are. Listen, there is a lot of evil in the world and people perpetrating heinous, truly awful acts of cruelty to others. However, one area where the pervasiveness of sin in this world is truly evident is how people take their blessings for granted. Even worse, many of them feel entitled to their blessings.

We know the "I'm gonna get mine" attitude is reinforced throughout our society. Sadly, the "I deserve my . . ." and "Don't keep me from my . . ." attitudes are also everywhere. But, let's be clear on what we deserve: "For the wages of sin is death . . ." (Rom 6:23). We all deserve death. Believers and unbelievers, alike. We don't deserve a thing from God. Period. So, the thought that we're owed anything is—at best—silly. At worst, it's filled with pride, one of the seven deadly sins.

Every day, multiple times, I thank God for my life and health. I will never take these things for granted, especially as I get older and see friends of mine pass away in their early 50s or combat any number of life-threatening diseases. I praise God for all the provisions in my life, including my family, home, job, car, and so on. Any of these things can be taken from you in an instant. So praise Him from whom all blessings flow and for what He has given you!

When Life's Troubles Makes It Hard to Thank God

Some of you may be experiencing difficulties in your life and—sadly—thanking God is either not on your mind or the farthest thing from it. Divorce, death of a loved one, employment problems, addiction, infidelity, crushing debt, chronic pain or health concerns, effects from the pandemic, depression and loneliness are just a few of the conditions that could cause you to lose hope and your focus on God. In these difficult times, you may pray to God for relief and do not receive it. Philippians 4:6 reminds us, "Do not be anxious about anything, but in everything by prayer and supplication with thanksgiving let your requests be made known to God." But it's hard not to be anxious or angry or worse when it feels like God is not answering your prayer or giving you relief from what affects you. There is a common misperception among many followers of God that—when He doesn't relieve you of the burden that afflicts you—He isn't listening to your prayers or didn't answer them. Nothing can be farther from the truth!

God always answers your prayers. We must remember that the answer may be "no," "not at this time," or "my grace is sufficient for you." In 2 Corinthians, the Apostle Paul asks God to relieve him from a "thorn in my flesh" and he got an answer:

> . . . in order to keep me from becoming conceited, I was given a thorn in my flesh, a messenger of Satan, to torment me. Three times I pleaded with the Lord to take it away from me. But he said to me, "My grace is sufficient for you, for my power is made perfect in weakness." Therefore I will boast all the more gladly about my weaknesses, so that Christ's power may rest on me. That is why, for Christ's sake, I delight in weaknesses, in insults, in hardships, in persecutions, in difficulties. For when I am weak, then I am strong.

There has been much speculation about what that thorn was. Some speculate that it was blindness or other visual impairment. Others say epilepsy. It was something severe for Paul to refer to it as "a messenger from Satan." Regardless, God did not remove the thorn from Paul, who lived with that thorn for many years before his death.

Paul's reaction to being stuck with his thorn? Delight. My guess is that Paul didn't arrive at that feeling of delight when God first answered his prayer for relief. Clearly, Paul wasn't happy about the answer. He prayed to God three times for relief. Either God answered with the "my grace is sufficient" response after the first prayer, and Paul kept at it, or God said "no" or "not at this time" to the first two requests, then gave His "final answer" on the third prayer. Either way, there was undoubtedly a period while Paul contemplated God's response, came to understand the reasoning, maybe even grieved over the situation, then moved forward with an upbeat response.

Your difficulty is your trial, and you are not Paul. It may be extraordinarily hard or downright impossible for you to realize delight or anything that vaguely resembles positivity about your difficulties. That's a fair response. However, in times of trial, it's very important to look at your troubles through the lens of God's power "made perfect in weakness." Your weakness.

Pastor and theologian A.W. Tozer expressed it this way: "God never uses anyone greatly until He tests them deeply."

If you are a follower of God, you must trust that He watches over you in your time of difficulties, never giving you more than you can handle (1 Cor 10:13). More important, there is a reason for your difficulties according to God's perfect plan. Here's the tough part. It is very conceivable that you will not understand how your suffering fits into His perfect plan until you're with Him in heaven. So often, we—as followers of God—have no understanding of the effect of our actions and lives on others.

Look at Matthew 1 and the genealogy of Jesus Christ. Starting with Abraham, there were 42 males cited in the lineage of the Savior. Some of them were well-known to us, like Isaac, Jacob, Jesse, David, Solomon, and Joseph. However, I dare say that few of you have heard of Matthan, who was Joseph's grandfather and Jesus' great-grandfather. Other than the Matthew 1:15 reference, his name only appears in Luke 3:24. His name means "a gift." And that's about all that we non-Bible scholars know about him. I have no idea what Matthan faced in his life, good, bad, or indifferent. Regardless, I'm fairly sure that he had no earthly idea that his great-grandchild would be the most important person ever born. What role did he play in Jesus' birth? It's pretty simple. He carried on the lineage according to God's plan just like his father, Eleazar. God worked through Matthan to bring about His plan, and he had no knowledge of his role in it.

It may be tough to find consolation in God's perfect plan and the wisdom it will produce while you are suffering, especially if it leads you on a path toward death. Just understand that you are not alone. The psalmist who wrote Ps 88 relates one of the most mournful passages in the entire Scriptures (verses 3–9):

> I am overwhelmed with troubles and my life draws near to death.
>
> I am counted among those who go down to the pit; I am like one without strength.
>
> I am set apart with the dead, like the slain who lie in the grave, whom you remember no more, who are cut off from your care.
>
> You have put me in the lowest pit, in the darkest depths.
>
> Your wrath lies heavily on me; you have overwhelmed me with all your waves.
>
> You have taken from me my closest friends and have made me repulsive to them. I am confined and cannot escape; my eyes

are dim with grief. I call to you, LORD, every day; I spread out my hands to you.

This is a difficult passage, as it portrays the psalmist's woeful sadness that the Lord has "overwhelmed him with troubles," "put him in the lowest pit," "made him repulsive to his friends," and "swept over him with His wrath and terrors." Not fun stuff. One of the most melancholy of all the Psalms, chapter 88 is the only one of the 150 that does not conclude with or include some sense of comfort or joy.

If you have lost any sense of comfort or joy like the psalmist, and perhaps any reason for thankfulness, my humble recommendation is that you call out to God in prayer. You may have already done so many times, but do it again. This time though, emphasize your willingness to be His instrument and thank Him for using you to carry out His will. You may have already done that, too. Do it again. Do it loudly! Tell Him how hard your suffering is; it's okay. He knows. Tell Him that you're scared or full of rage or profoundly depressed or mystified or whatever emotion you're feeling. He knows. Let it all out! Yell at God! He can take it. He wants to take it. Or, if it's a calm whisper, you can do that, too. Your perseverance in prayer will be recognized by God, either now or certainly in heaven.

Which brings us to the last point here: for believers in God's grace, no matter how badly you suffer in this world, even to the point of death, recognize that you have a heavenly reward that awaits you. It was bought by the precious blood of Jesus Christ on the Cross. As it says in 1 Cor 2:9: "What no eye has seen, what no ear has heard, and what no human mind has conceived—the things God has prepared for those who love him . . ."

That small but monumental fact alone is worthy of an eternity of thankfulness. All of this leads to the following questions: How do you demonstrate your gratitude to God for everything He has given you and has yet to give you? How do you praise Him for all of these blessings? How do others recognize your appreciation for His many blessings in your life? The answers to these questions will reveal how you glorify Him.

Chapter 11

Brand Attribute—Is a Member of God's Community / Church

> And let us consider how we may spur one another on toward
> love and good deeds, not giving up meeting together, as some
> are in the habit of doing, but encouraging one another—
> and all the more as you see the Day approaching.
>
> —HEB 10:24–25

DURING MOST OF MY preteen and teenage years, my family didn't own a car that ran. For the most part, that was okay because we lived in Washington, D.C., which—at the time—had a spectacular mass-transit system. We took the bus and Metro everywhere. I commuted to elementary school via bus starting in first grade. That involved three buses and two transfers to get from my home in Northwest D.C. to Calvary Lutheran School in Silver Spring, Maryland. When I went to junior high and high school, I took a bus, train, then bus to get there.

There were a lot of downsides to not having a running car, though. Coupled with no working washer and dryer in our home, that meant bicycling to the local laundromat. With grandparents who lived 40 and 100 miles away, respectively, it meant seeing them maybe once or twice a year. (They never came to our house; my father was a hoarder, and there was literally nowhere for them to sit.)

The lack of a running car also gave my father, a devout Christian, a convenient excuse to avoid going to church. To begin with, my father wasn't the most sociable individual in the world. He substituted physically going to a church assembly with watching several televangelists, Pat Roberson being the primary one. Robert Schuller was also on the list.

When I started college at American University, my father arranged for me to begin going to the InterVarsity Christian Fellowship chapter on campus. For a series of reasons, it wasn't for me. Instead, I gravitated toward the on-campus Lutheran Fellowship, where—during the first gathering I attended—the co-leaders of the group both ordered tall mugs of beer at the student union. While it'd be tempting to insert a joke here about the sharp contrasts between the two fellowships, let's just say that I felt far more at ease with the Lutheran students, and I became an active member of the group.

Eventually, I became a peer minister, which was a stipend position for on-campus outreach where the Lutheran Church does not have a resident pastor. My role was to touch bases with students who—on their admissions application—cited that they were Lutheran and invite them to weekly worship services at the campus' spiritual center. At a certain point, it became important to me and the role to get baptized. (In my non-denominational upbringing, baptism was done as a consenting adult.) My baptism was arranged for the day before my 19th birthday at Georgetown Lutheran Church, where the presiding pastor for the campus ministered.

When I told my father about my baptism plans, he was upset. Imagine that! He considered the Lutheran Church far too liberal for his taste, and it wasn't my childhood church, McLean Bible Church. My memory is a little fuzzy on the argument that ensued and whether he attempted to forbid me from getting baptized there. But the one detail that is lucidly clear to me is the statement I made to end the argument. At one point, I said to my father, "At least, I go to church." He looked at me, dumbfounded and ticked off, which was a big deal if you knew my father. He was an "always get the last word" guy. But, in his heart, he understood some truth in my statement. He understood that the personal community of the church that I attended was valuable, probably more valuable than the televangelistic experience that he had.

My father did attend my baptism. The punchline to the story though is that—shortly after this sordid episode—my father began attending Washington Baptist Church, which was easy walking distance of my childhood home. Again, we didn't own a car, so the church had to be close. And, when he could no longer tolerate the theology of the pastor and congregation there, he saved enough money to purchase an old Toyota Corolla and drove out to McLean to the family's long-time church.

During my life, I've attended a wide range of churches on the ideological and theological spectrum, from liberal to conservative. For many believers, what the church believes is important. But, in my experience, there are two infallible truths about churchgoing: 1) even if you were raised in a church or denomination from childhood, there will come a time when you disagree with at least one of its major beliefs; and 2) none of the ideology and theology matters if you do not feel accepted by the people there.

God followers are meant to attend church or be part of a worshiping community of Christ. Why? The relationship we have with fellow believers is an environment that God uses for us to grow in faith. It is a natural extension of one's belief in God to share your faith with others. There are more than 50 "one another" verses throughout the Bible (e.g., John 15:17, Gal 6:2, Rom 15:7) that reinforce the spirit of God's community.

There is an important distinction that we need to draw about what is meant by "church." In the Old Testament, believers were identified with the community of Israel and worshipped according to the offerings and feasts that were prescribed by the Law. The concept of modern church really began in the New Testament, where the word appears more than 100 times. Even more specifically, the idea of Christ's church starts in Acts 2 with Pentecost and the Holy Spirit coming on disciples:

> Suddenly a sound like the blowing of a violent wind came from heaven and filled the whole house where they were sitting. They saw what seemed to be tongues of fire that separated and came to rest on each of them. All of them were filled with the Holy Spirit and began to speak in other tongues as the Spirit enabled them.
>
> Now there were staying in Jerusalem God-fearing Jews from every nation under heaven. When they heard this sound, a crowd came together in bewilderment, because each one heard their own language being spoken. Utterly amazed, they asked: "Aren't all these who are speaking Galileans? Then how is it that

each of us hears them in our native language? Amazed and perplexed, they asked one another, "What does this mean?"

What it meant was the beginning of the spreading of God's Word across the whole world at the time. Following this passage, Peter addressed the crowd, explained about Jesus and His sacrifice, and delivered a call to action to "Repent and be baptized, every one of you, in the name of Jesus Christ for the forgiveness of your sins. And you will receive the gift of the Holy Spirit. The promise is for you and your children and for all who are far off—for all whom the Lord our God will call."

Christ's church kickstarter began with "about three thousand were added to their number that day." The rest of the Book of Acts details the evangelism performed by Peter, Paul, and the other apostles. In addition, the remainder of the New Testament is filled with epistles from Peter, Paul, James, and John on how believers should behave toward one another, including the Book of Romans, which is the Apostle Paul's masterful summary of Christian living in the church.

Rom 12 dives into our role as members of the body of Christ. Note that Paul elevates the conversation somewhat by talking about unity and humble service in Christ, both qualities of being in a church. However, Paul does not use the word church here:

> For just as each of us has one body with many members, and these members do not all have the same function, so in Christ we, though many, form one body, and each member belongs to all the others.

The pivotal verse here is ". . . in Christ we, though many, form one body, and each member belongs to all the others." We, true believers, belong to one body in Christ, both at a local church as well as a more universal church of a world-wide community of individual believers that spans different congregations, denominations, or geographies.

Being Inclusive

There's an old saying about the commonality of the people of God's church. It goes something like this: you have more in common with believer from another country who speaks a different language than you do with your unbelieving neighbor who speaks your language. Clearly, this expression must be kept in perspective. Most of us have friends who are unbelievers, and we get along well with them. We know them. We share our lives with them. They may be close family members or dear friends.

However, if you look at it as commonality versus knowing, the perspective changes. You do have more in common with the person from the other country: your faith, knowing Christ, reading and following His Word, salvation, celebrating others coming to faith, the nomenclature of the church and being a member of it, and more. One of them, you'll spend your life around; one of them, you'll spend eternity with.

Scriptures highlight that believers live in a diverse world and that God's kingdom is diverse. Rev 7:9 highlights the vast diversity of God's kingdom: "I looked, and there before me was a great multitude that no one could count, from every nation, tribe, people and language, standing before the throne and before the Lamb."

Rev 15 highlights that this diversity of God's people: "All nations will come and worship before you, for your righteous acts have been revealed."

Here, "the nations" refers to all the peoples of the earth, who represent the outcome of Jesus' last command while He was among us from Acts 1:8: "But you will receive power when the Holy Spirit comes on you; and you will be my witnesses in Jerusalem, and in all Judea and Samaria, and to the ends of the earth."

Since we are commissioned by Christ Himself to spread the Word of God to the ends of the earth, we must expect that believers from churches and backgrounds from all over the planet will cross our paths. When they do, how will you react? Will you see their differences and embrace the commonality you share as believers? And, if you do embrace it, will you be receptive to their culture, their voice, their differences?

Why does your willingness to be inclusive matter to your Godly brand? Many, if not most people, say they are open to diversity in their lives, but do not take active steps to integrate people from diverse cultures and backgrounds into their church, prayer groups, or business. The husband of a dear friend of mine got up and left the sanctuary of our church when they were visiting because we sung a hymn and alternated verses in English and Spanish. He didn't like singing in Spanish. Despite what you may think, this person is one of the nicest guys you'd ever meet. He just didn't like the unfamiliar in a church setting. The differences made him uncomfortable.

My friend's husband is not alone. A church I formerly attended had a food pantry to feed the area's homeless population. Some in the church were very open to serving the chronically homeless (mostly) men and (occasional) women that came by. But others were troubled by the ministry and concerned about having "that element" on or near the church grounds. Was the latter audience of concerned churchgoers wrong? Were their feelings inappropriate?

While many of us go to churches that support ministries in other languages and countries, some believers have a difficult time embracing others with differences or simply do not do so for whatever reason. If their church hosts congregations that perform their services in other languages or invoke other cultures, these believers are content as long as those ministries remain separate and not comingled with theirs.

Thing is, as a member of God's community, you are meant to follow the example of Jesus. He modeled acceptance of those who are different, spanning physical abilities, language and culture, religion and non-religion, and much more. The Gospel books are filled with examples of Jesus helping people with differences. In Matthew 9, Jesus heals two blind men who call out to Him. He heals the blind, mute, and demon-possessed in Matthew 12. Matthew 20, Mark 8, Mark 10, and Luke 7 offer similar instances of Jesus helping those who were impaired. In Matthew 8, Jesus helps a Gentile Roman centurion who asked Him to heal a servant. In Matthew 15 and Mark 7, Jesus has mercy on a Canaanite woman who shows great faith. In John 4, Jesus speaks with an outcast Samaritan woman. And, as John 21:25 tells us: "Jesus did many other things as well. If every one of them were written down, I suppose that even the whole world would not have room for the books that would be written." There are likely many, many more instances of Christ healing and helping people with different abilities that we do not know because they were too voluminous to record.

If you, your prayer group, your church or your business have difficulty being inclusive of those who are different from yourself, I'd encourage you to pray about it, dive into the Word on the topic, and ask God to provide you guidance. If you know someone like this, come alongside them in prayer and nurturing to help open their hearts so that the Holy Spirit can speak to them on this topic.

None of us can comprehend what heaven will truly be like. However, it'll be a place where all languages will be brought together again, like an anti-Tower of Babel, and we will all understand each other as we praise our magnificent God. I'm not sure if there will be a "language of heaven" or whether communication will occur in some other fashion.

But all voices will be joined together, and it will be beautiful beyond our wildest dreams. In anticipation of being citizens of heaven and as current members of the community of God on this earth, figure out one thing that you can do today to help yourself or others embrace those with differences in your life, then—with God's help—do it.

Chapter 12

Brand Attribute—Is an Agent of Change

> For we are God's handiwork, created in Christ Jesus to do good works, which God prepared in advance for us to do.
>
> —EPH 2:10

GOD PLACED YOU ON this planet to do His work, advance His plans, and make a difference for His kingdom. For some, this realization comes naturally, and they immediately spark to kingdom work, such as building a ministry, being a missionary, teaching in a religious school, being a Christian entertainer, or some other calling. For many others though, especially those who come to faith later in life, that difference-making for the kingdom may not be clear. In fact, many in faith don't realize that God calls them to change something as part of His kingdom-building. Or, they have not yet come to understand what change they should undertake.

One may call this notion the concept of purpose, and we'll explore that concept more deeply in the next chapter. Being a change agent goes beyond mere purpose. Being a change agent for God means praying about, receiving His discernment, then acting on His calling to enact a meaningful transformation of something on the Lord's behalf. That may involve creating something new or bringing a wholly new approach to something that already exists. There is an inherent newness to the change you take ownership over performing.

Let's say you were raised in the church, and you've been involved in the ministries of that church since you were a kid. You sang in the youth choir, went to youth group most weeks, attended every youth outing and summer camp, then—upon graduating into adulthood—you maintained that same level of commitment to serving in your church. During that time, you lived an example of God's gracious love. You undoubtedly touched the lives of others. You may have helped others find their way to the body of Christ. You advanced to the kingdom of God in ways that you know and don't know. Inherently, that is change, yes. You made a difference in His kingdom. Now what? How do you build on your prior work? How do you take the learnings you have from the life experience and spiritual gifts you have, and change something in this broken world? That's what being a change agent for the kingdom of God means.

There isn't a major figure in the Scriptures who wasn't an agent of change. Jesus didn't come into this world to preach a little bit, then leave. He came to change the world. Forever. Noah built an ark under God's guidance to save humanity. No matter how badly Moses wanted to remain a shepherd hiding in the hills of Midian and not return to Egypt, God compelled him to go to change the future of Israel. David wanted to build a first-ever temple for the Name of the Lord. Nehemiah returned to Jerusalem to rebuild it. Mary willingly turned over her life to God as a humble servant to be the mother of Jesus. Paul was the ultimate agent of change, second only to Jesus in his evangelical outreach. In the same way, God placed you on earth to change something according to His plan, then keep changing things.

Perhaps, the most evident example that Jesus offered regarding being an agent of change is the Parable of the Talents recorded in Matthew 25. In it, a master goes on a journey and entrusts his servants with his property. From verse 15, "To one he gave five talents, to another two, to another one, to each according to his ability." The first two servants doubled the talents given them; the third hid his one talent, fearing condemnation from the master if he lost it. When the master returns, he praises the first two servants for being good stewards with his property, telling each "Well done, good and faithful servant. You have been faithful over a little; I will set you over much. Enter into the joy of your master."

Things don't go well for the third servant. He admits his fear of the master as a "hard man" and hands back the one talent. The master answers him, "You wicked and slothful servant! You knew that I reap where I have not sown and gather where I scattered no seed? Then you ought to have invested my money with the bankers, and at my coming I should have received what was my own with interest." Then, the master casts the worthless servant into the outer darkness.

This well-known story conveys God's expectations of us: to multiply the "talents" he gives us. In the context of the story, a talent was a monetary unit worth about twenty years' wages for a laborer. This example extends beyond money, of course, to include *everything* God gives us: our time, our talent (i.e., skills or spiritual gifts), and our treasure.

What does being an agent of change for God entail? There are three qualities in Scriptures that point to how God activates us to carry out His will in this world. We need to be 1) faithful, 2) receptive to His call, and 3) willing to act. Let's take a look at each of these three qualities:

Being Faithful

There are many stories of individuals in the Scriptures being faithful in the Lord, but one of my favorites is Hannah.

In 1 Sam, we read that Hannah is one of two wives of Elkanah, who "year after year . . . went up from his town to worship and sacrifice to the LORD Almighty at Shiloh." The man's other wife Peninnah had children, but Hannah had none. Peninnah would taunt Hannah about not having kids, so much so that Hannah's despair led her to weep bitterly and refuse to eat. Her husband could not comfort her.

One time when visiting Shiloh, Scriptures tell us that "In her deep anguish Hannah prayed to the LORD, weeping bitterly. And she made a vow, saying, 'LORD Almighty, if you will only look on your servant's misery and remember me, and not forget your servant but give her a son, then I will give him to the LORD for all the days of his life.'" Think about this prayer for a moment and how awesome it is. Hannah was willing to give to the Lord any child that He gave her. And, as we find out a few verses later, she kept her promise.

She bore a son and named him Samuel, saying, "Because I asked the LORD for him." From verse 24, "After he was weaned, she took the boy with her, young as he was, along with a three-year-old bull, an ephah of flour and a skin of wine, and brought him to the house of the LORD at Shiloh." She gave him to the Lord. Then, in chapter 2, she offered a prayer of thanksgiving and praise to the Lord, starting with "My heart rejoices in the LORD; in the LORD my horn is lifted high." The Lord blessed her faithfulness, too. From 2:21, "And the LORD was gracious to Hannah; she gave birth to three sons and two daughters."

Many of us would've held onto our son, once born, even after making a solemn pledge to the Lord and justified our reasoning. As we consider Hannah's faithfulness that she would still pray to God to give her a child despite years of being barren, what are those difficulties in your life that you need to lift up to the Lord and turn over to Him, trusting in His boundless goodness?

Being Receptive to God's Call

In Williamstown, Kentucky, Answers in Genesis owns and operates Ark Encounter, a historical theme park with a 510-foot-long facsimile of Noah's Ark as its centerpiece attraction. The park's website (arkencounter.com) boasts numerous statistics about the ark they've built. It's 50 feet tall, which is "plenty of space for three extra-tall inner decks as the Bible describes." Another fun factoid is this: "The Ark had the same storage capacity as about 450 standard semi-trailers. A standard livestock trailer holds about 250 sheep, so the Ark had the capacity to hold at least 120,000 sheep." Lastly, the site states that "the Ark is near the maximum size known to be possible for a wooden vessel" and wonders whether it is literally the largest wooden ship ever built.

Now, imagine that God approached you today and said to build such a vessel and seek the help of three untrained workers. With power tools, motorized cranes, hydraulic lifts, and other such equipment at your disposal, you'd swallow hard and figure out how you're going to pay for all of the materials. Then, as you were frantically trying to wrap your mind around constantly building a vessel to withstand a cataclysmic flood, you were told that you only had to complete the task as soon as possible. I know this is the plot line of the 2007 movie Evan Almighty, starring Steve Carell and Morgan Freeman. But, in reality, it'd be nearly impossible.

Nothing is impossible with God, of course. This was the task given to Noah *more than four thousand years ago*. And he was 600 years old when he undertook this building project. Yet, Gen 6:22 tells us that "Noah did everything just as God commanded him."

In chapter 7, God instructs Noah to "Take with you seven pairs of every kind of clean animal, a male and its mate, and one pair of every kind of unclean animal, a male and its mate, and also seven pairs of every kind of bird, male and female, to keep their various kinds alive throughout the earth." Verse 5 tells us: "And Noah did all that the LORD commanded him."

Scriptures tell us that Noah followed God's commands without question, even when they seemed ludicrous, and out of his and his sons' skill sets. The question for all of us is: when God has placed a task, job, or other area of service on your heart, how have you responded? Noah did all the Lord commanded him. With God's help, he fulfilled his mission from God. How have you responded to teaching that bible study, joining the church council, doing the audio-visual duties during the worship services, or whatever opportunities have been presented to you? How have you prayed to God, if you need help? It's a very safe bet that Noah was praying for guidance and God's assistance throughout the entire construction of the ark. The Lord will be there for you, too, if you call on Him.

Being Willing to Act

The Old Testament books of Ezra and Nehemiah tell us about the return of the Israelites from Babylon through the stories of three men of action: Zerubbabel, Erza, and Nehemiah. About 50 years after Babylon destroyed Jerusalem, God moved King Cyrus of Persia to decree to the Israelites in captivity: "Whoever is among you of all his people, may his God be with him, and let him go up to Jerusalem, which is in Judah, and rebuild the house of the LORD, the God of Israel—he is the God who is in Jerusalem." The first six chapters of Ezra tell the story of Zerubbabel and a large contingent of Israelites (42,000+) that he led back to Jerusalem to rebuild the city.

Zerubbabel oversaw the building of an altar to God, then eventually the foundation of the Lord's temple. And the people praised the Lord. At this time, the descendants of the Israelites who were left behind during the exile approached Zerubbabel to let them help build the temple. He flatly refused. From Ezra 4:3, "You have nothing to do with us in building a house to our God; but we alone will build to the LORD, the God of Israel, as King Cyrus the king of Persia has commanded us." It's not clear from Scriptures why Zerubbabel denied their request, but the result was the descendants—stung from the rejection—appealed to the new Babylonian

King Artaxerxes to shut down the construction of the temple, which he did.

Later, the prophets Haggai and Zechariah encouraged Zerubbabel to return to the building of the temple, which he and the Israelites did in direct conflict of the King Artaxerxes edict. The local governor questioned Zerubbabel about restarting the construction and—empowered by God to keep going—he did not cave to the pressure. The governor appealed to the new Babylonian King Darius to halt the rebuilding efforts, but—led by God to find King Cyrus' original decree to rebuild Jerusalem—the new king instead instructed the governor to aid the rebuild efforts.

Ezra 6:14 tells us that Zerubbabel and "the elders of the Jews built and prospered through the prophesying of Haggai the prophet and Zechariah the son of Iddo. They finished their building by decree of the God of Israel and by decree of Cyrus and Darius and Artaxerxes king of Persia." Then, the Israelites celebrated Passover and "they kept the Feast of Unleavened Bread seven days with joy, for the LORD had made them joyful and had turned the heart of the king of Assyria to them."

Flash-forward about 60 years, once again moved by God, a new Persian King Artaxerxes sends another contingent of Israelites to Jerusalem to help instruct the city's inhabitants in the Mosaic Law. Ezra, "a scribe skilled in the Law of Moses that the LORD, the God of Israel, had given," led this next wave of Israelites with a letter from King Artaxerxes for the local governor to give Ezra whatever he required up to certain limits.

On his arrival to Jerusalem, Ezra found out that many of the exiled Israelites who had previously returned had intermarried with non-exiles who were living in the surrounding land, most of whom were not Israelites. Ezra tore his robes in despair, harkening to the Mosaic Law from Deut 23:2-4 that states "No one born of a forbidden union may enter the assembly of the LORD. Even to the tenth generation, none of his descendants may enter the assembly of the LORD."

Ezra offered up a pleading prayer to the Lord, acknowledging the sins of the people. The leading priests and Levites offered to get rid of their wives and children in response to the problem and called together all the men of Judah and Benjamin to do likewise. Ezra led the people, telling the men who assembled, "You have broken faith and married foreign women, and so increased the guilt of Israel. Now then make confession to the LORD, the God of your fathers and do his will. Separate yourselves from the peoples of the land and from the foreign wives." Most of them did divorce their wives, and the end of Ezra 10 tells us who did not.

Regardless of how you think about the course of action taken by Ezra and the religious leaders in Jerusalem (e.g., God opposes divorce in Malachi 2:13–16), he felt justified in his convictions because of the Mosaic Law. He carried out that conviction to its logical and faith-based extent.

You May Upset Some People, and That's Okay

An entrepreneur named Oliver Emberton (oliveremberton.com) wrote an opinion piece entitled (pardon the saucy wording): "If You're Not Pissing Someone Off, You Probably Aren't Doing Anything Important." In this piece, he writes:

> It's an uncomfortable truth. We're raised to be nice, and for good reason. Niceness is safe. It's excellent at maintaining the status quo. Nice people are conscious of what might upset others, and avoid such things.
>
> Which is deadly if you want to accomplish anything of significance.
>
> If your mission is to lead, create, or better the world, surrendering to the emotional concerns of others will paralyze and kill you. Leaders that can't make tough decisions can't lead. Artists that can never offend anyone can never delight anyone either.
>
> This is not to say that being [a jerk*] will make you successful. But an unwillingness to *occasionally* be one is an almost certain road to failure.
>
> * This word was changed to avoid offensive language.

First off, taking this philosophy to an unreasonable degree or using it to justify inappropriate, mean-spirited behavior is not right. Period. However, his sentiment is spot on.

The Apostle Paul said it best in Rom 1:16, "For I am not ashamed of the gospel, because it is the power of God that brings salvation to everyone who believes . . .»

Lest you think this ticking-people-off thing is only a modern-day thing, it's all throughout the Scriptures, starting with Jesus. The Gospel books are filled with instances of Jesus upsetting or enraging the Jewish leaders of the day. It's why they set out to kill Him on numerous occasions. Here's just one example from Matthew 12, verses 9–14:

> Going on from that place, [Jesus] went into their synagogue, and a man with a shriveled hand was there. Looking for a reason to bring charges against Jesus, [the Pharisees] asked him, "Is it lawful to heal on the Sabbath?"
>
> He said to them, "If any of you has a sheep and it falls into a pit on the Sabbath, will you not take hold of it and lift it out? How much more valuable is a person than a sheep! Therefore it is lawful to do good on the Sabbath."
>
> Then he said to the man, "Stretch out your hand." So he stretched it out and it was completely restored, just as sound as the other. But the Pharisees went out and plotted how they might kill Jesus.

Jesus showed them up through His righteousness. And He did so frequently. The tipping point occurs in John 11 with the raising from the dead of Lazarus and the subsequent aftermath. For years, one of the central questions in my personal faith-walk was, "How, after seeing all the miracles and wonders that Jesus performed, and knowing the prophecies in the Old Testament about where the Messiah would be born, did the Pharisees not realize that Jesus was the Messiah?" The Pharisees had to have pieced together that Jesus was born in Bethlehem. How did they not figure it out? The answer is: the Pharisees knew, yet they still killed Him. From John 11:49-53:

> Then one of them, named Caiaphas, who was high priest that year, spoke up, "You know nothing at all! You do not realize that it is better for you that one man die for the people than that the whole nation perish."
>
> He did not say this on his own, but as high priest that year he prophesied that Jesus would die for the Jewish nation, and not only for that nation but also for the scattered children of God, to bring them together and make them one. So from that day on they plotted to take his life.

Jesus pushed the Jewish leadership to the point where they felt they had no other option but to kill Him. Interesting thing is, verses 50-53 suggest that Caiaphas understood the power of Jesus and even prophesized about it, yet he still steered the others toward plotting to kill Him. Why? Because He threatened the status quo, and Satan-driven fear took hold of them.

Throughout the Scriptures, the prophets frequently upset other people, including kings and rulers, in the name of carrying out the Lord's will. Samuel had several corrective runs-ins with Saul. Elijah literally ran for his life from the wrath of Jezebel, who was upset at his killing of the 450 prophets of Baal (1 Kgs 18). King Ahab himself referred to Elijah as "you troubler of Israel." Nathan rebuked King David after his taking of Bathsheba. Isaiah confronted King Ahaz about putting the Lord to the test (Isa 7:10–13). John the Baptist was killed after he denounced Herod's marrying Herodias, his brother Philip's wife. And the list goes on and on . . .

If you follow the Word of God evidently in your life, you will come under fire from others because your Godly brand may cause others guilt and shame, even if you never say a word to them. People do not want to be reminded of their sin, even passively through a follower's Godly example. Therefore, the sinful heart condemns that evident Godly living, rather than face his or her sin and repent.

If you live a Godly branded life and lead, too, then the likelihood will dramatically rise that you will upset others, come under fire, and need to turn to the Lord to strengthen you. God places each individual in a place of leadership according to his or her Godly calling. That can be leadership over a single child, a team at work, a student group on a class project, CEO of a company, or the President of the United States. In each of those roles, there will be times of trouble and personal attacks against you. During these times, it's very important to remember the old adage: "Those who avoid criticism will never say anything, do anything, or be anything." Also remember to remain committed to the Lord, His ways, and the direction that you believe—through prayer and guidance from others—He has given you.

Chapter 13

Strengthening the Frieze

How Your Actions Define You

> Even small children are known by their actions, so is their conduct really pure and upright?
> —PROV 20:11

IN CLASSICAL GREEK ARCHITECTURE, the frieze is the portion that may be plain or patterned, or may contain reliefs (shallow images) like the eagles around the entablature of the Lincoln Memorial in Washington, D.C. Commonly, friezes were painted after being carved, which made them "pop" at the top of the temple and make people really take notice of them.

The frieze decorations depict scenes in a sequence, as if to tell a story. In the case of your Godly brand temple, the frieze tells your story. What are the events or things in your life that reflect and/or shape your Godly brand? Perhaps, you served in the military, are a cancer survivor, started your own business, became a parent, assumed a leadership position, are a recognized expert in your field, and the list goes on and on.

These happenings in our lives form us into who we are and, if we want, can help define our Godly brand. There are events and things in our past that can affect us deeply, like the loss of a loved one, being a victim of a crime, or suffering a setback in your career. You may not want to share that part of your background with others. You may or may not want to consider those types of events as part of your Godly brand. But, they most certainly are.

Ultimately, through prayer and the Lord's guidance, you should consider which parts of your background should be front and center as part of your Godly brand, enabling you to better fulfill the purpose He has given you.

Being an Example

Many people I know who came to their faith later in life seem to have one aspect of their individual testimonial in common. Somewhere along the line, they met a believer who "just acted differently" from everyone else. These late-faith bloomers will share how that person stood out to them and made them curious about why he or she acted that way. Eventually, they asked that believer about his or her behavior. Why is he or she always happy around the office? What makes him or her so patient at the parent-teacher association meetings? How does he or she always find time to listen to my troubles?

Very few validations of someone's faith walk are greater than when the Lord leads a nonbeliever to ask a believer about his or her behavior and why he or she behaves that way. These sorts of openings demonstrate that one's behavior can make a huge difference in the eyes of others and potentially bring them to the Lord. These opportunities for a believer to share the Good News in whatever manner God is leading him or her are a blessing unlike any other that the Lord may grant us in this world.

Being an example for the Lord begins with the life that Jesus Christ modeled for us while He walked with us. His example was clear to both his disciples as well as those believers who followed Him. In Paul's letter to the church in Philippi, he instructs the church to lead a life worthy of the gospel of Christ (Phil 1:27): "Whatever happens, conduct yourselves in a manner worthy of the gospel of Christ. Then, whether I come and see you or only hear about you in my absence, I will know that you stand firm in the one Spirit, striving together as one for the faith of the gospel . . ."

Note Paul's comment that he will "hear about you" to confirm whether the churchgoers in Philippi are indeed conducting themselves "in a manner worthy of the gospel of Christ." This passing comment brings up two common-sense but important aspects of brand: 1) people will talk [i.e., report] about how the people of Philippi act and 2) that talk—dare I say, gossip—will form a reputation about the church. Paraphrasing here, Paul tells the Philippians: "Act right, or I'll hear about it. Others will hear, too. And that's a big deal."

Later in the book, Paul extends this concept of following Christ's example to following his (Paul's) example. From Phil 3:17–20a:

> Join together in following *my example*, brothers and sisters, and just as *you have us as a model*, keep your eyes on those who live as we do. For, as I have often told you before and now tell you again even with tears, many live as enemies of the Cross of Christ. Their destiny is destruction, their god is their stomach, and their glory is in their shame. Their mind is set on earthly things. But our citizenship is in heaven.

This passage describes how to be an example by relating what NOT to do, namely setting one's mind on earthly things, focusing on personal glory, and being an enemy of the Cross of Christ. Paul emphasizes that a follower's "citizenship is in heaven," whereby we should conduct ourselves as if we represent a being who resides in heaven. Being a citizen of heaven means acknowledging that what you do in this world should serve the Lord and that acceptance on your part will merit a heavenly reward. We should live, knowing that we are already citizens in heaven. That knowing should enable us to endure life's challenges because something much, much better awaits us.

Paul implores the church in Ephesus in Eph 5:1–2 to "Follow God's example, therefore, as dearly loved children and walk in the way of love, just as Christ loved us and gave himself up for us as a fragrant offering and sacrifice to God." In 2 Thess 3:7–10, Paul advises the followers to follow his example:

> For you yourselves know how you ought to follow *our example*. We were not idle when we were with you, nor did we eat anyone's food without paying for it. On the contrary, we worked night and day, laboring and toiling so that we would not be a burden to any of you. We did this, not because we do not have the right to such help, but in order to offer ourselves as *a model for you to imitate*. For even when we were with you, we gave you this rule: "The one who is unwilling to work shall not eat."

What does Paul say about his example while working with the members of the church? First, he was not idle; he worked, avoiding anything that could be perceived as laziness or entitlement. Second, he didn't eat anyone's food without paying for it, meaning that he didn't take advantage of his position or role. In the positive, he states that he "worked night and day" to avoid being a burden to the churchgoers in Philippi. Paul concludes by referring to himself as "a model for you to imitate."

In his letter to Timothy, who at the time was a young preacher with his own church, Paul wrote in 1 Tim 4:12: ". . . be thou an example of the believers, in word (speech), in conversation (behavior), in charity (love), in spirit, in faith, in purity (in motives as well as act)."

Paul is saying that to win people to the Lord, that you should be an example in these ways. The Apostle hit on this again in his letter to the Galatians (chapter 5, verse 25): "If we live in the spirit, let us also walk in the spirit." Again, Paul's writings all map back to Jesus and His example.

These passages all relate to being an example for Christ. But what should you do or not do to reflect that example? Let's start with the easy one: what NOT to do.

The Bible is filled with commentary on how not to act or observations on people, their sinful behavior, and its ramifications. You can't tell the story of the fall of man and being saved through Jesus' redemptive sacrifice on the Cross without pointing out humanity's sin for which He died. Of course, the Bible starts with Adam and Eve, and the sinful act of eating the fruit from the Forbidden Tree in Gen 3. Shortly thereafter, Cain murders Abel in chapter 4. Then, the first reference of societal sin appears in chapter 6 with the story of Noah and the wickedness of the world. From Gen 6:5:

> The LORD saw how great the wickedness of the human race had become on the earth, and that every inclination of the thoughts of the human heart was only evil all the time. The LORD regretted that he had made human beings on the earth, and his heart was deeply troubled.

Given just how loving God the Father is, it is amazing to think that evil in the world was so great and pervasive that it led Him to regret his choice to create humankind. Think we live in evil times today? At that time, the whole world was corrupt with sin, and there was no beacon of hope except for one righteous man and his family. So, the flood happens. The world's population was wiped out. Through Noah's family, God builds back up the human race. However, it does not take long in Biblical time before humans are back to systemic, societal sin with the building of the Tower of Babel and the desire to "make a name for ourselves" (Gen 11:4).

Sodom and Gomorrah are destroyed in chapter 19. The Book of Exodus details repeated acts of sin by the Israelites during their journey from Egypt to the Promised Land, including sin so deep that it caused the Lord to wipe out an entire generation of them, save two faithful followers (i.e., Caleb and Joshua).

The history books of the Bible recount the progression of the Israelites as a people and culture, and record their repeated departures from the Lord that required Him to rise up a judge to save them. The Israelites asked the Lord for a king and—despite His warnings against the idea—they get one. It does not take long for the king concept to go astray. Saul sinned. After David, Solomon eventually falls into sin, followed by 32 to 34 of 39 kings of Israel and Judea "doing what was evil in the Lord's eyes."

The people's sin in Israel and Judea becomes so great that the Lord sends the armies of the north, wipes out the people, and sends a remnant into exile. The books of Isaiah, Jeremiah, Ezekiel, and Hosea go into deep detail on the sins of the Israelites and what not to do, including some very heinous behavior. From 2 Kgs 17:16–17:

> "[The Israelites] forsook all the commands of the LORD their God and made for themselves two idols cast in the shape of calves, and an Asherah pole. They bowed down to all the starry hosts, and they worshiped Baal. They sacrificed their sons and daughters in the fire. They practiced divination and sought omens and sold themselves to do evil in the eyes of the LORD, arousing his anger."

Today, no one may be sacrificing their children to the fire in a terrible religious ritual. However, today's humans are not far off. We are predisposed to sin. It is innate and unavoidable. If not the sins of the Israelites, there are other manifestations of society's sin that undoubtedly occur today.

One need not go very far to find examples. They're as close as everyday television. When *Law & Order: Special Victims Unit* premiered in 1999, my wife and I tried watching the show. We generally like episodic police procedurals. According to the website IMDB.com, the series "follows the Special Victims Unit, a specially trained squad of detectives in the N.Y.P.D., who investigate sexually related crimes." One of the early episodes involved heinous crimes committed against a child. More than 20 years later as I write this book, I remember—at one point about halfway through the episode, as the sordid details of the crime became more apparent—I looked up from my laptop, glanced over to my wife, and said something to the extent of, "This is pretty nasty stuff. We don't need to be watching this." There's something about crimes committed against kids that crosses the line, and it was a painful reminder of the horrors that exist in this world. Eerily, crimes like the ones portrayed on TV harken to the ritual murders committed by the Israelite people.

When Your Actions Don't Match Your Brand

For me, Solomon is easily the most enigmatic person in all of Scriptures. When you think about his Godly brand, what are the first two things that generally come to mind: 1) wisest person who has ever lived other than Jesus and 2) hundreds of wives. Boy, do those two things seem to contradict themselves.

In 1 Kgs 3, the young king of Israel does something amazing. When God says to him in a dream, "Ask for whatever you want me to give you," Solomon asks for "a discerning heart to govern your people and to distinguish between right and wrong."

In speaking with God, Solomon humbly refers to himself in this passage as "your servant king" (v7) and "your servant" (v9). The young king asks for something that will ultimately benefit his people, rather than something only for himself. And God responds by blessing him with abundant wisdom and knowledge, beyond anything Solomon could have comprehended. God also blessed him with the other things that he did not ask for, namely wealth and honor, so "that in your lifetime you will have no equal among kings."

This wisdom is immediately demonstrated in the second half of 1 Kgs 3 with the story of the two prostitutes who come to Solomon to resolve a dispute over a baby. One woman says that the other took her infant after accidently smothering hers while she slept. The other woman disputes her charge. Solomon asks for a sword to be brought to him. He gives the order: "Cut the living child in two and give half to one and half to the other." (v25)

The mother of the living child, moved by love for her child, tells Solomon, "Please, my lord, give her the living baby! Don't kill him!" But the other said, "Neither I nor you shall have him. Cut him in two!" Crazy bad response from the other woman, right? Solomon then renders his ruling: "Give the living baby to the first woman. Do not kill him; she is his mother."

The Scriptures tell us that "When all Israel heard the verdict the king had given, they held the king in awe." (v28) Awe, indeed. Not even the most hardened of us would consider hacking an infant in two to uncover which complete stranger loves that child more than the other. In doing so, Solomon uncovered the love of one woman and profound bitterness of the other.

Solomon fulfills what his father David intended to do, that being the building of a temple for the Lord. First Kings 9 tell us, "When Solomon had finished building the temple of the LORD and the royal palace, and had achieved all he had desired to do, the LORD appeared to him a second time, as he had appeared to him at Gibeon. The LORD said to him:

> 'As for you, if you walk before me faithfully with integrity of heart and uprightness, as David your father did, and do all I command and observe my decrees and laws, I will establish your royal throne over Israel forever, as I promised David your father when I said, 'You shall never fail to have a successor on the throne of Israel.'
>
> 'But if you or your descendants turn away from me and do not observe the commands and decrees I have given you and go off to serve other gods and worship them, then I will cut off Israel from the land I have given them and will reject this temple I have consecrated for my Name.'"

These words from the Lord are a clear promise followed by a warning. It's this passage that makes it so difficult to reconcile where Solomon goes in his leadership and eventual falling away from the Lord. At the end of chapter 10, we are reminded of Solomon's splendor:

> King Solomon was greater in riches and wisdom than all the other kings of the earth. The whole world sought audience with Solomon to hear the wisdom God had put in his heart. Year after year, everyone who came brought a gift—articles of silver and gold, robes, weapons and spices, and horses and mules.

Yet, in chapter 11, it all goes off the rails, starting with verses 1–4, 6:

> King Solomon, however, loved many foreign women besides Pharaoh's daughter—Moabites, Ammonites, Edomites, Sidonians and Hittites. They were from nations about which the LORD had told the Israelites, "You must not intermarry with them, because they will surely turn your hearts after their gods." Nevertheless, Solomon held fast to them in love. He had seven hundred wives of royal birth and three hundred concubines,

and his wives led him astray. As Solomon grew old, his wives turned his heart after other gods, and his heart was not fully devoted to the Lord his God, as the heart of David his father had been. So Solomon did evil in the eyes of the Lord; he did not follow the Lord completely, as David his father had done.

Unpacking this passage, it starts with "King Solomon, however, loved many foreign women . . ." That, right there, was a big problem. Verse 2 clearly states that they were from nations that the Lord prohibited the Israelites from intermarrying. He "held fast to them in love," clearly prioritizing them and their wishes over following God and His Word. Verse 3 is simply staggering: "He had seven hundred wives of royal birth and three hundred concubines, and his wives led him astray." I bet. One thousand women must've kept him quite busy, day and night.

These women turned Solomon's heart after other gods, and the most heartbreaking result was "Solomon did evil in the eyes of the Lord." God tried to bring the king back. Twice, He appeared to Solomon and forbade him to follow other gods. Yet, "Solomon did not keep the Lord's command." In these types of situations, there will be consequences for the king's sin. When it was clear that Solomon would not return to a righteous path, God told him: "I will most certainly tear the kingdom away from you and give it to one of your subordinates." And that's exactly what the Lord did. Later in chapter 11, "the Lord raised up against Solomon an adversary, Hadad the Edomite," who had fled to Egypt as a boy when Joab earlier wiped out all the other men of Edom.

From a Godly branding perspective, Solomon is seemingly full of contradictions. How can the man who authored "The fear of the Lord is the beginning of knowledge . . .» (Prov 1:7) and "Trust in the Lord with all your heart and lean not on your own understanding; in all your ways submit to him, and he will make your paths straight . . ." (Prov 3:5–6) also have written "I applied my mind to study and to explore by wisdom all that is done under the heavens. What a heavy burden God has laid on mankind! I have seen all the things that are done under the sun; all of them are meaningless, a chasing after the wind."? (Eccl 1:13–14)

Both Proverbs and Ecclesiastes feel as though they were written by two different people. In a sense, they were because Solomon's Godly brand evolved over the course of his life. I use the word "evolved" not "changed," because Solomon seemed to always prioritize certain things like women in his life. One of the young king's first missteps was taking an Egyptian wife. He did it for political and economic gain. But the choice directly conflicted with Mosaic law, specifically from Deut 17:16 that states "for the Lord has told you, 'You are not to go back that way again,'" referring to acquiring horses from Egypt, making the people return there, or any other dependency on that nation. Furthermore, verse 17 states another pitfall for the king of Israel to avoid: "He must not take many wives, or his heart will be led astray." Of course, that clearly happened in Solomon's later life. As if those two infractions were not enough, verse 17 continues: "He [the king] must not accumulate large amounts of silver and gold." Solomon violates the trifecta of "don't dos" here.

The big question is: how did Solomon reach the place where he became so disconnected from God that—despite two warnings, then the "I will most certainly tear the kingdom away from you" decree from the Lord (1 Kgs 11:11–13)—the king continued to worship the detestable gods of his foreign wives? Why did Solomon let himself fall in this way to this magnitude?

Potential cause number one: Solomon's emotions of love for his many wives and concubines overrode his profound wisdom. How many times in life do we know the right thing to do in our mind, but "follow our heart" anyway? Something "just feels right" or "my gut is telling me." So many times, we can be confronted with the logical awareness that what we're doing is a sinful act, yet we press forward with it anyway because 1) we simply want to do it; 2) we're feed up with always following the rules; 3) we're angry at God for something, and it's a form of lashing out; 4) we rationalize that the sinful act "isn't that big a deal" in the grand scheme of things; or 5) many other excuses we give ourselves to justify our willingly giving into temptation and sinning.

Somewhere along the line, Solomon let his feelings grab hold of him and justify worshipping other gods. These feelings were largely driven by wanting to please his many wives, I'd presume. Sadly, he became more interested in pleasing them, than God.

Potential cause number two: Solomon's saw the absolute worst that humanity had to offer. If the story of the two prostitutes who quarreled over the alive child is any indication of the types of cases he had to adjudicate, he had to apply his profound wisdom to the ugliest of human behaviors. Yes, the mother of the alive child showed tremendous love for her son by being willing to give him up to the other woman to spare his life. But the reaction of the other woman (i.e., "Cut him in two!") is deeply bitter and monstrous. One can only be exposed to such atrocious behavior before it takes a toll, and you find yourself writing for all posterity: "For with much wisdom comes much sorrow; the more knowledge, the more grief." (Eccl 1:18)

Potential cause number three: Related to the first two potential causes but slightly different, Solomon simply stopped caring about following God's ways. In his profound wisdom, Solomon had a lucid understanding of the law and following the Lord's decrees. The king did it for a portion of his life, then he just gave up, perhaps because he found it unsustainable, especially in light of the distraction of the women in his life. I've personally wondered whether Solomon treated the worshipping of other gods as a form of expansion of his wisdom, as if he was experimenting with them for pure reasons of discovery. Was that a justification to stop being vigilant in following God's ways?

Potential cause number four, and this one feels the most likely: Solomon fulfilled his purpose early in life and didn't come up with a new one. In 1 Kgs 9:1–2, we read: "When Solomon had finished building the temple of the LORD and the royal palace, and had achieved all he had desired to do, the LORD appeared to him . . ." There are a couple telling things here. First, Solomon had completed what he set out to do with building the temple for the Lord as well as his own palace. The temple took seven years to build and required ongoing diligence from him to ensure that it was built to his satisfaction. Those two construction projects were Solomon's purpose for 20 years during his tenure as king. And, when they were completed, that was it. The rest of chapter 9 tells us about other construction projects that Solomon set in motion: a palace for his first wife, fortifying towns, and building ships to haul back gold from Ophir. Nothing recounted in this passage seems especially inspiring, almost as if these tasks were "the next thing on the laundry list."

The second telling part of the first two verses of chapter 9 is that God chose this time to—once again—remind Solomon that "if you walk before me faithfully with integrity of heart and uprightness, as David your father did, and do all I command and observe my decrees and laws, I will establish your royal throne over Israel forever," as well as repeat the warning that "if you or your descendants turn away from me and do not observe the commands and decrees I have given you and go off to serve other gods and worship them, then I will cut off Israel from the land I have given them and will reject this temple I have consecrated for my Name."

Chapter 9 only records this promise and warning. Nothing else. No other instruction, no other action items for the king to fulfill. Why does the Lord repeat this vision to Solomon? It is a cautionary tale to us that the Lord could see that the combination of Solomon finishing the work he perceived for himself with the distracting women in his life was going to be a big problem in the future. It's also interesting that—unlike like their prior exchanges—the Scriptures do not record Solomon speaking with God at this point. God delivers His opportunity and warning, and there is no response from Solomon. It feels as though a minimum response from the king may have been something along the lines of the following: "Lord, you are great! You have blessed me beyond measure. Thank you for blessing your humble servant. I'll keep what you said in mind."

It's difficult to comprehend when you read in chapters 9 and 10 just how much gold Solomon was receiving as tribute and revenues. Conservative estimates in today's monetary exchanges place the value of the gold he received at $500,000,000 or half a billion dollars. Solomon received so much gold that he "made two hundred large shields of hammered gold" (9:16) and "a great throne covered with ivory and overlaid with fine gold. (9:18)" In Bible studies about Solomon, I have personally wondered what he may have done with all that wealth, rather than simply gathering it for himself. Instead of amassing gold, accumulating chariots and horses (9:26), or importing horses from Egypt (9:28), all of which were prescribed sins recorded by Moses in Deuteronomy, could he have fed the poor or helped those in need? In Eccl 4:1, Solomon writes "I saw the tears of the oppressed—and they have no comforter." Could he have paid his forced labor a fair wage? (Yes, I know that's complicated given that they were the peoples of Canaan who should have been wiped out, per God's instructions to the Israelites.) Should he have placed that gold in the Lord's treasury?

Should Solomon have asked God to reveal to him what to do with the gold? Oddly, it seems as though Solomon knew that his riches were eroding his soul. Eccl 4:8 states ". . . yet his eyes were not content with his wealth." Then, later in verse 13, "Better a poor but wise youth than an old but foolish king who no longer knows how to heed a warning." Of course, that warning is God's warning from 1 Kgs 9.

Here's the real question: if we were in Solomon's shoes, would we have gone down the same path? How would we handle literally everyone in the world seeking us out for our greatness, wanting to be around us, sending us shipments of gold that weighed in the tons, or—in Solomon's case—having any woman of our choice? While Solomon had all the wisdom in the world, he did not have the example of Jesus to follow, as we do today.

What can we learn from Solomon from a Godly branding standpoint? First, your purpose is inextricably tied to your Godly brand.

Without a making-a-difference purpose for God in your life, you are prone to idleness, sinking deeper into sinful behavior, and departing from God's ways and likely God Himself. Second, your actions define your brand. Yes, we remember Solomon's wisdom. However, in the same thought, we remember his many wives. Most people consider this aspect of his life before they consider the amazing temple that he built for God, and that sad fact detracts from his brand.

Third, your brand changes over time, but is rooted in your true self. There were signs early in Solomon's life with the marriage to Pharaoh's daughter—even if it was for political reasons—that he was not fully aligned with God's Word. If your true self compromises your brand today, ask God for help in managing it. As an example, I grew up in a home with a father whose temper frequently got the better of him. I, too, share that type of temper or—at least—anger. I pray for calming all the time when I get upset.

Fourth and arguably most important, having profound, unparalleled wisdom still doesn't protect you from the insidious reach of sin. There are two sides to this coin. On one hand, it's a cautionary tale of the power of sin in our lives and its capability to corrupt even the most discerning among us, including the wisest person who has ever lived. On the other hand, for those who struggle with repeated, willing sinfulness then suffer with the guilt and fear that accompany it, there may be comfort in knowing that even "the best" succumbed to sin, fell hard, challenged God's patience and willingness to forgive many times over, and still arrived at the point where he wrote in Eccl 11:13: "Now all has been heard; here is the conclusion of the matter: Fear God and keep his commandments, for this is the duty of all mankind."

Ultimately, in Solomon's later years, his actions neither followed his Godly brand of wisdom nor God's laws. Remembering that branding is the alignment of what you say about yourself with what you actually do, Solomon unwound his Godly brand later in his life. Considering what happened to the wise king, when have you been challenged with sin and been tempted to walk away from God for the long term? If that has happened to you, know that—through God's everlasting grace—you can always come back to Him. If you're currently grappling with ongoing sinfulness like Solomon did, turn to God in prayer, listen to what He speaks to you, and know that—through repentance—you can overcome what may seem like insurmountable sin in your life. With Him, nothing is impossible.

Chapter 14

Things that Harm Your Godly Brand

> So then, I myself in my mind am a slave to God's law,
> but in my sinful nature a slave to the law of sin.
>
> —ROM 7:25

POP QUIZ: HOW DO you destroy a $100-billion, 29,000-employee company in one year? A company that *Fortune* magazine named "America's Most Innovative Company" for six consecutive years?

Harder question: how do you do that *and* completely wipe out a 79-year-old, $9.3 billion, 85,000-employee company in the process?

Answer: systemic corporate fraud and corruption that brought down the first company and—due to the greatest audit failure in the history of the U.S.—effectively dissolved the second company.

Those of you who are 35 or more years old may remember the players here. The first company was called Enron, a former energy, commodities, and services company based in Houston, Texas. The second company was Arthur Andersen LLP, formerly one of the "Big Five" accounting firms with PricewaterhouseCoopers, Deloitte Touche Tohmatsu, Ernst & Young, and KPMG.

In 2001, the widely publicized scandal involved the corporation's key executives using accounting loopholes, special-purpose entities, and poor financial reporting to hide billions of dollars in debt from failed deals and projects. These executives overtly deceived Enron's board of directors and audit committee on the company's financial operations and pressured Arthur Andersen to go along with the charade. When the fraud and corruption were exposed, the company's stock price that had sold at US$90.75 per share in mid-2000 cratered to less than $1 by the end of November 2001. On December 2, 2001, the company filed for Chapter 11, making it the largest corporate bankruptcy in U.S. history at the time.

The groundwork that led to the failure of Enron was laid well before its collapse in late 2001. However, when the executive corruption was revealed, the brand's demise was swift and decisive. Caught up in the wreckage, Arthur Andersen was found guilty of illegally destroying documents relevant to the U.S. Securities and Exchange Commission (SEC) investigation, thereby voiding its license to audit public companies and effectively closing the firm.

What does Enron's failure mean to you? No brand is immune to the effects of sin. In the case of Enron, it was the sinful acts of its executives, all of whom landed in jail. We know we live in a sinful world and that the majority of people on this planet are not God followers. The big problem is, people who do not know God have no higher authority to whom they are answerable. Without that higher authority, even if they understand or respect the concept of sin, rationalizing it and performing sinful acts become all too easy. For unbelievers, gossip, lies, cheating, malicious ambition, advantage-taking, disrespect, and lack of integrity are just a few of the many fruits of their sinful selves. We, as God followers, are commanded by Jesus through the Great Commission (Matt 28:16–20) to enter into this sinful world and bear Godly fruit ourselves:

> Jesus came to [the eleven disciples] and said, "All authority in heaven and on earth has been given to me. Therefore go and make disciples of all nations, baptizing them in the name of the Father and of the Son and of the Holy Spirit, and teaching them to obey everything I have commanded you. And surely I am with you always, to the very end of the age."

As God-followers go into this world and co-mingle with unbelievers, we come face-to-face with the sinful acts of others as well as our own sinful behavior in relation them. How do we steel ourselves from the effects of a sinful, fallen world? And how do we cope with the other things that will harm our Godly brand, if we let them? Things like fear, inconsistency, and—believe it or not—too much idle time all can hurt your Godly brand. Let's take a look at each of these brand-assailants, starting with our own sin.

Our Own Sin

Put simply, sin affects your brand. In fact, sin is a huge part of your brand. Just as consumer brands have weaknesses or gaps in their offerings that competitors try to exploit, we have weaknesses. And, just as consumer brands find ways of positioning their value over their weaknesses to remain compelling to people who buy their products or services, we, too, must reflect the value of our Godly brand to counteract the effects of our sin.

Because sin is inherent, it cannot be defeated or removed from your Godly brand. We will always be sinful all the time, no matter what we do. However, we can do things to help overcome it or position our Godly brand to positively affect other people. We cannot do this on our own! We need the strength and guidance of the Holy Spirit to make our Godly brand more prominent than our sinful nature. The tough part is, it's a constant work-in-progress. It is never-ending. For the entire duration of your life as a God follower, you will need to rely on the Holy Spirit to position your Godly brand ahead of your weaknesses.

A great example of this need to be vigilant with the Holy Spirit in your life is King David from the Old Testament. God called him "a man after my own heart" (Acts 13:22). He was God's anointed king. He was responsible for writing more than 75 highly inspirational and moving psalms. However, he got caught up in what is arguably the second-worst display of sin in the Scriptures, behind only to the Jewish leaders' persecution of Jesus on the night before His death.

The story of David and Bathsheba that is recorded in 2 Sam 11–12 is well-known to most believers. In summary, David stayed home "in the spring, at the time when kings go off to war," and—one evening when he was idly walking on the roof of his palace—he noticed Bathsheba bathing. He was struck by her beauty and sent someone to find out who she was. David discovered that she was married to one of his elite soldiers, Uriah. Despite this, he sent messengers to her home, brought her into the palace, and slept with her.

Bathsheba became pregnant and notified David. His response was to attempt to cover up his sin by recalling Uriah from the front lines for a little R&R with his lovely wife. Being a good soldier and loyal to his fellow soldiers, he instead slept at the entrance to the palace with all his master's servants. So, David's plan didn't work. When he confronted Uriah, the soldier explained his reasoning. David's response? Try to get Uriah drunk, then send him home to Bathsheba. It still didn't work, as the soldier spent the night at the palace gate again.

Desperate to cover up his sin, David did one of the most heinous acts recorded in the Bible (2 Sam 11:14–15):

> In the morning David wrote a letter to Joab and sent it with Uriah. In it he wrote, "Put Uriah out in front where the fighting is fiercest. Then withdraw from him so he will be struck down and die."

Uriah literally carried his death sentence back to the front line, gave it to Joab (the commander of the armies), probably watched as he read it, then left the tent when Joab dismissed him, not having any idea what fate awaited him.

Uriah did fall in battle, and David took Bathsheba as his wife after she mourned for the appropriate amount of time. As the Scriptures point out though: "But the thing David had done displeased the LORD." (verse 27)

There are a lot of lessons to be learned about the effects of sin on your Godly brand from this story, and from chapter 12 when the prophet Nathan confronts David about his actions:

- *Sin makes you do things that are inconsistent with your Godly brand*—One thing about this story that is so interesting and disturbing is how much David tried to scheme his way out of his sinful actions. He knew the penalty for what he did was death. So, to cover it up, he undertook a grievously premeditated approach to bring back Uriah, get him to lay with his wife, and hope that no one would notice the conspicuous timing of when the child would ultimately be born. When Uriah didn't go home that first night, David had to double-down on his cover-up by coercing Uriah through drunkenness. That didn't work, of course.

    Now, at this stage, David's sin only involves him and whoever was helping him try to send Uriah home to Bathsheba. In continuing his deeper descent into sin, David dragged Joab and maybe others on the battlefield into his deceit.

    David has a lot of brand qualities. However, up to this point, deception, dishonor, and abuse of power had not been among them. He exhibited all these qualities and more due to his sin.

It's as the old saying goes, "Sin will take you further than you wanted to go, keep you longer than you wanted to stay, and cost you more than you wanted to pay."

- *No matter had bad your sin is and how it affects your brand, you can come back from it, but only if you repent*—Another alarming part of the story is how content David was to go along his merry way once learning of Uriah's death. After Bathsheba mourned for her husband, David married her, and they had a baby together. David believed he got away with his crime. That is, until the prophet Nathan was sent by God to confront him.

    Nathan relates a story of a rich man with many sheep who stole the one and only lamb that belonged to a poor man to feed a traveler. The prophet did this to help David understand the depths of his sin. He was so upset at the telling of the story that he "burned with anger against the man and said to Nathan, 'As surely as the Lord lives, the man who did this must die!'" (2 Sam 12–15)

    Nathan immediately told David that "You are the man!" Uh-oh. David just pronounced a death sentence for himself and rightfully so. Nathan recounts all the consequences of David's sin, including "the sword will never depart from your house" (verse 10); "one who is close to you" will sleep with his wives in public, humiliating David (verses 11–12); and "the son born to you will die." (verse 14)

    At this very pivotal juncture, David has many ways to respond. His predecessor Saul was keen to giving any number of excuses for his sinful behavior. David could deny the wrongdoing. He could throw Nathan out for his insolent accusations. Instead, David repented immediately in verse 13: "David said to Nathan, 'I have sinned against the Lord.'"

    David did suffer the consequences of his sin. His kingdom was under constant strife for the rest of his life, including coup attempts from two of his own sons. He lived to see four of his sons die, harkening back to his comment to Nathan after hearing the lamb story when he referred to himself, saying "He must pay for that lamb four times over." Lastly, Absalom slept with 10 of David's concubines in a very public daylight exhibition of power. The consequences of David's sin were an absolute horror show.

    However, God still restored David. He comforted Bathsheba, and they had another child, Solomon, whom the Lord loved.

Absalom tried to take the throne and drove David into exile. Yet, through some machinations involving God turning Absalom's trusted advisor's very smart counsel to attack David while he was on the run into "foolishness," David was able to recover and win the ultimate battle for the throne.

Despite his sin, David was able to recapture the kingship through God's grace and mercy. All of it occurred because of David's repentance and humility (see 2 Sam 16:5–14 and David's reaction to Shimei's curses). To borrow another old cliché, "always 'fess up when you mess up."

- *There will be consequences and harm to your brand*—It's unavoidable. There will be consequences for your sin. The effect of those consequences on your Godly brand can be proportional to the severity of your sin. While all sin is equal, society does perceive them differently. Rightly or wrongly, murder is generally regarded by people as worse than using obscenities, to use an extreme example.

As my wife and I entered our forties, we began to see numerous Christian couples in our social circles get divorced due to one of the three As: abuse, adultery, or addiction. Noted talk show host and author Dr. Laura Schlessinger deserves credit for the concept of the three As that lead to the demise of many marriages. Of the three, adultery seemed to be the biggest culprit as a marriage-wrecker among the Christian couples we knew. The varied reasons behind the adultery are not relevant. The consequences of it are.

With divorced parents myself, the situation gets ugly for the kids, family, and friends real fast. Sides must be taken, and usually it's against the parent who committed the adulterous act. Depending on the proceedings of the separation and eventual divorce, houses are sold, kids change schools, older kids have to care for younger kids like pseudo-parents, the couple's family and friends are divvied up, and the list goes on and on.

One big consequence for the adulterer is that his or her brand is associated with the act as well as other not-so-likeable attributes, such as untrustworthiness, betrayal, stupidity, selfishness, and being a wretch. This stink on the brand sticks with that person, too. If the adulterer begins dating again after the marriage has been destroyed, he or she has to explain how and why the adultery occurred and provide some assurance that it will not happen again. It's bad all the way around.

As mentioned earlier, David faced the consequences for his sin numerous times. The story of Bathsheba is one thing. However, in 1 Chr 21, David commits a foolish sin against the Lord by counting the fighting men of Israel without following the law. His motivations for doing so are unclear, although the first verse of the chapter states that "Satan rose up against Israel."

Ultimately though, David's act—which he did over the protests of Joab, the commander of his armies—costs the lives of more than 70,000 Israelite men when God sent a plague in the form of an angel carrying out the punishment among David's kingdom. And it would've been more men had the Lord not shown mercy and stopped the angel from entering Jerusalem at the threshing floor of Araunah the Jebusite.

Again, David repented of his sin, built an altar at that threshing floor, and worshipped God for showing mercy, and the Lord forgave him. But, you can see through David's life, that there were always consequences for his sin. Some of those consequences were harsh. The same holds true for us today. If you feel as though the hand of God is against you, do some self-reflection and honest assessment of your current walk with Him, and identify whether there is some unrepentant sin in your life. If there is, turn to the Lord in humility and ask for forgiveness, and call out to Him for guidance on what you should do to avoid further entrapment to sin.

Fear

What's the greatest hazard of sin? There are a lot of answers to this question, including pride, self-centeredness, and self-justification, just to name a few. These are real hazards. But the real danger is fear and everything that comes with it (anxiety, impatience, desperation, separation, depression, etc.).

There's a great quote from Frank Herbert's masterpiece novel *Dune* about fear: "I must not fear. Fear is the mind-killer. Fear is the little-death that brings total obliteration." So true! The terms "mind-killer" and "little-death" are perfect descriptions for what fear does to us, when it truly grips our lives.

According to the Merriam-Webster dictionary, fear is "an unpleasant often strong emotion caused by anticipation or awareness of danger." The publication *Psychology Today* refers to it as "a vital response to physical and emotional danger—if we didn't feel it, we couldn't protect ourselves from legitimate threats. But often we fear situations that are far from life-or-death, and thus hang back for no good reason."

Fear affects us all. We fear things such as not finding a life partner; not achieving your life's goals or perceived purpose, basically failing in life; being criticized, especially in front of others; being poor or not being able to provide for your family; people you love dying or becoming seriously ill; becoming seriously ill yourself; being the victim of a violent crime; being out of work, especially in your older years; growing old or retiring; or dying. Everyone has some measure of fear, whether they want to admit it, even if it is fear of having fears. Yes, that's a thing.

Josh 1:9 tells us, "Have I not commanded you? Be strong and courageous. Do not be afraid; do not be discouraged, for the Lord your God will be with you wherever you go." Being strong and courageous may seem simple, but the act of doing it may not be. It requires complete *trust* in the Lord that everything will be okay, even though you may have no idea how things will play out. It's not easy to say, "Lord, I have no idea what's going on here, but I trust that You will make all things good and right, according to Your perfect will." But you must. Paraphrasing Ps 91:2, the Lord wants you to look on Him as a "refuge and fortress, placing your trust in Him."

What does deep trust look like? Looking at the story of King Hezekiah from 2 Kgs 18:5: Hezekiah trusted in the Lord, the God of Israel. There was no one like him among all the kings of Judah, either before him or after him.

In the 14th year of Hezekiah's reign, the Lord put him to the ultimate test. The king of Assyria, Sennacherib attacked Judah and captured all its cities. Attempting to appease him, Hezekiah offered him anything he wanted, then—at Sennacherib's request—gave him three hundred talents of silver and thirty talents of gold. To scratch together this amount of gold, Hezekiah emptied the Lord's temple and the treasuries of the royal palace, and even stripped off the gold with which he had covered the doors and doorposts of the Lord's temple. But Sennacherib wanted more.

Sennacherib sent his supreme commander, chief officer, and field commander with a large army to Jerusalem to bully Hezekiah into submission. When they arrived, the field commander began speaking with

Hezekiah's high officials, essentially trash-talking about how they were going to wipe out the city.

From verse 23, "I will give you two thousand horses—if you can put riders on them! How can you repulse one officer of the least of my master's officials?"

Then, from verse 25, "Furthermore, have I come to attack and destroy this place without word from the Lord? The Lord himself told me to march against this country and destroy it."

You can imagine Hezekiah's response when his officials reported to him what the field commander said. From 2 Kgs 19, first verse: "When King Hezekiah heard this, he tore his clothes and put on sackcloth and went into the temple of the Lord." At this point, Hezekiah had a number of choices: give into the field commander's demands to capitulate, ready his troops for one last stand, do what the people of Masada did when confronted with the Roman armies, or turn to the one source of his strength and his people's deliverance: God.

In verse 2, Hezekiah sent his palace administrator, secretary, and all the leading priests—all wearing sackcloth—to see the prophet Isaiah. They humbled themselves before the man of God with a simple message: ". . . pray for the remnant that still survives." Isaiah told the officials not to be afraid and that Sennacherib's armies would withdraw, and that the Assyrian king would be cut down after returning to his country.

On receiving this good news from Isaiah, Hezekiah went to the Lord's temple and prayed himself: "It is true, Lord, that the Assyrian kings have laid waste these nations and their lands. They have thrown their gods into the fire and destroyed them, for they were not gods but only wood and stone, fashioned by human hands. Now, Lord our God, deliver us from his hand, so that all the kingdoms of the earth may know that you alone, Lord, are God."

The Lord responded quickly (verse 35), "That night the angel of the Lord went out and put to death a hundred and eighty-five thousand in the Assyrian camp. When the people got up the next morning—there were all the dead bodies!" Sennacherib withdrew to his home country and soon was killed by his two sons.

What is so marvelous about this story is the size of the army and God's delivering Hezekiah and his people from it. This was the Death Star hovering over Aldaraan from *Star Wars* or Sarumon's orc armies standing outside Helm's Deep in *The Lord of the Rings*. It was an insurmountable force. It was seemingly certain doom. One's natural tendency may be to attempt to make peace and hope the conquering king doesn't annihilate you and your people. That would be trusting yourself and your judgment, verses God.

For believers who have been through any measure of hardship in their lives and come through it with the Lord's help, trust was vital, and it had to be complete and unrelenting, just like Hezekiah's. The king knew he could not beat the evil hordes of Sennacherib, and he didn't try. His first recourse was to humble himself, trust in God, and seek help from Him in prayer. And the Lord heard his prayer, and kept him and his people safe. Remember Ps 27:1, "The LORD is my light and my salvation—whom shall I fear? The LORD is the stronghold of my life—of whom shall I be afraid?"

Where are you dealing with fear in your life? And how have you turned that fear over to the Lord? Have you turned to Him in prayer? Ps 34:4 tells us, "I sought the LORD, and he answered me; he delivered me from all my fears." Don't let fear or any consequential sinful behavior overwhelm you. In the Lord, you will find the love that helps prevent fear. From 1 John 4:18, "There is no fear in love. But perfect love drives out fear."

Being Inconsistent

Lack of consistency in reflecting your brand will kill it. People need to see your brand properly functioning over time before they perceive what it is and that it works. Think of it like training a dog. If you give a dog a treat after he fetches a ball, then slap him the second time he fetches the ball, the dog will not understand what you're going to do next. The trust in what to expect will not exist. Same concept exists with your brand. People need to see consistent proactivity and reactivity with your brand.

In 2 Kgs 11 and 2 Chr 23, we find the story of Joash. As an infant, he was hidden away from his grandmother when she killed the royal family after her son, King Ahaziah, died. For seven years, Joash was concealed in the Lord's Temple by his aunt Jehosheba and her husband, the high priest Jehoiada. Joash was raised in the ways of the Lord and, during a coup staged by Jehoiada, he was anointed king and took the throne upon the execution of his grandmother.

Second Chronicles 23:16-17 tells us that "Jehoiada made a covenant between himself and all the people and the king that they should be the LORD's people. Then all the people went to the house of Baal and tore it down." The next chapter tells us that "Joash did what was right in the eyes of the LORD all the days of Jehoiada the priest." Joash restored the house of the LORD through a proclamation "made throughout Judah and Jerusalem to bring in for the LORD the tax that Moses the servant of God laid on Israel in the wilderness." With the money gathered, Joash gave it to masons and carpenters, and bronze and iron workers to restore the temple.

All that sounds great, right? So far, you may be thinking, "Hey, Joash has a nice ring to it. Wonder why more kids aren't named after him." Well, it's because of a brand shift that began once Jehoiada, the high priest, died at the age of 130 years old. Second Chronicles 24:17–18 relates that "after the death of Jehoiada the princes of Judah came and paid homage to the king. Then the king listened to them. And they abandoned the house of the LORD, the God of their fathers, and served the Asherim and the idols. And wrath came upon Judah and Jerusalem for this guilt of theirs."

To compound matters, when Zechariah, a prophet of the Lord and Jedoiada's son, called out Joash for forsaking the Lord, the king had him stoned to death. As the prophet was dying, he said, "May the LORD see and avenge!" A short time later, Joash was assassinated and *not* buried in the tombs of the kings. Interestingly, Joash is one of four kings omitted from the genealogy of Christ that is recorded in Matthew 1.

That's quite a fall from grace, and that's how quickly inconsistency can ruin a brand. Joash served the Lord and did great things for the temple for the first 30–40 years of his life. However, after being led astray by others then not remembering the kindness of Jehoiada in killing his son, Joash suffered the ultimate penalty: being not gathered to his fathers and "redacted" from the line of Christ.

Too Much Idle Time

This threat to your Godly brand may be the sneakiest of all, because most of us generally do not equate down time with lapsing into sin. In fact, most people want free or idle time to recuperate from a long day, week, or busy season in their lives. Yes, people need down time to rest. Of course, God mandated that time for rest in our lives through the Sabbath. It's also the concept of sabbaticals, if you're in a profession that enables you to take one. However, it's the adverbs "too much" that are important to note. Too much idle time presents problems, because of how we—as sinful creatures—will fill that idle time. And there are repeated examples of the effects of too much idle time throughout the Bible.

When King David experienced idle time in his palace after not going off with his men to war as he always did, he fell to temptation with Bathsheba. Then, in his spare time, he doubled down on his sin with schemes to bring home Uriah to sleep with her to hide the conceiving of a child. As mentioned in the previous chapter, Solomon got into a world of hurt when he finished the building of the Lord's temple and his own palace, and all he had left to do was fortify towns, build ships, and amass more gold. He became more engaged with his 1,000 wives and concubines, who led him astray. The people of Israel turned to idol worship when Moses left them in the desert for 40 days to meet God up on Mount Sinai. Too much idle time in the Garden of Eden for Adam and Eve gave Satan an opportunity to sway them into temptation with eating the fruit from the tree of knowledge of good and evil. You get the idea: too much time on your hands is not a good thing because our tendency is to fill that time with idle pursuits, or—more aptly—*idol* pursuits.

Research repeatedly points to idle time as a cause of boredom among teenagers. With nothing else to do, this boredom leads many of them to experiment with drugs, binge drink, engage in sexual pursuits or turn to inappropriate activities via the internet. These things become idols that distract teenagers from focusing on God and living a Godly branded life. Guess what? Teenagers aren't the only ones for whom boredom produces these things. Adults will do the same things, perhaps even more than teenagers.

If you chronically have a lot of free or idle time and grapple with these types of behaviors, there are two Godly brand attributes that may help put you on the right path: being a member of God's church and being an agent of change in the world. Both entail active involvement in the world outside of your home. Both may involve you volunteering for service. You should find a ministry that speaks to your spiritual gifts and do it. Or perhaps, try something a little out of your comfort zone to expand your toolkit for God.

Regarding making a difference in the world, this one can take many shapes and sizes. However, when the Lord blesses you with wisdom and insight into what He calls you to do, you can devote time and energy into fulfilling it, thereby reducing too much idle time down to a reasonable amount of free time.

What to Absolutely, Positively Avoid

Because some people need to know both the positive (i.e., what should I do) as well as the negative (i.e., what should I *not* do), there are two passages that outline actions, behaviors, and thoughts that the Scriptures instructs us to absolutely, positively avoid. Perhaps, the most obvious place to start is the 10 commandments found in Exod 20:1–17: have no other gods before me, do not misuse the name of the Lord your God, remember the Sabbath day by keeping it holy, honor your father and your mother, do not murder, do not commit adultery, do not steal, do not give false testimony against your neighbor, and do not covet your neighbor's house.

In addition to the commandments, as well as the many, many other verses throughout the Bible that provide guidance on what not to do, four short verses in Prov 6 cover the sins that God truly hates (verses 16–19):

> There are six things the Lord hates, seven that are detestable to him: haughty eyes, a lying tongue, hands that shed innocent blood, a heart that devises wicked schemes, feet that are quick to rush into evil, a false witness who pours out lies and a person who stirs up conflict in the community.

Note that they are *hateful* to the Lord. It's important to stop and take a moment to ponder the word hate here. It's a very strong word and emotion. It isn't that the Lord is annoyed, displeased, or exasperated with these things. He *hates* them. God hates these sins so much that He even turned away from His own suffering son when Jesus bore all our sins on the Cross.

To be true to your Godly brand, you must define it and understand how your brand attributes apply to your life. That's the purpose of the next section: Defining Your Godly Brand.

Section 3

Defining Your Godly Brand

In this section, you will perform warm-up exercises to begin to shape how you think about your Godly brand. Then, you will perform exercises to help define it, including your core brand values, personal tagline, and elevator speech. Lastly, you will look at how to aspire to a new Godly brand, if you want or need to change others' perception of you.

Chapter 15

Prep Work

Personality Tests, Spiritual Gifts, & Role of Diversity

IN THIS CHAPTER, WE'LL explore three key aspects of your personal makeup that will set the stage for and get you thinking about your Godly brand, which you'll define in the next chapter. Consider them warm-up exercises to help get you ready by performing some initial self-analysis. Here's the real important part: *the keys to ensuring you get the best results through these exercises and the ones that follow are being honest and realistic with yourself and about yourself.* If you do not approach these exercises with honesty and realism, you will generate results that do not align with what you actually do and say in life, and people will recognize that mismatch. As a result, you will be less effective in fulfilling your purpose for God.

Just a reminder, you can change your brand, and chapter 19 on Aspirational Branding covers that topic. For now though, let's see where you currently stand with your Godly brand.

This chapter is meant to serve both individuals and organizations. While much of the content leans toward individuals, if you own a God-following business, these steps apply to you, too.

The Impact of Your Personality Type

If you've ever worked in a corporate environment, you've probably taken one or more of the different personality tests to help inform how you interact with others in your organization. There are several popular ones: Myers-Briggs, StrengthsFinder, Enneagram, DiSC, and Insights Discovery, to name a few. Each of them has a different methodology to reveal different aspects of your personality. Personality tests can be good at uncovering certain drivers that affect how you relate with others, and their findings may help inform some aspects of your brand, but the results do *not* define your brand.

Personality tests tend to reflect how you innately respond to things in your life—good, bad, and everything in-between. The key word here is "innately." Your personality is hardwired into your being; you cannot help but to feel the way that you do when different life circumstances arise. However, your Godly brand is more controllable and can be presented for an effect. For example, your personality test results can indicate that you are introverted, prefer to work alone, and get your energy from self (versus others). You can still speak at a networking event, then mingle with the crowd of attendees afterward, thereby giving the appearance that you're extroverted, love being around people, and receive your energy from others. In these types of cases though, you put on a persona for a limited amount of time and—after it is over—you are typically exhausted from maintaining that appearance of being extroverted.

People who don't know you well will think that you're very social, because that's how they perceive you. Your personality didn't change. How you present yourself is what defines your brand, and—as in the example above—can run somewhat counter to your natural personality.

It can work in the reverse, too. Really extroverted people who may not be "good with numbers" may have a job that compels them to balance P&L statements, create and manage departmental budgets, and parse data and metrics all the time. It may take them much longer to do that number-crunching, but—to the outside world—they look like real "number-crunchers."

We as humans do this type of thing all the time, depending on the context of our lives and our audience at the time. How many of you recognize that you behave differently at work than at home? Ultimately, creating your Godly brand will factor your personality into the equation, but does not need to be dependent on it. If you have never taken a personality test, it's a good idea to take one, and all of the above-mentioned tests are available online via a simple search.

Spiritual Gifts

The concept of spiritual gifts is primarily viewed as something that pertains to individuals rather than businesses or organizations. Let's change that mindset to include both.

For individuals and organizations, God has blessed you with spiritual gifts that offer an invaluable dimension to better understanding your brand attributes. You may be thinking, "Hey, God gave me these spiritual gifts . . . they are so pervasive in everything I do in life . . . they must be my brand, right?" And you'd be somewhat correct. Your brand attributes may indeed dovetail with your spiritual gifts in some ways.

Spiritual gifts are God-given and Holy Spirit-empowered abilities that each believer receives when he or she turns over his or her life to Christ. They are meant to help a God follower fulfill God's plan on this earth, advance His church, be in His service, or help give the Holy Spirit the opportunity to enter the hearts of other people. Spiritual gifts are not natural abilities or talent, such as being a singer or musician, athlete, craftsman, or successful business professional, although they may manifest through your abilities.

There are many books and websites that offer full explanations of the 20 or so spiritual gifts that are cited by the Apostle Paul in Rom 12, 1 Cor 12–14, and Eph 4, along with tests to ascertain your gifts. This section of the book is meant to familiarize you with the various spiritual gifts, get you thinking and praying about which may apply to you and your Godly brand, then—if you're interested—refer you to one of the many spiritual gifts tests that you can find online.

In Rom 12:6–8, the Apostle Paul writes "We have different gifts, according to the grace given to each of us. If your gift is prophesying, then prophesy in accordance with your faith; if it is serving, then serve; if it is teaching, then teach; if it is to encourage, then give encouragement; if it is giving, then give generously; if it is to lead, do it diligently; if it is to show mercy, do it cheerfully." These verses not only indicate several of the spiritual gifts that we may have, but they also show us that we are to go above and beyond with the gifts we have. It's adopting an attitude to use well what God has given us. The Scriptures offer 20 or so spiritual gifts, listed here in alphabetical order:

- *Administration / Organizing*: Organizing people and resources for greater efficiency, effectiveness, and success.

- *Apostleship:* Seeking out others with the intent of revealing God to them, encouraging a deeper relationship with Him and His community of followers.
- *Discernment / Distinguishing Spirits:* Seeing the "big picture," being intuitively in tune with people to know what is motivating them or situations to offer guidance or insights.
- *Evangelism:* Sharing one's faith and proclaiming the gospel of Jesus Christ to people you meet.
- *Exhortation:* Offering encouragement, wise counsel, unflagging support, and empowerment.
- *Faith:* Believing in Jesus Christ as Savior and knowing in your heart that God has a perfect plan and works all things together for good.
- *Giving:* Freely committing your time, talent, and treasures to carry out God's will and plan.
- Healing: Less about removing someone else's pain or disease, and more about imparting God's healing power and grace to those who are suffering physically, emotionally, or spiritually.
- *Helping:* Lending your time and talent to support others, especially friends, family, and church.
- *Hospitality:* Making visitors, guests, and strangers feel at ease, often opening your home to entertain others and helping to integrate others into the Body of Christ.
- *Interpretation of Tongues:* Understanding what someone who is speaking in tongues is saying, then interpreting it for others across different languages, age groups, and societal groups.
- *Knowledge:* Analyzing data, facts and figures, and information, then translating it into meaningful knowledge.
- *Leadership:* Seeing what God has planned for people, churches, organizations, or communities, then leading them toward God's intended purpose, remaining focused on the big and little things along the way to make it happen.
- *Mercy / Compassion:* Helping others who are in need.
- *Miracles:* Less about performing miracles, and more about helping others see God's awesome power and how He performs them in our day-to-day lives.

- *Prophecy:* Being open for God to speak through you, then sharing it with others.
- *Servanthood:* Serving others ahead of oneself.
- *Shepherding / Mentoring:* Mentoring and offering spiritual guidance to others to help them develop their faith and discipleship.
- *Teaching / Pastoring:* Instructing others based on personal knowledge, experience, and wisdom.
- *Tongues:* Speaking in foreign languages to convey things not previously known to him or her.
- *Wisdom:* "Reading between the lines" and realizing the deeper meanings of things in everyday life, then applying that understanding on behalf of yourself or others.

These spiritual gifts can be grouped into three broad categories, with some overlap between them:

- *Ministry Gifts:* Includes gifts to help grow churches, such as administration, apostleship, faith, helping, leadership, and wisdom.
- *Serving or Supporting Gifts:* Includes how a believer views life, interrelates to others, and grows the church of Christ, such as administration, encouragement, giving, hospitality, leadership, mercy, servanthood, and teaching.
- *Manifestation or Sign Gifts:* Includes supernatural demonstrations of the Holy Spirit, such as discernment / distinguishing spirits, healing, miracles, prophecy, speaking in tongues, and interpreting tongues.

While some gifts seem more important (e.g., prophecy) and some less (e.g., speaking in tongues), the Holy Spirit gives and empowers one or more of them to each believer in relation to how he or she will work to help fulfill God's perfect plan on this earth. These gifts are tailored for each believer, and they take time to develop into fully mature usefulness.

To be clear, just because a God follower may have one or more gifts but not others doesn't mean he or she is "off the hook" from performing them. For example, you may realize that neither evangelism nor giving are among your spiritual gifts. Yet, you still must fulfill Christ's Great Commission (Acts 1:8) to spread His Word. Likewise, in Deut 14:22, the Scriptures tell us to tithe (i.e., give 10 percent of what is ours to God's ministries).

There are plenty of online tests to help determine your spiritual gifts. Here are a few websites that I found when writing this book:

- https://spiritualgiftstest.com/
- https://giftstest.com/
- https://mintools.com/spiritual-gifts-test.htm
- Any number of ones developed by churches across the country. A simple online search will uncover a long list of them.

One cautionary note on these tests that you'll find online, via a mobile app, or in a published book: they are manmade tools to help guide a believer to assess him- or herself with the goal of discovering his/her unique spiritual gifts. God works in mysterious and wonderful ways that manmade tests cannot evaluate. Treat these tests as guidance, not absolute truths. If the Holy Spirit works in you to cultivate a particular gift, do not dismiss it merely because a test did not confirm it. Also, avoid letting a test guide you toward relying on your natural abilities or talent to serve God, versus your spiritual gifts.

Beyond the tests, here is a simple list of questions that you should prayerfully consider to determine your spiritual gifts:

- Looking at the list of spiritual gifts above, do any of them speak to you or resonate with you? Do you have a "gut feeling" about any of them in your life?
- Do you find yourself gravitating to any of these gifts in your current service to the Lord? Do you enjoy doing any of them? Is the Holy Spirit blessing a current ministry that you're involved with?
- What do others say are your strengths or areas where you excel in your service for the Lord?
- After prayer and looking at God's Word, is the Holy Spirit leading you toward any of them?

For the sake of preparing to determine your brand attributes in the next chapter, find a spiritual gifts test that works for you and take it, if you feel called to do so. Otherwise, spend some time on your own to consider these questions, pray about them, and write down your answers. Then, keep those answers handy as you read the next chapter.

If you're considering your spiritual gifts as an organization, have each of your team members take an online or mobile app test, share the results (if each person is willing), then look for patterns and holes in your "coverage" of spiritual gifts. For example, if you're organization performs a lot of community outreach, you'll need people blessed with Ministry gifts. You'll either need to recruit or hire new team members, if you do not have any currently among your volunteers or on the staff. Or, you may want to redeploy team members who identify themselves with Ministry gifts, but are not in a role that requires or optimally uses them.

The Role of Diversity in Your Godly Brand

Diversity can play a large role in your Godly brand, depending on your interest in incorporating what makes you diverse into it. When thinking about diversity, we consider things such as age or generation; cultural background, differences in ability (disabilities); gender and sexuality; health; heritage; language; military veteran; nationality, ethnicity, or race; religious affiliation; socioeconomic status; and more.

Incorporating diversity into your Godly brand looks different for individuals than for businesses. For individuals, diversity involves personal choices about your Godly brand, whereas for businesses, there are operational and marketing choices that must be considered.

Whether for individuals or business, one universal truth exists with regard to incorporating diversity into your Godly brand: be authentic. Including diversity in a brand should never be done solely as a public relations move, to attract certain types of consumers, or counteract a bad reputation in the area.

Individuals

Ultimately, incorporating diversity into your Godly brand involves storytelling, which means that you need to determine why and how your diversity plays a part in the uniqueness of your personal story. The emphasis here is on uniqueness.

In the next chapter, you will go through exercises to narrow down five core values about yourself, then define your brand messaging (talking points, elevator speech). These exercises should help you tell the uniqueness of your personal story and the role diversity in your life.

Your personal storytelling will extend far beyond labels, as in "I'm a 52-year-old Cambodian combat veteran who is deaf and a cancer survivor," for example. Your story will involve the significance of these aspects of your diversity and will be told through the lens of your attitudes, behaviors, character, differentiated experience, expertise, and style. In this example, what about your Cambodian heritage makes you unique from others of Cambodian descendent? How did your military service shape your outlook? How has being deaf affected you? What does it mean to you to be a cancer survivor? What is your attitude toward these aspects of who you are? How do they impact how you express your voice?

One thing that a Caucasian male in his 50s like me simply cannot understand is how the world looks at and impacts people with differences—whether they are a person of color, have a different sexual orientation, or have differing abilities. I am treated differently by this world, given who I am, than those with differences. This is undisputable. Given this reality, I can only address the incorporation of your diversity into your brand *conceptually*.

Conceptually, your attitudes, behaviors, character, differentiated experience, expertise, and style will enrich and amplify your personal story in your own unique way. Some may call this your voice. It is the effect that being a person of diversity has affected your life journey and faithwalk. It will be informed by everything that being a member of a diverse population means to you. But it is also highly individualized. You can come from a first-generation family of Mexican immigrants, and your story will have parallels with other first-generation Mexicans. Along with those similarities, your story will be different.

Finding your unique voice and using it may require you to overcome your fears in sharing your Godly brand. But doing so will bring to life your core purpose and values, which you will define in the next chapter.

Businesses

For businesses, many articles and books have been written on incorporating diversity into a company's operation and offerings. Professional organizations exist solely to promote diversity in corporations and throughout society in general. Companies of varying sizes, but especially large ones, already have an internal infrastructure in place to ensure DEIJ (Diversity, Equity, Inclusion, Justice) initiatives occur for employees, and virtually all those organizations have a C-level executive to strategically design and implement those initiatives.

Because this book targets faith-based small- to medium-sized businesses that may not have the capability to hire someone to specifically preside over DEIJ functions, this section is meant to cover some basics to consider as it pertains to speaking about diversity in your brand.

Let's start with the argument for incorporating diversity into your Godly brand. Market research shows very clearly that brands that promote diversity and equity create far more awareness and get more noticed by diverse populations, younger audiences, and consumers in general. A 2021 Deloitte Global Marketing Trends indicates that 57 percent of consumers are more loyal to brands that commit to addressing social inequities in their actions.

Most business owners/leaders recognize that diversity in their company is a strategic priority; the issue is the extent to which the organization tailors its operations to promote it. If diversity is important to your Godly brand, there are several ways to reflect it across an organization:

1. *Figure Out Your Comfort Zone:* As a business owner/leader, you may recognize the importance of diversity and want to fully support it in your organization. However, it can come with hard questions for people who are faith-based. For example, are you okay hiring someone who is gay or transgender, Muslim or Buddhist, or other trait that takes many Christians out of their comfort zone? Are you open to hiring someone who is blind or visually impaired, or deaf or hearing impaired?

    Very important: never hire someone thinking that exposure to you or your organization's Christian values will "convert" or "save" them. You either accept the person for who they are or you do not hire them.

    You, as the business owner/leader, need to decide and commit to whatever level of diversity you want to embrace. Hiring a person who is Christian and African American, Hispanic, or Asian may be as far as you have gone. Including specific time-off, childcare, or health benefits for moms may be another thing you've done or considered.

    You need to pray about and discern your approach to diversity. And, if it includes embracing more diverse populations, then the next few steps should help.

2. *Bring Diverse Voices into Your Organization:* Besides hiring people from diverse backgrounds as team members, you need to seek out vendors, suppliers, and like-minded co-branding partners. If you are marketing a diversity brand, bringing diverse outside perspectives is vital to the success of your promotional efforts. These various parties should reflect your target markets or customers. If you are marketing to Latino populations and do not have a member(s) of your team who is Latino, you are very much at risk of not fully understanding how to properly message to that target audience, even if you have an outside marketing agency to help.

    If you use diversity influencers in your marketing campaign, make sure you vet their channels of influence (e.g., website, social media, videos) to ensure their brand is aligned with yours and—if it is—seek to establish long-term working relationships with them.

    Make sure that your materials are transadapted. Note that I say transadapted, not translated. Translation is a verbal exercise; transadaption is for the written word. Frequently, English words or axioms do not translate easily into other languages and need to be adapted.

    I have managed multi-million-dollar campaigns that included outreach in more than a dozen threshold languages. I enlisted transadaption services to convert my English materials into those respective languages, then sought trusted messengers (i.e., influential members of their community to whom the people listen) to take those transadapted messages, make them their own, and share them with their constituents via video, e-newsletters, in-person events, or other communications tools.

3. *Listen to those Diverse Voices:* You must give your team members and partners a platform to share their diverse views and genuinely listen to their input. Encourage them to express their needs and those of underrepresented communities.

4. *Create a Written Diversity Plan:* It's very important to get down on paper how your business plans to approach diversity in the workplace so that it can be shared with employees. This plan should address the employee experience and how they see diversity actualized in everything your organization does. That may sound intimidating, but it just means looking through the eyes of diverse populations as you make business decisions.

Also, as the old axiom goes, "think global, act local." Your efforts in diversity are meant to address opportunities that are close by and in your community or industry. Make the objectives of your plan achievable.

5. *Make Your Outcomes Measurable:* Your plan should include some measurable actions that will ultimately demonstrate progress toward a diverse workplace. These measurables may include a target number or percentage of employees, vendors, suppliers, etc.; an increase in the number of diverse members of your senior management team; performing a certain number of company-sponsored service projects in the community; celebrating holidays beyond the "traditional" ones; and more. These ideas are only the tip of the iceberg.

As your business grows, be ready to update and adapt what DEIJ means in your company, to your employees, and with external audiences, especially those to whom you are marketing.

Chapter 16

Defining Your Core Purpose and Values

IN THIS CHAPTER, YOU will define your Core Purpose and select your three to five Core Values. Why only three to five? Both with individual and organizational brands, three to five values are all that can be reinforced adequately by a person or people within the organization. Trying to remember and market more than five values becomes a difficult exercise for consumers of the brand to accept, internalize, and recall. In other words, if you stand for too much, people may get confused about your brand or will not pick up all the things you want them to.

When an organization goes through the process of selecting its brand values, all its stakeholders / decision-makers gather to go through a facilitated exercise with a branding professional. It's always interesting to watch these leaders describe their organization in words or phrases. There can be up to 25 people in the room who have worked there for years, and they will invariably use different words or phrases to describe the organization's values and attributes. They will be close to each other in concept. However, each one will articulate the value or legacy of the organization slightly differently.

Every branding professional has a slightly different process, but they all eventually ask the decision-makers to describe the organization with a word or short phrase. For years, the process that I used involved giving each of the decision-makers a sheet of paper with a list of attributes to complete on their own. This list typically included 50 or more words, with a few empty slots to add words that were not provided.

The decision-makers offered their respective feedback on the list. After they were finished, I collected the sheets of paper, and began to aggregate and categorize the feedback. For some organizations with well-trained workers where corporate messaging had been devised, the groupings of words would be similar and easy to discern. In these cases, the process mostly codified what the decision-makers already knew and served the purpose of committing the brand values to paper for all to share.

However, for some organizations, especially ones that grew from mergers and acquisitions or increased their headcount very quickly, there would be more misalignment when the decision-makers selected their values. Again, it was pretty rare when a decision-maker would call the organization "night" when everyone else called it "day." The misalignment usually took the form of one or two decision-makers listing a value that they wanted the organization to embody, while the others did not see it going in that direction. For example, one or two decision-makers may list the term "price conscious," thereby implying that the organization provides or will provide low-cost products or services. However, the other decision-makers may stand firm that the brand should remain a "midrange" brand, whereby it appeals to consumers who want a higher standard of quality, delivery of services, look and feel, customer experience, etc.

In these cases, the branding professional should facilitate a discussion among the decision-makers on what they want. Remember, branding is the alignment of how an organization or person markets itself (says about itself) with what it delivers and how that shapes people's perceptions. The branding professional will remind the decision-makers that—based on their choices—other aspects of the organization may need to be reshaped to fulfill the brand values.

Only one time in 20-plus years of performing these types of facilitated discussions did I come across an organization with a truly "split brand personality" that was nearly impossible to reconcile. For this one organization, its lack of ability to reconcile this split personality kept it from achieving national prominence, despite having a very worthy corporate mission. The organization serves the homeless by building nice, state-of-the-art shelters that empower those who reside in them toward self-sufficiency. Sounds worthy, right? But the organization served the homeless through the help of companies in the homebuilding industry. Those companies wanted the organization to focus its attentions on being the "white hat" the homebuilding industry. Therein lies the misalignment within that organization that could not be reconciled.

Said another way, if there is brand misalignment among the key decision-makers, it will affect its ability to deliver its products or services in the long term. By the way, there was nothing wrong with this homeless organization. It did and still does fine and worthy work to help disadvantaged individuals and families. The national organization and its affiliates are content to do the good work of helping the homeless in their respective communities without wanting the national spotlight.

Core Purpose

In their best-selling book *Built to Last*, Jim Collins and Jerry Poras refer to a business' core purpose as "the organization's fundamental reason for being. An effective purpose reflects the importance people attach to the company's work—it taps their idealistic motivations—and gets at the deeper reasons for an organization's existence beyond just making money." In describing the profound importance of a core purpose, the authors wrote: "Leaders die, products become obsolete, markets change, new technologies emerge, and management fads come and go, but core ideology in a great company endures as a source of guidance and inspiration."

In his best-selling book *Start with Why: How Great Leaders Inspire Everyone to Take Action*, Simon Sinek describes core purpose this way: "It is *who* you are as a company and *why* you exist. As such, an organization's core purpose has to be completely idealistic. Your ability to prosper as a company is not about what you sell, *it's about what you believe.*"

Your Core Purpose is meant to last a very long time, typically measured in decades. It is meant to inspire change, generate excitement among employees, or focus your organization, aligning it toward a common reason for existing. It is not a Big Hairy Audacious Goal (BHAG) or business strategy, both of which can change numerous times over a span of decades. Also, while you can achieve a goal or complete a strategy, you cannot fulfill a purpose. Sometimes, you see people refer to a Core Purpose as the "soul of an organization" or—for individuals—a "personal vision statement."

Whether for business or personal use, writing a Core Purpose statement takes time, a fair amount of thought and soul-searching, and honest assessment.

Defining Your Core Purpose and Values

Determining the Core Purpose for an organization tends to be easier because there was—at some point—an inspiration or mandate to start it. That inspiration carried the organization through its entrepreneurial stage of initial growth, if not longer. When I go through this exercise with organizations, I use Simon Sinek's *Start With Why* approach. It works for people, too. I ask What the organization does, then How it does it. Every entity with which I've ever worked has been able to articulate What and How. Then, I ask the Why-oriented questions:

Business / Organization	Individual
Why are you in business?	Why do you exist? What are you meant to achieve with your life?
Why is that important?	Why is that important?
Why should anyone care about your brand?	Why should anyone care about what you're doing?
What problem(s) does your organization solve?	What problem beyond yourself are you trying to solve?
Why should investors, donors, etc. consider funding you?	What would you do if many millions of dollars were gifted to you right now? How would you use it?
If you have an existing brand/identity, why isn't it working for you?	If you have an existing brand/identity, why isn't it working for you?
What would the world miss if you never existed?	What would the world miss if you never existed?

There are follow-up questions to these initial thought-starters, but answering them gets the conversation going. I capture the responses, looking for answers that resonate with most of the people in the meeting (when working with a group of business leaders) or the individual him- or herself. I take these answers and write an entire brand platform that includes the Core Purpose and Core Values.

If you're doing this exercise for yourself or your business, this is where honest assessment is critical. You can be honest at this stage because your Core Purpose is for you, not others. Different marketers disagree about whether to share your Core Purpose with the others outside of yourself or your business. Some marketers say, "share it; let external audiences know why you exist." Others, like me, say, "your Core Purpose is an internally facing tool, not meant to be shared with others." Your Core Purpose isn't a secret. It's just generally something the outside world cannot process or has very little relevancy to them because it pertains specifically to your business or person. This is not to say your Core Purpose doesn't manifest itself in everything you do. It should! And because it will, people will eventually begin to discern a general sense of your Core Purpose. But, being upfront with it before demonstrating it consistently over a very long period of time is a little like repeatedly telling someone you want to date that you plan on asking him or her out, but never doing so.

When I write a Core Purpose for someone, I ask myself the following questions as a litmus test before I share it with the client:

- Will the Core Purpose stand the test of time? Will it be true about the organization or person decades from now?
- Is it inspiring? Can people rally around it? Does it instill a sense of pride (the good kind) among employees and stakeholders?
- Will it direct the organization's or person's decision-making about business opportunities, staffing hires, partnerships, etc.?
- Is the Core Purpose genuine to the person or organization? Has the person or organization embodied it, or is on a path to embody it?
- Is it about some business objective, whether it's making money, growing into a new industry sector or with a new target audience? If the answer is yes, then it is NOT a Core Purpose.
- Can the Core Purpose be achieved in the next 5 to 10 years? If the answer is yes, then it is NOT a Core Purpose.
- Is the Core Purpose transformative in some respect? Will it make a difference in the world?

When I'm satisfied with the answers to these questions, I share the draft of the Core Purpose statement with the client to get feedback. Then, the editing process begins. Using an example from a former client, Africa New Day / Un Jour Nouveau (French for "A New Day"), a Christian ministry working in the Republic of Congo that I referenced earlier in the book, the following Core Purpose was derived from interviewing its Board of Directors along with several other influencers in the organization:

> In Congo, one of the most desperate places on earth, God has placed an opportunity to change the culture of a nation through modeling and teaching the sacrificial love of Christ and His

servant heart to a new generation of Congolese men, women, and children. Africa New Day and Un Jour Nouveau work at the center of this opportunity to educate, foster leadership skills, and peacefully oppose pervasive violence and corruption to instill respect for all people, especially women and children, and offer hope for better tomorrow. According to God's perfect plan, we know that "A New Day" in Congo is possible.

This statement was approved by Africa New Day's board in 2016. Since that time, the organization has hired a new executive director, members of its board have come and gone, and the ministry in Congo has evolved dramatically. But this Core Purpose remains evergreen and clearly guides the future direction of the ministry.

To write your Core Purpose, ask yourself the Why-oriented questions above, write down your answers, then distill the important parts into a 100-word or so statement. When you get a first draft completed, ask yourself the litmus-test questions to make sure the statement stands up as an inspiring, decades-long Core Purpose, then edit and fine-tune your statement accordingly.

Core Values

Your core values (or principles) direct everything that you do. Whether for a person or an organization, they define what you believe and stand for. They should guide your behavior and help discern what is right or wrong for your life or business. They are the driving force behind your brand. Core values are inwardly focused; like the Core Purpose, you *only* share them among your workers, not the outside world. You will have brand messages that are externally facing; they are meant to deliberately shape how people perceive you or your organization. We'll cover brand messaging in the next chapter.

When you define your core values, you'll realize some specific benefits that will help define your brand messaging; make better decisions in life for yourself or your business; better understand which relationships (both personally and in business) are best for your life; and better evaluate new opportunities that come into your life. In a business, properly defined and communicated core values will have a direct bearing on your business' credibility in the market; your ability to hire the right team members; and boost morale and corresponding worker productivity.

For organizations or companies, when core values are properly defined and incorporated into the corporate culture, they can align a large employee or volunteer base around specific behaviors or goals. Employees who understand an organization's core values more positively interact with and respect each other; mitigate or prevent conflicts; ideate and innovate more productively; and better serve the customers, which affects the bottom line.

The key is aligning your life or business with your core values and reinforcing them in everything you do. In a business context, that means incorporating them into your internal messaging, collateral, and team meetings.

When creating your core values, you will want to create ones that are unique to you and not what you think someone else would want you to be. It's best to be honest to yourself or business, because not doing so will lead to confusion with people with whom you come into contact and eventual brand mis-alignment. Core values should have other characteristics:

- *Exclusive:* Some or all your core values must be individual to you or the culture of your business. Although there may be other people or businesses with similar values, create your own; don't copy anyone else, even those you admire or aspire to be.

- *Virtually Unchanging:* Once defined and promoted, core values should not change. That consistency will serve you and your business well, especially when attracting customers who align their values with yours, which is the ultimate objective for business success. Whether personally or in business, you should never change your values without a great deal of thought and consideration.

- *Important:* Core values should be something that you or the members of your team in a business are driven by and holds special meaning. As an individual, you need to believe in them; as a company, your workers must buy into them.

- *Clear and succinct:* Core values should be easy to understand with nothing left vague or ambiguous. As we proceed to defining your core values in the next section, you'll have the option to make them a single word or short phrase.

- *Action-oriented:* Because core values are meant to guide everything you or your business does, they should be directive and imply an action of some sort. You can choose single words for your core values, like "caring." If defining core values for yourself, you will understand what a word like "caring" means. However, a word like this one is open to interpretation by others, if determining values for a business. It's better to narrow-down what the concept means with phrases like "Show others we care," "Ensure customers feel well cared for," or "Go the extra mile for customers." Each of these phrases has an action word to kick it off.

Now that we understand what core values should be, it's time to create them. Listed below is an exercise to help you identify your core values or those of your business. Whether for personal or business use, the process is largely the same, except for one big factor: the involvement of your team members.

6 Steps to Define Your Core Values

Defining your core values is an exciting and considerate exercise. It starts with being completely open-minded about the process, though. This is important if doing it for yourself. It is vital if doing it for a business. The process requires the elimination of preconceived notions, prejudices, or long-held beliefs about yourself or your business. Why? Core Values are discovered through deep self-awareness and introspection; they are not chosen from a list on the Internet.

When I lead this exercise for an organization or business, sometimes I'm asked how long the process will take. It depends on a few variables: how many people are involved; how young or old the organization is, and how much some may want to hold onto "the old" ways of doing things; the personalities of the people in the room and their interest in the work; and more. For businesses, it should take 6 to 12 weeks, but can take months if internal conflicts occur or the corporate culture is slow-moving. For individuals doing this exercise, it could take a few hours or days of careful, prayerful consideration.

Step 1—Uncover All the Possibilities

Either by yourself for personal use or with a group of experienced, invested employees for an organization, list all your greatest strengths;

personal or corporate priorities, beliefs, and ideals; current skills you do well and ones you hope to do well in the future; and any areas where you feel passionate or want to make a difference. Try to refrain from generalities, such as reliable, integrity, caring and so on, *unless* they are truly and deeply woven into who you are.

Whether yourself or with a team, do not limit or constrain this process. If you think or speak it, write it down. If you have difficulty thinking through this process or getting your employees to speak up, here are a few starter questions:

- What are my/our greatest strengths?
- If someone asked you what you/we believe, what would you say?
  [Note: This question doesn't just pertain to faith; it can include ideology, business practices, cause-related or philanthropic beliefs, and more.]
- What do I/we stand for? What makes me/us tick?
- When I/we face challenges, describe how we overcome them?
- What are the top few behaviors I/we should expect from myself/ourselves?

Besides these questions, there are two other ways to consider this exercise. First, think about brands or people that you love or admire and want to follow, either individually or in your business. Write down the qualities about those brands/people that you believe match yours or that you aspire to be. Second is the "eulogy test" where you write down all the values that you would want people to say about you at your funeral. This exercise forces you to be both introspective to think about your own values, but it also compels you to put yourself in the shoes of others and reflect on how they may perceive you. Honesty with yourself and others is key during this process.

When I perform this values-discovery exercise with an organization, I write down the words, phrases, and statements on butcher-block paper with an adhesive on the back and—as I fill up each sheet—I tear it off, then stick it to the wall. The more people involved in the process, the more sheets you'll use. During one session with a non-profit organization that had about 25–30 participants, I placed at least 15 sheets of values around the room with at least 120 different words and phrases.

Note that in corporate brand development, a marketing firm will perform primary research through polling individuals or focus groups to ascertain how target audiences perceive your brand. The findings from this research are then presented to you or your business as part of this process. However, this research takes time and is typically more expensive than most small- or mid-sized companies are willing to pay, so they forego it. Most if not all organizations and their marketing teams recognize the importance of having data-driven insights from target audiences to guide the branding process. But when they see budgets in the tens of thousands of dollars, they will rely on their own insights, generally.

For individuals, the only decision-maker who will determine your brand values is you. While you may not have the benefit of a brand professional to facilitate a dialogue with you to isolate these concepts, the process is easy to undertake. On the following pages, you will find a list of 150 personal attributes. These are words that describe a quality about yourself; they do not describe your vocation or role in life. Of course, being a CEO, mother, high schooler, sorority president, actor, or other role is very important to your brand. But your role is not your brand, even if people largely know you for your role.

We'll discuss your role and how it relates to your brand in Chapter 18, Verifying and Applying Your Godly Brand. For now, review the list of personal attributes and check all of them that even remotely apply. Do not limit yourself on the first pass. Also, don't be afraid to select a value that you think may reflect poorly on you. If you are picky, demanding, intolerant, or any other perceivably "negative" attribute, so be it. It is who you are. And if you are concerned with this value being an identifier for your brand, then you can aspire to alter it (more on that later).

Selecting Your Core Values

Review the list of attributes and select all the values that apply to you. If you need to list a value that is not provided, or want to combine words (e.g., game-changing creativity), use the "Other" space(s).

Absent-minded	Curious	Happy
Accessible	Cute	Hard worker
Achiever	Cynical	Health conscious
Activist	Daring	Hip
Adaptable	Decisive	Honest
Adventurous	Demanding	Honorable
Aggressive	Determined	Humble
Ambitious	Disciplined	Ideator
Arrogant	Disorganized	Imaginative
Articulate	Diverse	Impatient
Artistic	Dominating	Impersonal
Athletic	Dreamer	Impulsive
Attractive	Driven	Independent
Authoritarian	Dutiful	Innocent
Awkward	Eager to help	Innovative
Balanced	Educated	Inquisitive
Beautiful	Emotional	Intelligent
Believer	Energetic	Intense
Best Among Friends	Enthusiastic	Introverted
Big-Picture Thinker	Extroverted	Intuitive
Caring	Faithful	Inward-facing
Cautious	Family-focused	Irreverent
Charming	Fashion conscious	Joker
Challenging	Finicky	Judgmental
Cheerful	Fit	Justice-minded
Classy	Flexible	Leader
Clever	Focused	Liberal
Coach	Forceful	Listener
Compassionate	Forgiving	Logical
Competitive	Friendly	Loner
Complex	Frugal	Loving
Confident	Fun-loving	Loyal
Conscientious	Generous	Maverick
Conservative	Genuine	Methodical
Contrite	Good listener	Multi-cultural
Cooperative	Good natured	Musical
Cosmopolitan	Gracious	Naive
Creative	Guilt-ridden	Neat
Cultured	Handsome	Nerdy

Defining Your Core Purpose and Values

- Observant
- Old-fashioned
- Open-minded
- Optimist
- Organized
- Outsider
- Patient
- Perfect
- Perceptive
- Persuasive
- Pessimist
- Planner
- Playful
- Polite
- Political
- Popular
- Practical
- Precise
- Predictable
- Principled
- Proactive
- Problem-solver
- Procrastinator
- Professional

- Punctual
- Quiet
- Quirky
- Reactive
- Relaxed
- Reliable
- Religious
- Resourceful
- Responsible
- Rich
- Rigid
- Romantic
- Sad
- Sarcastic
- Sardonic
- Secure
- Self-centered
- Self-critical
- Self-denying
- Selfless
- Sensitive
- Sexy
- Skeptical
- Smart

- Social
- Sophisticated
- Spirited
- Spontaneous
- Strict
- Strong-willed
- Stubborn
- Studious
- Suffering
- Temperamental
- Thorough
- Tough
- Troublemaker
- Trusting
- Trustworthy
- Unyielding
- Vivacious
- Weird
- Well-read
- Woke
- Worried
- Other: _____
- Other: _____

Step 2—Group Similar Values Together

Once you have a master list of values, begin to group them together. This portion of the exercise is an inherently visual one; you have to see all the options to connect similar ones. This is where having all the values on butcher-block paper around the room really helps. You can step back and see everything at once. I use different colored markers to highlight each group, drawing lines across the papers or boxes around words/phrases.

Eventually, you group like concepts together, and it makes sense. For example, if you have values such as reliable, dependable, consistent, accountable, "always there on time," and "there for our customers," they can be grouped together into one group.

As you go through this process, you may have a few outliers that cannot be grouped with other values. That's okay. If you feel they are important, keep them for now.

Step 3—Narrow Down and Focus the Groupings

Once you feel as though you've grouped the master list words and phrases, attempt to narrow down the number of values to 10–12. If you can cut the list to less than that, great. But really force yourself to focus the groupings to a maximum of a dozen values. In an organizational setting, this step can be a hard one if you do not have a facilitator to preside over the process. If you need help though, once all the words/phrases are grouped, choose one from each group that best represents it.

For example, if you have a group that includes timely, responsive, "quick to solve problems," fast, "always there," "operates 24/7," and "never let you down," all of them may be worthy choices, but choose the one that ideally fits your personality/corporate culture, sums up how you or your organization actually behave, or encapsulates all of them. Just looking at these words and being in a professional service industry myself, the term "responsive" is one that many clients gravitate toward. You could help the term by adding a modifier like "ultra," so the term becomes "ultra-responsive." If that still doesn't quite capture the essence of the value, add a noun like "service" or "people," resulting in "ultra-responsive service." You may see that you can combine or support another value such as "caring" or "customer-centric" by adding the word "customer" into the value, so it becomes "ultra-responsive customer service." You get the idea . . . these things are flexible, but it's important to land on the right word or phrase.

After you've narrowed down the master list to groups then down to 12 or fewer values, the hard work begins.

Step 4—Choose the Final Words/Phrases

If you thought cutting the list to 12 or fewer values was difficult, further narrowing down the list to 5 will be even harder. If you're doing this exercise individually, the process will require a great deal of self-awareness, reflection, and prayer.

For organizations, this process will require a lot of give-and-take, compromise, patience, sacrifice, and commitment to generate results that are uniquely the organization's. During this process, see if you can add more impact to the value by emphasizing a desired outcome, an emotional reaction, an easy-to-remember or catchy phrase, or all of the above.

This finessing of your values may take a little time. When I've written brand platforms that include these types of values as a central piece, I labor over every single word, and it can take days and—more often—weeks to truly get it right. One important reason is that the creative process requires time and distance to write something, let it lie, then come back to it to see if what you have still works. Collaboration with clients and their internal review processes add time to the process, too.

One question that arises is how many values you should have. The natural default during these sessions where an organization will narrow down its values is to say "why limit ourselves to only 5; let's do 7 or 8 or 9." I'm a firm believer in getting this number down to 5 values. It just makes things more focused and enables you to spotlight the uniqueness of your values, then train your employees more effectively. It's hard for team members to keep track of and balance more than 5 values in my experience. However, others in my profession will say 5 to 10 values is okay. That's fine. The important point here is that you arrive at a set of values that uniquely describe you or your organization, get you excited about your future, and establish a strong and lasting persona (for individuals) or culture (for organizations).

Drilling Down to Your Core Values

After selecting five values, place them in the five left-hand boxes below, then write one sentence to accompany each word or phrase that describes how it is reflected in your life or business. These sentences should explain or provide justification for the value that you chose. The important thing here is to be honest.

Two things to consider as you approach this exercise:

1. Writing a comprehensive statement for each value that captures the different ways that you personify the word or phrase may be a hard exercise for you. When I write these statements for organizations, I labor over them for many hours, choosing just the right words for proper impact or to capture the exact nuance of how the value applies to the company. You don't need to work on these statements for hours (unless you want to), but—if you give them the measure of thought they deserve—it may take you an hour or two to fine-tune them.

    Use your best judgment. If you're not gifted in writing, do the best you can or seek help from someone you trust.

2. Because it's sometimes easier to see how others view us than how we view ourselves, your sentences can either state *your perception of yourself* (e.g., Caretaker → I enjoy caring for people in my life, with a priority on my family, but also including friends, co-workers, fellow churchgoers, and more) or *how you believe others perceive you* (e.g., Caretaker → My family, friends, co-workers, and others see me as the person who will always be there to take care of them, get them what they need, or be there to help, rain or shine). It's a small difference in how you describe the value. Whichever way works best for you, use it.

Use this grid to describe how each value applies to your life, using specific examples where possible:

Defining Your Core Purpose and Values

Core Value	Statement Sentence(s)

To give you an example of how your values and statement sentences may look, here are the five Core Values for the previously mentioned Africa New Day / Un Jour Nouveau:

- *Christ-Centered:* Bringing hope and instilling personal value among the Congolese men, women, and children who are affected by UJN's ministries is possible through their understanding of Christ's love in their lives. His love sets the stage for all equipping, educating, and healing that occurs through UJN. AND and UJN understand that true transformative change in Congo can only occur through the awesome power of the Holy Spirit, working in and through UJN as well as those people who have been touched by the organization.

- *Agents of Change:* Making Congolese men, women, and children aware of Christ's love and engaging them through education and leadership programs are only the start. People must act to make a difference in their village, city, or country. UJN programs are specifically designed to enable and provoke problem-solving. In this way, people realize success, gain confidence, and are active contributors to societal change.

- *Fearless Leaders:* God chose the Ntotos (the founders) and their team to minister in one of the most desperate locations on earth. Like Isaiah who answered the call "Here I am. Send Me!", they went and work there because of their steadfast belief that they will transform a nation, despite the surrounding cruelty and corruption. They model fearlessness in fulfilling their call so that their ministry can relentlessly stamp out the greatest barrier to personal and cultural change in the country: fear among the people.

- *Empowering Others:* To remove fear, one must be empowered, first through faith, then through education and eventual action. At the core of UJN's ministry is the concept of preparing the next generation of Congolese men, women, and children. They are equipped, educated, and led to contemplate and embrace respect and love for themselves, then others. This empowerment starts with self, but very quickly multiplies to affect a village, a city, a nation . . . for generations to come.

- *Trusted:* In a country rife with corruption and distrust, UJN has earned a reputation for its passionate, consistent program delivery and repeatable outcomes, that being an ongoing flow of graduates from the organization's ministries who enter society with a new outlook on life and purpose. So profound are these outcomes in Congo that secular and non-Christian people and organizations alike support AND/UJN with funding based on their belief in the organization's work. Lastly, perhaps most important, residents of Goma who have spent their entire lives dwelling on fear and anger view UJN as a safe place to go and grow.

Yes, these short paragraphs are longer than a sentence. If you feel emboldened to expand your descriptions, please do so.

Step 5—Test Your Values

Once you've created your list of values, it's time to test them with external audiences. This testing process can take many forms based on how extensive you want it to be. For yourself, asking a few trusted friends, work colleagues, fellow church members or your minister, mentors, and any other important influencers in your life what they consider to be your five values will help you understand how you appear to others and the brand persona that you live out every day. At this stage, I would avoid mentioning or showing the preliminary values that you have determined to others. It's much more important that you listen rather than tell during this process, take notes, and ask follow-up questions if their feedback is unclear. It's vital that you do not attempt to explain yourself or—heavens forbid—defend yourself as you receive feedback. Take their feedback seriously.

Lots of times, unless you're really dialed into your thinking, attitudes, and behaviors, you may be giving off certain vibes that you are unaware of. And that's okay. It's always better to be aware of how people perceive you, than not. Lack of knowing makes it nearly impossible to self-correct.

An important point here, asking family members about your values can be a loaded proposition given just how much your mother, father, or siblings may know and love you. Since they've seen you more than anyone else in the world—warts and all—there may be an inclination to either be too loving and therefore avoid being totally honest, or the reverse, be brutally honest. Either way, family members' viewpoints on your core values may be skewed.

For organizations, this testing process may involve internal employee or external customer surveying to understand how your core values are perceived. Another option is focus-group testing. With surveys or focus groups, you can ask open-ended questions that enable participants to give you their perceptions and feelings about your organization's values and brand. For this work, you will want to consider hiring a third-party research firm or marketing agency to help create and administer the survey, conduct the focus groups, or perform both. This way, the findings that you receive will be impartial and accurate.

If you choose a marketing agency, it will likely want to help handle the entire process of defining your brand values as well as your brand messaging, which is covered in the next chapter. This is natural. Any good marketing agency will say "if we're doing this one piece, it only makes sense to help you do it all."

If your business cannot afford to conduct surveys or focus groups, borrow a page from how an individual would seek feedback from others whom he or she trusts and ask your business partners, suppliers, or trusted clients. You can do this in the guise of a client satisfaction survey, if you want. Ask current or former employees, especially those who had manager roles. Take these folks out to coffee or lunch and pick their brains. Besides helping you understand how they perceive your business' values, it's a great business development and networking exercise.

Step 6—Write Down Your Values

Whether for yourself or your business, after you have received feedback from others via your testing, go ahead and adjust your values in whatever ways seem appropriate. Do not rewrite your preliminary values. There should only be tweaks to the language. Also, balance the feedback you receive. Just because one or two people may have cited something doesn't mean you must change your values. Remember, they're your values. You must trust the original process of defining them.

The only time you may shift a value significantly is if the majority of your feedback givers cite an observation that you had not considered. For example, if you believe that you are caring for others or open-minded, but most of the people you asked say that you "really want things your way," you need to consider that feedback. It will compel you to either modify the value or—if that value is truly important to you—change your behavior.

I've got plenty of God-following friends and colleagues who are wonderful, caring people and relentlessly stubborn, principal-focused antagonists when you disagree with or cross them. Can those qualities reconcile in a person. You bet! I have dear friends who are deeply religious who self-sabotage their lives with drinking, sexual misconduct and poor dating choices, foul language and other vulgarities, and the list goes on and on. People are complex beings who sin, including you and me. Part of the point of writing this book is to help those who want a means to recognize when their brand and values are not aligned with how God wants them to act, especially in front of others.

If the feedback on your values surprises you or reveals some aspect of your values and behavior that is less flattering, pray about it, seek guidance from your minister or religious leader, and work toward rectifying the issues you may have. It may involve seeking professional help or therapy.

The last part of this process is writing down your brand values. For individuals, write down what each value means to you personally and keep them somewhere accessible, so that you can refer back to them during difficult times in your life or when important decisions must be made. For organizations, you may create a one-sheet hand-out or posters that list your values, then give them to employees to post in their workspace or around the office.

Whether for yourself or your business, keep your values handy; you will reflect on them as you determine your brand messaging in the next chapter.

What If Any of Your Core Values Are "Negative"

Determining your Core Values can be an interesting exercise. Sometimes, if you are truly honest with yourself during your self-analysis, you may realize that one or more of your concepts can be deemed as "negative." In this context, the term negative means a value that other people may conventionally hold as undesirable, not necessarily bad, harmful, or destructive.

The thing with the use of the word "negative" is that the term is relative. What may be a negative term to one person may be a source of pride to another. Take the word "nerd" for example. I have heard my oldest son refer to himself and his friends with this term. As someone who grew up when the movie "Revenge of the Nerds" appeared in theaters, that label has had a negative connotation of being overly studious, maybe even socially awkward. Yet, for younger generations, that term has a different meaning, one with which kids self-identify.

Let's take the spectrum of "self-assured," "confident," "in command," "knows what I want," or "arrogant" next. Are these brand descriptors negative or not? It depends. A person can certainly be self-assured. That's a very healthy aspect of an individual's personality. But taken to an unreasonable, maybe stubborn, maybe prideful point, that self-assuredness becomes a negative. If you self-identify as arrogant, you need to think and pray about that one. By its very nature, arrogance involves being self-important and superior, and those things are attributes that God does not want for us. Remember the eight Godly brand attributes. One of them is a servant mindset. It's very hard to reconcile arrogance with prioritizing a servant mindset.

Some values can be tricky in their negative context. One of my values is "dreamer." On the surface, the term dreamer may not seem overly negative. In fact, it may seem aspirational. However, as a dreamer, I can tell you firsthand how I struggle with translating all the dreams, ideas, and vision I have into action. To be honest with you, I should've finished this book at least three years earlier than I did. Now, it'd be easy for me to rationalize and justify the delays due to a busy life filled with work, teaching, being a good husband and father, being involved at church, and more. However, my dreamer quality kept me from finishing this book earlier. I kept adding things to it. I kept noodling new content in my mind. I'd dream about writing other things that were not this book. I found new and inventive ways to keep from writing this book. As you can see, I eventually got it done. But my "dreamer" value allowed me to both complete this book with hopefully some insightful content as well as delay its publishing through distraction. Point being, be mindful of brand values that keep you from carrying out your service to God and how you can overcome them through prayer and action.

There are other brand descriptors that may be cause for prayer and seeking help in your spiritual walk from God and others in your life. If you chose words like aimless, sad or depressed, alone or lonely, drifter, unhappy, angry, bitter, resentful, or bad, please look to God through prayer to strengthen you. If you chose brand values like loser, worthless, wicked, or suicidal, please get immediate help from your spiritual leader or other trusted religious advisor.

Defining Your Core Purpose and Values

If you associate any negative concepts with your brand, there are three vital points to remember:

1. *You can change these negative concepts:* All you need is time and clear direction on how to change your brand. That direction comes from introspection, prayer, and reading God's word, trusting God that He will help you and accepting the help of others.

    The Bible is replete with examples of figures who were God followers with clear Godly brand attributes who mis-stepped and sinned, realized their sin, asked for forgiveness, then were redeemed. Moses, David, Judah, and Solomon were explored in earlier chapters. Others include Adam, Jonah, and Samson.

2. *Seek guidance from a trusted friend or spiritual advisor/leader:* Seeking guidance is especially important if you feel as though you do not deserve a "second chance." No sin is too great for God to forgive, regardless of what you've done or to whom. The one thing you *must do* is turn to Him for help. If you do not, you are relying on your own power to solve your problems. Scriptures tell us repeatedly that—if we return to God, if we call out to Him for help—He will care for us (e.g., David, Hezekiah, Jacob, and more). If we don't, we stand apart from Him and His awesome grace. In these situations, your pastor or other religious leader are other great resources for help.

3. *Pray to God for guidance on how to change your brand:* If you have clarity on your purpose, this should be achievable through reading God's word and prayer.

Chapter 17

Defining Your Brand Messaging

WHEREAS YOUR CORE PURPOSE and Core Values are largely internally facing, messaging determines how you articulate your or your business' market uniqueness, differentiators and positioning, target audiences, and stories that engage others about you. This chapter will help you identify four critical tools of messaging that will help you relate what you or your business does quickly, effectively, and with impact. The four tools are your 1) USP, or unique selling proposition to highlight how you're different than anyone or anything else; 2) tagline to very quickly sum up who you are; 3) elevator speech to communicate your need-to-know story in 30 seconds or less; and 4) talking points that expand your narrative storytelling about your background and experiences, when you have the time to get into deeper detail about yourself.

The four tools build upon each other and arm you with messaging that can be delivered in short snippets, like an introduction during a meeting or networking event, or in longer form when you have a conversation with someone. After completing the exercises to create these four tools, you'll see how that can be used together to laser-focus your communications with others.

USP (Unique Selling Proposition)

A Unique Selling Proposition (USP) is an advertising term that refers those features, characteristics, or properties that make a product, service, or organization better (or, at least, different) from its competition. That specific benefit(s) of those features must be unique; no other competitor can or does offer it. A clear USP helps a product or service stand out from the other offerings in its category and enables consumers to form a positive attitude towards the brand. Products or services that do not differentiate themselves risk being ignored by consumers.

Some well-known examples of a clear USP include Disney's "The happiest place on earth," Federal Express' "When it absolutely, positively has to be there overnight," or BMW's "The Ultimate Driving Machine." Each of these taglines communicates a specific quality about the product or service, versus more emotive ones like Nike's "Just do it" or McDonald's "I'm lovin' it."

The USP term was co-opted in the practice of personal branding to refer to an aspect of a person's makeup that differentiates him or her from other people. USP is sometimes called a "wow factor" or "freak factor." In sports, seeing a person's USP can be easy: Tiger Woods, greatest golfer; Michael Jordan, best basketball player; Tom Brady, most accomplished football player; and so on. The same can be said for entertainment: Meryl Streep, most decorated actress; Steven Spielberg, greatest director; John Williams, best-ever composer of movie scores; and so on.

Bringing things closer to home, think about your church. If I were to ask you to name the best musician, best singer, best with kids in youth ministries, best church leader, most charismatic member, or most devoted through his or her volunteer time, the names and faces of individuals in your congregation would come to mind.

Whether a member or your church or a celebrity, these unique identifiers were cultivated over time. No one sprung from the womb as the greatest in anything, except Christ! Your USP is something that is identified then nurtured during your lifetime as part of your Godly brand.

You may be thinking, "Hey, there are more than 7.5 billion people in the world; how can I do something unique that no one else can do?" The answer is: because God made you that way. He has a plan for your life. Your fingerprint isn't the only unique thing about you. I'll give you a personal example. Do you think that I'm the only one in the world who knows how to brand people, places, or organizations? No. In fact, there are people in the world with more knowledge of branding in their pinkie finger than I have in my whole body, as the ol' expression goes. Am I the only person in the world who believes in God and has devoted years of his (or her) life to studying the Word? No. The senior pastor at my church can recite dozens of Bible verses from memory. Am I the first person to take the concept of personal branding and apply it to biblical figures to help people better understand the importance of demonstrating a Godly life to others? Yes, to my knowledge.

Listen, if you're reading this book—first—thank you! Second, I hope to meet you someday, either here or in heaven. And when we meet, what you'll see about me is that I'm no one special in the grand scheme of the world. But I am in God's eyes. He uniquely qualified me and blessed me with failures and learnings to reach the very point where I just typed this *word* at 8:26am on Wednesday, May 29, 2019.

There are examples throughout the Bible of God uniquely preparing His followers to play their part in His perfect plan. Moses was raised in Egypt; fled after killing a soldier who was abusing his people; spent 40 years in the desert, leading sheep through the wilderness; then spent 40 years leading God's chosen nation though the wilderness. Those 40 years in the desert stripped him of whatever pride or royal privilege he may have had from his days in Egypt, as he spent long nights alone with his flocks, no doubt contemplating his life. By the time God called him via the burning bush on Mount Horeb, Moses' confidence was rock bottom, to the point where he was terrified of his mission and begged God to send someone else. God knew that request was coming, which is why He had already sent his brother Aaron to meet Moses. Flashforward a few decades, Moses' humility with dealing with the worse elements of the Israelite people earned him great favor with God, and—by the end of his life—he was in complete command of the Israelite nation. His fear of speaking before the people was gone, and the result was a long and comprehensive discourse on how they should live and honor God as they entered the Promised Land that is found in the Book of Deuteronomy.

If I were writing a USP for Moses, it would go something like this: An Egyptian-born Jewish leader born into royalty, I possess a deep awareness of Pharaonic politics and the enslaved Israelite nation there, making me ideally suited to help free its people with God's assistance. Forty years of working experience in the desert has ideally prepared me to lead those people to their Promised Land, a distance of hundreds of miles, across that very same wilderness, again relying heavily on my personal relationship with God.

While this USP for Moses may sound silly, you get the idea. There are several unique properties included in this overall USP statement that demonstrate how God specifically guided Moses, versus another like his brother Aaron.

God uniquely qualified Samuel through his upbringing in a temple, exposure to the corruption of Eli and his sons, his love of the people he served, and the gift of prophecy to preside over God's formation of the nation of Israel under Saul, then David.

Samson was uniquely qualified through the gift of strength that God gave him, his hubris, his love for women that led to his fall, then his ultimate humility to turn back to God to restore his strength to commit his one final act of bringing down the Philistine temple of Dagon.

These examples and many more throughout the Scriptures detail how God gave each one of His followers unique abilities that were derived from their God-directed upbringing and life. As a result, each one had their own USP in God's perfect plan.

It's time for you to write you own USP. The process is different for individuals versus businesses. For individuals, follow this step-by-step process to determine your USP:

- List all the things you do well, including skills you have, education and training, job experience and learnings, volunteer experience, hobbies, and any other area or thing no matter how small that you feel your strength is.

- List those things in your life that you feel passionate about, you really enjoy doing, or you get excited about. Also, list things in your past or background that make you different.

- Conversely, list those things in your life that you do NOT enjoy doing, you try to avoid, or you know are things that negatively impact you. Be honest here.

- If your purpose is creating a USP specifically for your business or professional life, list what value you bring to an organization or client, what problems do you solve, what outcomes can someone expect to receive from you, and how you are worth whatever investment of time, talent, or resources that an organization or person will place in you.

- Review all the factors that you have written that make you who you are. As you do, try to uncover what you feel gives your life meaning and direction. Where do you excel or want to excel? Here, you are trying to isolate your purpose, that thing God has called you as a unique child of His to fulfill as part of His plan. Don't be too concerned if this step in the process takes you some time of self-reflection and prayer to determine. It should.

  Here are several helpful questions to ask yourself to move along this step if you're stuck:

  - How do I make the world a better place?
  - How do I help others fulfill their purpose or make a difference?
  - What would be missing from the world if I were not in it?
  - Where have I felt that God has blessed me and my work?

- With your inventory of strengths and passions as well as purpose, write a short USP for yourself. You're looking for two sentences that sum up your unique differentiator in God's kingdom like the Moses example.

  As you write your USP, try to add a little of your own personality to it, again to make it uniquely yours. Also, try to include either a direct or implied promise of what someone who hears your USP can expect to receive from you. You can include terms that assure another person that they'll get from you the best thinking, fastest responsiveness or service, highly creative or strategic input, highest-quality work or service, innovative approaches, interpersonal or high-human-touch communications, business leadership, excellent financial oversight, strong people management, and so on.

- Once you have a first draft of your USP, trial-test it with a few trusted people in your life who know you personally and professionally. Take the feedback that you receive from them and finesse that first draft into a more refined version.

- Lastly, once you have a version that you're ready to use, look back at your inventory of personal strengths and passions, and apply them as evidence points when you share your USP with the outside world. What should happen is—when you share your USP at a networking event or other meet-and-greet opportunity—the person to whom you are speaking will ask questions that compel you to support your

USP with facts about yourself that validate it. Be prepared for this by thinking through how God has uniquely prepared you to be where you are, what unique experiences you have, and what expertise you have garnered through that experience. Ultimately, you need to be a storyteller, and the story is uniquely yours. Your USP is the title of that story. The supporting evidence points are the details. Make it interesting and unique.

For organizations, here is a step-by-step process to determine a USP:

- List characteristics of your customers or target audiences.
- List all the ways that your product, service, or organization meets their needs (i.e., the selling points of your organization).
- List all the ways that your competitors meet the needs of your customers / target audiences.

  If your organization is a church or religious organization, you must do something that goes against every fiber of your being: you must consider other churches or religious organizations as competition, even if only as a conceit to help this exercise. The fact is, if your church or organization doesn't differentiate itself against other churches, it will affect your ability to attract new members and keep newer ones who visit.

- Delete of any selling points from your list that match ones from your competitors. Again, you're looking for something uniquely yours.
- Compare those selling points that are left with things that your organization does well and how you want it to be perceived by your customers / target audiences.
- Test your USPs with a sampling of your customers / target audiences. Select 8–10 of them and ask their opinion to choose the best one. If you're a church, this may be your members.
- Sanity-check that USP to make sure that it's memorable, you can deliver it, and it's something that absolutely no one else offers the same way that you do.
- Use this USP to develop your market strategy and launch plans for your product, service, or organization.

Your Tagline

Creating a tagline will seem very familiar to identifying your USP. A tagline is a phrase or small group of words that is associated with a brand, whether it be for an individual, company or organization, product, or service. The purpose of a tagline is to create a memorable or dramatic phrase that sums up the tone, personality, premise, or promise of a brand that is typically used in marketing materials and advertising to a target audience(s). When properly marketed, the catchiness of a tagline evokes or reinforces a target audience's mnemonic response with a brand.

Some famous taglines that sum up a brand expectation or experience into a simple one- to five-word expression include Apple's "Think different," Burger King's "Have it your way," McDonald's "I'm lovin' it," and Nike's "Just do it."

All taglines should connote a certain type of engagement that consumers will have with the brand. For individuals, taglines can give an immediate sense of who you are and what benefit others can expect from you. They can be great conversation starters when someone asks you about yourself or in a business setting when you engage a prospect. If you meet people at an event or conference, a well-crafted tagline can quickly sum up in seconds who you are, what you do, and why you do it. That latter part around the why harkens back to Simon Sinek's Golden Circle model. It's your mandate, that larger-than-life reason for doing what you do that beckons others to join you or do business with you.

> **Tagline versus Slogan**
>
> Many times, people use the terms tagline and slogan interchangeably. They do mean different things. A slogan typically refers to a marketing campaign or business initiative that lasts only a few months or even a couple of years, whereas a tagline has a much longer lifespan, typically many years as a seemingly permanent fixture in a brand's marketing. Slogans change regularly; taglines do not.

The proper tagline will boost your confidence as you speak with others because you will assertively and authoritatively describe that awesome benefit that you deliver. It will answer in seconds the following questions:

Defining Your Brand Messaging

- What area of expertise do I offer?
- What problems do I help solve?
- How do I help others achieve their goals, either personal or business?

It's important to remember that taglines are only meant to shortcut a longer personal introduction and get a conversation between you and another rolling. You're not necessarily trying to wow people with it or close a deal on the spot.

At this stage, you may be asking yourself, "do I really need a tagline?" It depends. You may not. For personal use, I would highly encourage you to create one for no other reason than to focus your thoughts and delivery when meeting people in a business or job-hunting context. Even if you do not use your tagline, it will help you get started with your longer personal narrative. Imagine if—when you meet a prospective employer or customer—and he or she asks you about yourself, you say "I help local nonprofits raise money with high net-worth individuals across Los Angeles" or "I'm a Microsoft Certified IT Professional who helps companies with the database administration." More personal descriptors than traditional taglines, these short statements may be far less engaging than the consumer taglines above; however, they ideally sum up your professional expertise in a conversational way. You can do this for your personal life, too, if it'll help focus how you speak with people. Examples can be: "I work full-time as a parent of three wonderful kids"; "I have a heart for the homelessness"; or "I volunteer in youth ministries at my church, working with junior-high kids."

For business, you should absolutely consider one if the name of your company does not connote what you do. Many people name their business after themselves. That's great for name recognition, but does very little to explain what you do. In these cases, you need some time of explanatory device (i.e., a tagline) to tip people to the nature of your products or services.

If you're considering a tagline for a small business, you may not want to take the time to create one, consider it a novelty with little bottom-line benefit, or consider it a distraction to the design or other messaging on your website, social media, printed collateral, etc. That's okay. If you're a print shop or surfboard manufacturer, it's easy to say, "I own a print shop in Cypress, California" or "I craft custom surfboards in Southern California." Consider though, you have the opportunity with a tagline to add an emotional punch to those statements that evokes a response from a prospective buyer. The print shop example becomes something like: "One-Stop Shop for All Your Small-Business Printing." In one brief statement, you communicate that you'll handle everything a small business needs. By derivation, you imply that—because you're targeting small businesses—that your culture, physical storefront, pricing, and offerings will be tailored to them. The surfboard manufacturer example may be: "Shaping Your Future." For the uninitiated, a surfboard shaper is someone who builds and designs surfboards by hand.

Here are the steps to create a memorable tagline:

1. Create a list of descriptive words, phrases, or sentences that communicate your unique skills, areas of expertise, top qualities, and anything else that identifies you. Borrow from the USP brand-attribute exercises in previous chapters.
2. Look for overlaps to consolidate your list down to 8 to 10 options phrases or sentences.
3. Narrow your list down to three or so options.
4. Now comes the hard work. Refine these final options into a concise, punchy phrase that aligns with your work or business and the benefit you offer to others.
5. To be most effective, your tagline should do one of the following:
   - Contain a benefit (e.g., FedEx' "When It Absolutely, Positively Has To Be There Overnight")
   - Describe your brand, product, service, or organization (e.g., Bounty's "The Quicker Picker Upper")
   - Make a call-to-action (e.g., Apple's "Think Different")
   - Evoke an emotional response (e.g., Coca-Cola's "Open Happiness")
   - Include an aspirational statement (e.g., Nike's "Just Do It.").
6. Your tagline should be short, no more than 8–10 words in length. Frankly, for ease of use, you should consider trimming it down to 6 or fewer words. Don't make it clever, cute, general or vague. Use precise language, making every single word count.

Once you have a tagline, test it with some trusted friends and/or professional colleagues. Get their opinion to see if what you've created aligns with who you are, what you do, and what you deliver. You can edit your tagline as needed, based on the feedback that you receive.

Your Elevator Speech

An elevator speech (also elevator pitch or statement) is a quick verbal overview of you or your business' background and experience that is meant to convey—at a minimum—credibility. It is a longer extension of your tagline. Optimally, your elevator speech will persuade someone to agree to a call-to-action (e.g., take a follow-up meeting, review a resume, etc.). An elevator speech may also apply to products, services, ideas, or anything else that you're trying to sell.

One quick note, an elevator speech is not a sales pitch, which overtly attempts to convince someone to buy something, and always involves a person who is trying to sell and a person who is a prospective buyer. While an elevator speech may persuade, it doesn't always involve that seller-buyer dynamic.

The conceit of an elevator pitch is that it can be delivered during an elevator ride from the ground floor to an executive's top floor. In New York City, the average elevator ride is 118 seconds. Nowadays, the recommended length for an elevator speech is 30 seconds, give or take. You should aim for somewhere between 30–90 seconds to craft your elevator speech. Of course, it is not just meant for elevator rides; you should deliver it anywhere you meet people.

The key to an effective elevator speech is brevity. Words and phrases should be concise, direct, and rehearsed. Get to the point quickly. What should a speech include? I've found that the most effective ones offer the "who, what, where, why, and next step" of the story you're trying to tell. Note that it says "next step," not "next steps." You should go with one call-to-action to keep your objective clear and succinctly make an ask to the other person.

During the telling of your story, make sure to weave in you or your business' specialties and goals, and why they are relevant to the person to whom you are speaking. Know your audience, too, and customize your elevator speech accordingly. For example, if you're an engineer speaking to another engineer, using technical jargon is appropriate. If you're talking with a non-technical person, like a recruiter, minimize it.

Don't speak too quickly as you deliver your speech. Do not ramble. Speak with inflection in your voice. Maintain positive body language with a smile, no slouching, and a casual tone. Lastly, have a business card ready to give to the contact, if he or she responds well, and follow up accordingly within 24 hours.

5 Steps to Create the Perfect Elevator Pitch

Here are five steps to create an effective elevator pitch:

1. *Start with a HOOK*

   Start with your unique selling proposition (USP), but take it a step further, adding an element of vision and/or larger-than-life purpose.

   Using an example from Africa New Day / Un Jour Nouveau, a Christian ministry working in the Republic of Congo, with fundraising arms in the U.S. and Europe, its hook was literally nation-changing due to its grassroots efforts to educate the men, women, and children to break the cycle of violence in that country that dated back centuries:

   In one of the most desperate countries on Earth, God has placed a very special ministry to achieve the seemingly impossible: eradicate the pervasive cruelty and corruption of a nation.

   By the way, this hook was dialed down a bit from the organization's initial thoughts when I began working with its leaders. At first, the leaders' hook was to change all of Africa, starting with Congo being in the center of the continent and working its way out. As the 11th largest country on the planet, we narrowed the immediate focus down to just Congo. That was large enough by itself.

2. *Identify areas of specialization*

   Cover those areas of expertise where you excel or that are especially relevant to the person to whom you are speaking. What qualified Africa New Day to pursue the above-stated hook? Its three areas of specialization are the key:

   - Spiritual formation provides hope and eliminates fear among the people
   - Education offers the fundamental tools to discern and communicate change

- Leadership development equips and activates the next generation of change agents.

3. *Describe typical customers*

   Mention the types of people or businesses to which you offer your products or services. Africa New Day's audience is twofold given its programming in Congo and fundraising efforts:

   - Men, women, and children of Congo who must cope with anger, depression, guilt, and fear brought upon by centuries of violence and corruption as well as cultural biases that excuse cruelty to women and children
   - Funders who believe in the effectiveness of Un Jour Nouveau's work and provide monetary support.

4. *Describe a relevant situation where you created end user value*

   Give an example of a success story or achievement that you personally managed and resulted in tangible return on involvement (ROI). Because the ministry had existed for a handful of years when I began working with it, Africa New Day / Un Jour Nouveau already had a proven track record of success. It merely needed to be honed down for the purpose of the elevator speech:

   - Thousands of program beneficiaries who have given testimonials about the transformative power of Un Jour Nouveau ministries to their lives
   - Graduates of Sons and Daughters of Congo and the Leadership Academy [two programs that Un Jour Nouveau runs] hold important societal roles (chief of police, magistrate, government tax agency, MONUSCO) and make a difference every day of their lives
   - Religious and secular organizations (Jewish World Watch, MONUSCO) that believe in the effectiveness of Un Jour Nouveau's programs and work, and fund them.

5. *Propose follow-up opportunity (if appropriate)*

   End with your call-to-action, whether it is a follow-up appointment, review of information that you leave behind, or some other action. Here are several opportunities that we identified for the organization:

- While 80 percent of Congo's population is Christian*, much work is required to activate that base to reverse the tide of cruelty and corruption in the country
- Africa remains the leading mission field on the planet, as the fastest-growth region for Christianity in the world
- Congo rests at the center of Africa; spark the Refiner's fire there, and change throughout the continent is possible.

* CIA World Factbook and Pew Research, both in 2013.

Note in the last bullet under follow-up opportunities that we did mention the possibility of the organization's mission and work spreading throughout the rest of Africa. If the Lord wants Africa New Day and Un Jour Nouveau's ministry to grow in that capacity and at that scope, it will occur. That's why we left that concept in the messaging mix.

Okay, we have all the elements of the 5 steps to create an elevator speech. What was the final product? Here's how it all came together, and you have to imagine that you are a member of the organization speaking to another person:

> I work with Africa New Day, a nonprofit organization that supports Christian ministries in Congo. It's a tough part of the world, but we're called to work there. We operate a school and chapel, conduct live radio broadcasts, and perform a lot of other Christian programs. Our goal is to equip and empower a new generation of Congolese men, women, and children to be Christ-like leaders in their village or city. We're very blessed. The programs work. We're 10 years old and have ministered to more than 35,000 people, some of whom are leaders in the local community. Others have noticed our success, too. In fact, we recently received monetary support from a couple of humanitarian organizations and the U.N.

This elevator speech can be delivered comfortably in 30 seconds. I performed training with the members of Africa New Day's Board of Directors, including the two founders, to help them internalize this speech and make it their own. I worked with them to help transition to the boarder storylines if the person hearing the elevator speech was interested in hearing more. In addition to this elevator speech, they were armed with talking points that dove deeper into the Africa New Day / Un Jour Nouveau story and could be delivered in under 5 minutes. After that, if the person is still interested, the board members were instructed to simply have a conversation and—at some point when it felt right—circle back to a call-to-action.

Your Talking Points

If a person is receptive to your brand and story after your elevator speech, you should be prepared with 3 to 5 talking points that further expound on you or your business and enable you to get a listener more invested in what you're doing. Besides telling your story, these talking points should clearly communicate key messages, priorities, differentiators, positioning, and target audiences for your or your business' purpose.

For Businesses

For businesses, talking points help get all your employees and especially spokespeople on the same page when articulating the value of what the organization does. Talking points should provide supporting facts that validate what you say. If you say, "we're the best in our industry at customer service," you need to offer supporting evidence that proves that statement to be true. Otherwise, you're just a cheerleader for your organization and can be easily dismissed by a discerning customer or prospect.

Imagine though, if you said, "Each year, we conduct a customer satisfaction survey and ask our customers to rate us on responsiveness, quality of service, and follow-through. Last year, we scored very good to excellent scores with 87 percent of our clients. I'd be happy to put you in touch with one." Perhaps, you're thinking, "This is so obvious. Doesn't every company have these types of metrics?" And the answer is "no, not by a long shot." In fact, very few small- to medium-sized businesses take the time to consider gathering these types of fact-based metrics.

When I'm engaged to write messaging for an organization, writing the descriptions, positioning, umbrella statements, and top stories take time but are relatively easy compared to drawing out the facts that support those stories from a client. Inevitably, many clients will not have the types of metrics that can be used, and I need to perform research to uncover third-party metrics that are derived from industry publications and magazines, academic institutions, industry analysts, financial analysts, government agencies, or other sources. It's not as strong as having organizational metrics, but third-party insights and facts are better than nothing.

What happens if you don't have any facts to support your talking points? You'll need to use anecdotal evidence in the form of detailed storytelling to convince a listener that you know what you're talking about.

Once the talking points are created, they should be used across all external marketing and communications channels to ensure consistency of message. They should be used in news releases, presentations, interviews, website and social media content, collateral materials, advertising, partner or supplier communications, internal employee and shareholder communications, and more.

You want to keep the number of talking points at 3 to 5 key messages, and each one should be about one concept only. Avoid being clever and writing long, complex sentences with multiple concepts to squeeze every last detail into your talking points. You will need to prioritize those 3 to 5 top messages and stick to them to start. Why only 5 or fewer? Because people cannot retain more than five new concepts, if that many. Frankly, most people may remember 3 things you say about yourself in an initial meeting, if you're lucky. Don't worry, if a person is still listening after you complete your 5 taking points, you have a conversation going and you can get to the lesser points if you believe it's important to do so.

When it comes to writing your talking points, they should build on each other to tell an overarching story about your business, product, or service. That story should be told in a "Situation, Problem, Solution, Results" format. The Situation states the situation or context for a Problem to the status quo. The Problem indicates some factor that caused difficulties or challenges in the Situation. The Solution covers one or more ways that you or your business solved the difficulties associated with the Problem. The Results are the data-driven outcomes of the Solution and frequently offer an insight based on how well the Solution worked or a future-oriented recommendation.

The Situation can either apply to your business, the industry you're in, a product or service line, your target audiences' life circumstances, or the customer's business. When I wrote the talking points for Africa New Day / Un Jour Nouveau, the organization's Situation was:

Defining Your Brand Messaging

> God is on the move in Congo. In 2005, Camille and Esther Ntoto founded a Christian ministry called Un Jour Nouveau (French for "A New Day") in Goma, the country's sixth largest city and epicenter of some of the worst cruelty and corruption perpetrated in the country. UJN has brought the love of Christ and accompanying hope to Goma, with a mandate to educate, equip, and empower each man, woman, and child in Congo to bring about cultural change.

This Situation clearly states what the organization does: to educate, equip, and empower each man, woman, and child in Congo to bring about cultural change. It also sets up the Problem. In your business' case, what problem are you trying to solve and for whom? Is it an industry or regulatory issue, an operational or business-performance matter, product- or service-oriented, or employee- or stakeholder-related? In the case of Africa New Day, its Problem was cultural:

> Changing a nation's culture that has been reinforced over hundreds of years is the grandest of tasks. It's measured in decades, not years; only through the awesome power of the Holy Spirit is it possible. UJN's ministries involve three strategic areas that create opportunities for the Holy Spirit to work in the lives of the people they reach: 1) spiritual formation, the heart of the ministries; 2) education; and 3) leadership development.

The Problem here is massive and seemingly insurmountable: changing a nation's culture that has been reinforced over hundreds of years. When writing this, what I did not get into are the unwholesome aspects of that culture that includes systemic corruption, rape and subjugation of women and children as objects, murder, and a lengthy list of completely demoralizing societal behavior by men. These are details that—if a listener sticks with the story and talking points—he or she will be prepared for those gruesome facts. This Problem talking point hints at part of the Solution (i.e., power of the Holy Spirit). The Solution talking point explains the tangible way that Africa New Day has made a difference:

> Congolese men, women, and children are first introduced or reconnected to the Word of God to increase self-worth and purpose, remove fear, and inspire hope. Congo is a wounded nation, from centuries of colonialization and war. People must know Christ as the central focus of their lives. Only then can UJN educate and train a new generation of leaders to affect positive change.

UJN's programs are specifically designed to enable and provoke problem-solving as a means to active societal change. As examples, Sons of Congo requires each graduate to form a new discipleship group to pass along the relationship education he has learned. Daughters of Congo teaches women leadership skills. Generation Hope offers children leadership training, mentoring, and family care. The Leadership Academy requires the planning and implementation of a community project to earn a certificate of completion. All of these ministries serve to stamp out the root causes of violence and corruption in the country.

Here, there are two talking points to cover the various ways that Africa New Day addresses the violence and corruption in the country. In considering your business' solution, ask yourself how you've solved your customer's Problem. Was it a combination of products and services, combined with excellent customer service? That's a typical solution for many companies. Then, you have to ask yourself, how well did my business' Solution work? Those are your results. The Results talking point should bring home your story. In the case of Africa New Day, it sums up how others perceive the work of the organization:

> These ministries work! Seeing the results, a dedicated group of believers formed Africa New Day, a U.S. nonprofit organization that supports UJN through financial and organizational assistance. Individual donors, religious institutions (Mariners Church) and secular organizations (Jewish World Watch, MONUSCO) all support AND/UJN because they believe in the effectiveness of UJN's programs and work.

Note, this Results talking point does not have evaluation or measurement metrics; the organization was in the process of gathering those when these messages were written. To validate the efficacy of the ministry, we used the investment dollars that other well-known organizations poured into UJN's programs. The implicit concept here is that "if the ministries are good enough for them, they should be good enough for you."

You may be wondering, "where's the call-to-action or next-step appeal?" You do need to understand what you'd like the listener to do when you're done, whether that's swapping business cards and being receptive to a follow-up from you, agreeing to a product or service demonstration, joining you for lunch, etc. You can get to those things in the endgame of your conversation. To start though, you never make an ask without first telling the story.

As part of this messaging work, I trained the Board of Directors, the primary ambassadors for the organization, on how to discuss the ministries in Congo and discern whether to begin laying the groundwork for a monetary donation or—even better—take a trip and witness the effectiveness of UJN's work in person. Having worked in and with nonprofit organizations, few things lead to a monetary contribution from a donor like experiencing the organization's work for themselves, *especially* if it involves vulnerable populations like children. However, getting a substantial monetary contribution or taking an international trip can take months, maybe years, to get a person to do. For this reason, I armed the Board with a 6th talking point that I called "The Ask:"

> Right now, we're raising funds to complete an Empowerment Center on the UJN campus that will house a grade school for the local residents. We have the first and second grades running now, but lack the space to build out the remainder of the school. Of course, when the kids are not in school, that facility will be used for a wide range of ministries on campus. We're [25 percent] of the way toward raising the [$xx million] that we need.
> Would you be willing to . . .

Actually, it's two talking points. The first involves growing the Empowerment Center; the second was the actual ask depending on how deeply invested the listener seemed to be in the conversation. Some people may be willing to visit the UJN campus in Goma, if they travel a great deal or had a special connection to the ministry (e.g., adopting a Congolese child). But most people will not make that trip. This open-ended path enabled the Board member to play things by ear and adjust the ask accordingly. Most likely, that ask entailed swapping contact information and agreeing to a follow-up communication.

By offering metrics or compelling anecdotes in your Results talking point, you should be able to lead the conversation in the direction of how your business solves the needs of people or entities that face the Problem you laid out. That transition can be as simple as asking the listener, "have you ever had to deal with anything like that?"

For Individuals

For individuals who develop talking points for themselves, their background, and abilities, they should employ the same process as a business.

Your tagline, USP, and elevator speech will get you started in a conversation about yourself with another person. Then, diving deeper into your experiences, you'll want to weave your prior jobs, volunteer roles, hobbies, or skills with stories from your life that follow the "Situation, Problem, Solution, Results" format.

Establishing credibility is the name of the game when speaking with someone. People want to hear stories about you. To the extent that you can make those stories compelling by adding a little conflict around and uncertainty in solving the Problems you have encountered and your Solutions to them, that will further strengthen your talking points.

If you struggle with determining which stories you want to tell, think about the facets of yourself, whether they are skills or problem-solving experiences, that you want to relate, then build your stories around those facets. In my case, I want people to know that I'm a creative problem-solver. My career is filled with examples of helping clients solve marketing and communications challenges.

My firm was retained by the County of Orange in Southern California to perform outreach for the 2020 Census. Our primary objective was to exceed the 75-percent self-response rate that the county achieved during the 2010 Census. My firm began work in February 2020, months later than the other firms that had been retained for outreach. My team pitched our county contacts on performing springtime egg hunts that would span the county's five districts, with people searching for a golden egg that had in-kind donated tickets and prizes from some of the county's leading brands (Los Angeles Angels of Anaheim, Disneyland, Knotts Berry Farm, Anaheim Ducks, etc.). I bought the golden eggs, which were about the size of a small watermelon. Our intent was to have egg hunts in each of the five districts as a kickoff to the Census and the search, then drive interested parties to county locations (parks, libraries, etc.) to get clues to find the eggs. We had an early April launch date, so we had to move fast. Just as we began our outreach to local partners to secure in-kind donations, COVID-19 happened.

On March 13, shutdowns began. At first, it wasn't clear how long the pandemic would last. The initial closures of events, schools, public locations, etc. were only for a matter of weeks. By the week of March 23 though, it was clear that we were not going to be performing any community-outreach events, let alone in-person egg hunts. Weeks of planning were wiped out. At this point, three realities existed for me and my team: 1) the 2020 Census was still launching in early April; 2) the goal remained unchanged at 75-percent self-response rate; and 3) we had to completely reconceive our approach due to COVID-19. The largest pillar of our campaign by far, in-person community event-driven outreach, was no longer an option.

We had to get creative! Very quickly, we had to isolate what we could do, given the restrictions of the pandemic. We leaned heavily on digital outreach using videos from "trusted messenger" spokespeople in 15 different languages; hyper-local geo-targeted digital advertising; creating a digital communications toolkit for the county's public information officers (PIOs) with dozens and dozens of sample ads, social media posts, web and newsletter copy, and more; and targeted bus and gas-station advertising in hard-to-count areas with non-English-speaking residents.

Ultimately, through the work of my team, the 2020 Census realized a 76.6-percent self-response rate, thereby achieving the objective despite the limitations from the pandemic. The County of Orange finished 5th among all counties in the State of California in self-response rate, which was a huge deal for our county contacts. Lastly, the campaign won a top award from the local Orange County chapter of the Public Relations Society of America as well as the Best of the West Award from the regional PRSA Western District.

How does all of this pertain to talking points? If I'm speaking with a prospect about creative problem-solving, I say something like this:

> When I worked on the 2020 Census, we had to pivot from an events-heavy community-outreach campaign to a largely digital campaign in a matter of days when COVID hit. We were all geared up to do these countywide egg hunts across each of the five districts, which would've been cool. Then, we shifted to a lot of video with trusted messengers who could relate to our hard-to-count audiences, hyper-local digital advertising, and traditional bus, outdoor, and gas station advertising. We even did aerial advertising via a plane flying over the county. The key though was creating a digital toolkit to arm our county PIOs with in-language materials to connect with their stakeholders. It was an awesome, crazy time, but we hit our target of having a better response rate than the 2010 Census, despite COVID upending everything.

In six sentences, this recap addresses the Situation, Problem, Solution, and Results of the story. Actually, the second and fourth sentences are a little gratuitous and could be removed. But I leave them in there to relate the big-picture thinking behind the campaign. "A countrywide egg hunt? Wow." is the thought I want the person thinking. "Aerial advertising? He/they thought of everything." is another thought for the fourth sentence. Again, I want people to think that I'm a creative problem-solver and—while these marketing approaches may not be the most ingenious ideas in the world—they do reflect creativity given the circumstances. And, at the time, they were successful. We provided our county contacts with detailed metrics reports on the effectiveness of the various portions of the campaign that they forwarded to their state contacts, who—we were told—were amazed at the results. Most important, we made our county contacts look good, and that fact has garnered us referral work from them.

For your talking points, you'll want to recount these types of stories from your own personal background; think about them in the Situation, Problem, Solution, and Results format; and create short narrative stories that can be expanded, if needed. If thinking back on your prior successes is a challenge for you, contact a fellow worker or friend who knows the details of your professional achievements. Ask him or her to help you remember how you overcame the Problem with a Solution that you conceived, then reported the Results. Get a few of these narrative stories down on paper, rehearse them, then roll them out at a networking event, job interview, new-business lunch, or other such occurrence, and watch how well people respond to your storytelling. I guarantee that you'll differentiate yourself from the crowd.

Chapter 18

Verifying and Applying Your Godly Brand

To this point, you have identified your Core Purpose and Core Values, unique selling proposition (USP), tagline, elevator speech, and talking points. The next step is to verify with others that what you developed truly represents your brand. The key here is to ensure that others perceive your brand the way that you want them to see it. That requires a little bit of testing. Depending on what feedback you receive, you may find that there is some confusion about your brand that you will need to address.

When it comes to living out or applying your Godly brand, regular reflection and maintaining consistency will be vital to ensure that others properly perceive and articulate it. We will explore all these concepts in this chapter, starting with testing your brand.

Testing Your Brand

Once you have identified what you believe to be your Core Values, it is important to find out whether your brand translates to others. You cannot assume that it does, regardless of your intentions or actions. Because your personality and actions weigh so heavily into how people perceive your brand, you need to verify how others see you. The process will be different for individual people versus businesses.

For individuals, testing your brand means sharing it with trusted people in your life who will give you honest, non-agenized feedback. Find professional colleagues to walk through your core purpose and values, tagline, and elevator speech, asking for feedback. If you have mentors, either in business, at church or at school, go to them first. Here's the trick: you must not be defensive in receiving that feedback, and you absolutely cannot take it personally. You can and should ask clarification questions if some aspect of the feedback confuses you or does not track with the rest of the person's comments. But being defensive or showing frustration because you do not like what the other person is saying is the fastest way to ensure that he or she stops speaking honestly.

You should choose people you trust. If you select someone who starts giving you inappropriate, harsh, or non-applicable feedback, disengage immediately and move on. The litmus test is whether the other person is truly interested in helping you or hearing him- or herself speak.

How many trusted colleagues should you interview? That depends on how deep you want to go to verify your brand, how much time you have to conduct the meetings, how much budget you have to pay for people's coffee or lunch (you always pay!), where you are in your career, and how dramatically you want to define or shift your Godly brand. Another factor is how divergent is the feedback that you are receiving. If you are interviewing colleagues across different walks of your life and you are receiving substantially varied feedback on your brand, you will want to add more contacts to your brand-verification process. To give you a starting point though, pick at least three people who know you in different contexts (work, professional network, church, school, volunteer organization, etc.) to begin the interviewing.

One note: if you are a freelancer or solo practitioner, be very careful about including your customers in this process. It's very important that—with your customers—you present your brand in the best light. Speaking with your customers may give them the type of access to yourself and your brand to which they are not accustomed. You don't want them wondering things about your brand that may confuse them or give them pause for thought in doing business with you. Only speak to those customers that are very trusted and "locked in" as clients about verifying your brand. For those trusted, locked-in customers, they will likely give you the best feedback and will appreciate being part of your process. Just use good judgment as you proceed.

For businesses, testing your brand can involve a wide range of research and analysis that depends on the size of your organization. Large organizations will commit a lot of budget and resources to perform attitude and usage surveys that compare how their target audiences perceive their brand, products, or services, measuring the customer attitudes against their usage behaviors; focus groups that garner input from target audiences on key drivers behind their perception of the brand; message testing that evaluates the effectiveness of how key value propositions (i.e., top benefits of using the products or services) are communicated and understood by target audiences; persuasion testing that measures whether target audiences' attitudes toward your brand led to a change in behavior; and recall testing that evaluates whether target audiences remember your key messages from advertisements, public relations, digital marketing, etc. and whether those messages stood out from your competition.

This is the extent of brand testing that sophisticated companies with the budget and willingness to spend it perform. If you're a small- to medium-sized business, you could perform a single "sentiment survey" of target audiences to better understand how they perceive your brand. Primary research of this kind will cost $25,000-$50,000 depending on the scope of the polling. There are other solutions that cost far less involving incentivized polling using tools like Survey Monkey. In these cases, you can conduct a giveaway whereby all respondents are eligible for a prize (i.e., iPad, GoPro camera, etc.) for participating. Point being, there is a scale from do-it-yourself surveying to very robust research that companies can perform. In all cases though, even if your company has a research arm, you are best served to engage a third-party firm to perform the outreach, aggregation of data, and reporting of the findings.

If you are a small business, church, or nonprofit organization, your marketing budget will not likely be able to afford doing any of these types of data-driven testing. As an entrepreneur, you've been doing business as you are, your customers know who you are, and it's been working for you. That's fine, *until* you begin to lose revenue, market share, or customers, or you want to grow to whatever the "next level" is. In those cases, you'll want to re-address your brand to either identify what's causing brand erosion (loss), opportunities for growth (gain), or both. You will want to seek out a marketing partner with a proven background in branding and messaging to help. Like performing research, that will involve engaging a third party to help, whether it's a local marketing firm, solo practitioner / freelancer, or a person you know from church who'll help for low to no cost.

If you go to the local firm or freelancer route, a great place to start is the local chapter of the Public Relations Society of America (PRSA). A list of nationwide and international chapters can be found at www.prsa.org. The site offers a searchable database of marketing professionals and firms to get you started.

Addressing Brand Confusion through Reflection and Consistency

Sometimes, there can be confusion about one's brand when an organization or person either acts in an inconsistent manner or is perceived by others in a certain light based on his or her role. Recalling that branding is the alignment of what you say about yourself with what you actually deliver, if you do not consistently reinforce your Core Purpose and Core Values through what you say and do, there is virtually no chance people will believe your brand messaging and therefore become emotionally engaged with your brand.

When managing young professionals who are having trouble keeping up with day-to-day tasks or ascertaining the meaning behind things, I always ask them if—at any point after work—whether they self-assess their actions or the significance of the happenings of the day. In essence, I ask whether they have reflected on the day. In an overwhelming number of times, I ask this question, I'm met with a blank stare or quick head shake "no." By the way, lots of older professionals don't do it either.

The reason for asking about reflection is that—if one cannot or does not evaluate what happened to him- or herself during the day—one cannot be truly self-aware. And, if one isn't self-aware, it's virtually impossible to improve one's position in life.

When you reflect, you think through the day, what you could have done differently, what you did well, what you could have done better. When processing the day in this manner, you invariably consider "strategic improvements" in how you'll do things in the future as well as behaviors you'll avoid. In short, without reflection, you don't know what to improve because you're not really in touch with what you need to improve.

The reflection process is vital to discerning one's brand because it is impacted by the world. We live in a sinful world, and that sin constantly and pervasively bombards your mind, body, and soul. The result is an ongoing sometimes obvious, sometimes subtle assault on your Godly brand.

Reflection is not just a daily thing. It can and should be done for longer periods so that you can look back at the bigger things that happened during a month, year, season of difficult times, or life. Every year, during the week between Christmas and New Year's Day, I reflect on the past year, ascertain what I accomplished and what I didn't, and set goals for myself for the next year. That reflection and goal-setting was the only way I finished this book; I held myself accountable.

You should constantly ask yourself and God through prayer what could you have done differently or better to build your Godly brand, draw closer to God in your personal service to Him, and improve your life circumstances. Ensure that you reflect for yourself first, then you can consider others, like your family.

Your reflection can prompt you to change some aspects of how you lead your life. Because you are a change agent for God's kingdom-building in this world, you should always be advancing, progressing toward a new personal milestone that plays your part in His perfect plan. If, after several attempts at reflection, you remain uncertain what the Lord wants you to achieve in your service to Him, continue to pray for guidance and seek out assistance from a spiritual leader.

Another key to effective branding is consistency. Maintaining a consistent delivery of your brand through packaging, ordering, and delivery of products or services; customer support and call centers; employee interactions with customers; problem-solving when customer complaints come or during crises; use of marketing channels; sales engagements with prospective customers; poor quarterly earnings; and every other force that impacts your brand is the *hardest part* of branding. It is why large brands employ a dedicated person and team to singularly monitor the brand experience across all the company's customer and stakeholder "touch points" to ensure the highest standard of service or whatever other metrics drive the brand perception among target audiences.

If you're a small business owner, think about all the times that you have had to answer a customer's question or solve a problem for a customer, either before or after they find out about it. For service-oriented businesses like mine, this is an hour-by-hour role and responsibility. It never stops and can strike at any time of day. How do you maintain brand consistency under these circumstances? First, you must identify and build a strong brand, reinforce it when things are going well, then remain true to your brand promise (e.g., speedy response, high-quality results, honest pricing, "get it done right" mindset) when things don't go well.

Your experience has probably taught you that—if you have goodwill in the bank for your brand—it will earn you some grace from customers when you need it. How you handle a challenge to your brand from any number of external factors will further strengthen or weaken it, depending on how your customers perceive your response. If an operational challenge arises that requires you to visit a customer's site and you don't go in a timely manner or try to charge the customer for the onsite visit, unless those cost stipulations are part of your contract, the result will be a negative brand experience for that customer. Conversely, if you exceed the customer's expectations by even the smallest amount, you will create a raving fan of your brand.

Effectively Handling Crisis

You know the old saying from novelist James Lane Allen, "Adversity does not build character, it reveals it." Nice sentiment, but it's not entirely true for people of faith. For followers of God, adversity both builds character *and* reveals it. James 1:3 frames it: ". . . because you know that the testing of your faith produces perseverance."

Truth is, we face a continuum of crisis virtually every day. Some crises are small (e.g., I'm late to work *again*, my son won't get dressed for school, I got a flat tire on the way to the birthday party), and some are large (e.g., the biopsy was positive, visiting a divorce attorney, a parent or child dies suddenly).

Regardless of where your daily troubles fall on your continuum of crisis today, realize that God has placed them in your life for a reason, and every one of them informs and affects your Godly brand. On the smaller side, perhaps God wants you to mind what you say. Nothing gets you to stop swearing in traffic like hearing your three-year-old son gleefully repeat an inappropriate word or phrase from his car seat. On the larger side, perhaps the biopsy, divorce, or sudden tragedy enables you to lend comfort to others in the future.

One complication is that frequently the reason God tests you isn't always immediately clear. Maybe your three-year-old doesn't parrot your swearing. Maybe no one enters your life for comforting after a large crisis. Sometimes, the "cause and effect" of a crisis and consequential Godly brand-building are not evident. If the "cause and effect" of a crisis in your life becomes clear and you can positively affect someone else, that's terrific. Offer a prayer of thanksgiving and praise to God for using you as His instrument. However, if it is not clear, always remember that crisis shapes your Godly brand.

God tested Job with the loss of his kids, wealth, and health, and his brand withstood the many crises that afflicted him. Job characterized these crises as a form of refinement, as if to help purify him: "But He knows the way that I take; when He has tested me, I will come forth as gold." (Job 23:10)

Numerous passages in the Bible refer to testing and crisis as a form of refining, likening the strengthening of one's spirit through crisis to removing the impurities from fine metal. Ps 66:10 says, "For you, God, tested us; you refined us like silver." And Prov 27:17 says, "As iron sharpens iron, so one person sharpens another."

Jesus was repeatedly tested, whether it was 40 days alone in the desert, being tempted by Satan; constant attempts by the Pharisees to trap Him with questions; non-stop people pressing Him to heal or perform miracles without taking the time to understand who He was and why He was there; and—the greatest test—the anticipation of and eventual death on the Cross.

Followers of God must try not to turn inward to themselves to solve a crisis, but always turn to Him, and remain consistent in your Godly brand, relying on your faith and prayer to "weather the storm." Trust me, even if you do not know the effect of a crisis that you've experienced on your life or another's, God will use it for good.

Chapter 19

Aspirational Branding: Evolving Your Godly Brand

FOR COMPANIES, ASPIRATIONAL BRANDING involves strategies that are designed to reposition a brand for the purpose of organizational change and/or modifying consumer opinion about the brand. For individuals, aspirational branding can be a calculated process to shift people's perceptions of you, or it can happen accidentally, randomly, or as a result of external forces upon you.

I can't think of a better example of aspirational branding than the singer, songwriter, and actress Miley Cyrus. As a father of a daughter who watched a lot of Disney Channel programming in the 2005–2010 timeframe, I knew her from the *Hannah Montana* show, where she played the very wholesome character Miley Stewart/Hannah Montana. I also knew her from her voice-talent role in the animated feature, *Bolt*. During her time on Hannah Montana and shortly after, she released albums, went on music tours, and starred in feature films.

In the early 20-teens, Cyrus changed her image and brand toward a more adult look with her *Can't Be Tamed* album that featured a more dance-oriented sound than her prior releases. She appeared in a movie called *The Last Song*, based on the Nicholas Sparks novel. Then, in 2013, Cyrus hired as her manager the same person who had represented Britney Spears, who went through a similar "escape from Disney" brand shift. Soon thereafter began a series of actions that were designed to bury forever her Hannah Montana persona. At the 2013 MTV Video Music Awards, she performed with Robin Thicke, simulating sex acts with a foam finger. In the same year, in the video for her popular "Wrecking Ball" single, she swung naked on a wrecking ball. She was figuratively and literally taking a wrecking ball to her former brand and creating a new edgy adult one. During this time, Cyrus' brand officially "grew up."

Since then, Cyrus was quoted in *Time* magazine that she identified as gender fluid. She's dated men and women. She is a huge advocate and supporter of the LGBTQIA+ community, tattooing an equal sign on her ring finger in support of same-sex marriage and founding her Happy Hippie Foundation, which works to "fight injustice facing homeless youth, LGBTQ youth and other vulnerable populations."

Cyrus has become one of the most successful entertainers on the planet. In the span of six or so years, she completely recast herself and her brand, and—while the process may have had some rough edges—she did it rather brilliantly to arrive where she is today. Cyrus is an example of how an individual with help from others reshaped her personal brand. It doesn't really matter whether you like the brand she reflects; her transformation was crafted and the results she wanted were achieved.

The Bible has several good examples of individuals who have done this, too, but—in their case—it wasn't a music manager or agent who helped them aspire to a new brand. It was God. There are three fantastic examples of aspirational branding in the Scriptures with the lives of Moses, David, and Paul.

In the case of Paul, like Abraham, Sarah and Jacob, he went through the ultimate aspirational branding experience: he changed his name. Like the other three, his new name was given to him by God; it was not a human choice. Also, his and others' name change marked a decided course-correction in their lives, directed by God, whereby they would never be the same again. Looking at Paul though, his transition was by far the most dramatic.

Paul went through at least two definitive brand evolutions in his life, and I could argue a third one, too. Here they are:

1. *Road to Damascus Conversion:* We first meet Saul as a young man in Acts 7 at the stoning of Stephen. The Scriptures recount how Stephen stirred up the members of the Sanhedrin with his testimony about Jesus, and they hauled him out to stone him. Saul was there, and the people stoning Stephen laid their coats at Saul's feet. There

is a direct implication that Saul was responsible in some part with actions of the people stoning Stephen. At the very least, Acts 8:1 tells us that "Saul approved of their killing him."

That stoning began "a great persecution [that] broke out against the church in Jerusalem, and all except the apostles were scattered throughout Judea and Samaria." (8:2) And Saul? He "began to destroy the church. Going from house to house, he dragged off both men and women and put them in prison." (8:3)

In Philippians 3, Paul referred to himself as "a Hebrew of Hebrews; in regard to the law, a Pharisee; as for zeal, persecuting the church; as for righteousness based on the law, faultless." He considered stamping out the followers of The Way, as it was called, his personal and God-given mission.

Saul clearly did a good job, too. His brand and reputation proceeded him to the extent where, when—in Acts 9:13—Ananias is commissioned by God to "go to the house of Judas on Straight Street" and place his hands on Saul to restore his sight, the elder disciple says, "Lord, I have heard many reports about this man and all the harm he has done to your holy people in Jerusalem." At this point, Saul's brand attributes could be characterized as zealous, persecutor of the church, Pharisaical knowledge of Jewish law, angry (Acts 9:1), and uncompromising.

2. *Recognized by the Council of Jerusalem:* After his conversion, Saul preached in Damascus, until a plot to kill him compelled him to flee the city (Acts 9:24). He went to Jerusalem, met Peter and James, and preached there until another plot to him forced him to flee to Caesarea (Acts 9:30). Some time later, Barnabas found Saul in Tarsus and brought him to Antioch. For a year, they stayed there, preaching to the people. In Acts 13, the Scriptures tells us that "the Holy Spirit said, 'Set apart for me Barnabas and Saul for the work to which I have called them.' So after they had fasted and prayed, they placed their hands on them and sent them off."

Saul and Barnabas went to Cyprus first. About this time, Saul began going by the name Paul. After Cyprus, they went to Pisidian Antioch, then Iconium, then Lystra, where Paul was stoned so badly by a mob that they left him for dead. They eventually went back to Antioch. There, Paul and Barnabas came into sharp dispute with "people [who] came down from Judea to Antioch and were teaching

Aspirational Branding: Evolving Your Godly Brand

the believers: "Unless you are circumcised, according to the custom taught by Moses, you cannot be saved." In Acts 15:2, the Bible tells us that "Paul and Barnabas were appointed, along with some other believers, to go up to Jerusalem to see the apostles and elders about this question." Bible commentators suggest that it had been 14 years since Paul's conversion when he made this return to Jerusalem.

Paul, Barnabas, and Titus arrived in Jerusalem and—in a moment that seems like those rare occurrences when 4 or 5 U.S. Presidents are gathered for a state occasion—there were the leading apostles of the faith all gathered in one location. Peter, James, and John were there. James spoke on the topic at hand. After hearing Paul and Barnabas speak "about the signs and wonders God had done among the Gentiles through them," the Council cleared the path for the Word of God to be brought to the Gentiles.

The apostles and elders in Jerusalem sent a letter "to the Gentile believers in Antioch, Syria and Cilicia" that resolved the circumcision issue and dispatched Paul and Barnabas, along with Judas (called Barsabbas) and Silas, men who were leaders among the believers, to encourage and strengthen the believers in Antioch.

Besides resolving the issue of circumcision to be saved, that letter served another important function: it legitimized Paul and Barnabas with the Council at Jerusalem. From Acts 15:25-26, the letter states, "So we (the Council) all agreed to choose some men and send them to you with our dear friends Barnabas and Paul—men who have risked their lives for the name of our Lord Jesus Christ." Think of it as a hub church recognizing the leaders of a satellite church, agreeing with their position, and sending delegates to verify that support.

Furthermore, in Gal 2, Paul writes that, while he and Barnabas where in Jerusalem, "they (the Council) recognized that I had been entrusted with the task of preaching the gospel to the uncircumcised, just as Peter had been to the circumcised. For God, who was at work in Peter as an apostle to the circumcised, was also at work in me as an apostle to the Gentiles." Here, Paul became an apostle.

Where did Paul's brand attributes stand at this point? He was still zealous, possessed a Pharisaical knowledge of Jewish law, and remained uncompromising. The word zealous encompasses several attributes that Paul demonstrated in his new role; specifically, he became *emboldened* and *driven*.

On the emboldened front, Gal 2 relates a confrontation between Paul and Peter over Jews eating with Gentiles. Paul called out Peter in front of the church of Antioch, saying "You are a Jew, yet you live like a Gentile and not like a Jew. How is it, then, that you force Gentiles to follow Jewish customs?" Since Paul is writing the epistle, we don't get the benefit of Peter's response to the rebuke. Among biblical scholars, there is some debate over this confrontation. Some say that Peter took his medicine in stride. Others point out that this calling out, where Paul also condemns Barnabas who was "led astray," so polluted the waters in Antioch that Paul was estranged from that church for the rest of his days.

Regardless of what happened with Peter and Antioch, Paul was clearly emboldened in his role. That attribute reared its head again when Paul and Barnabas had a falling out over John Mark (Acts 15:36–41) that caused them to go their separate ways.

Starting in Acts 16, Paul sets out on his second and third missionary trips across Asia and Macedonia, with a two-year break between the two journeys in Corinth. These travels lasted 8–9 years and covered more than 5,200 miles on foot and by water. If you ever read the accounts of these travels in Acts 16 through 23, it becomes clear that Paul was *driven* to fulfill his role as "an apostle to the Gentiles."

Reflecting Paul's suffering from 2 Cor 11, only someone who was relentlessly driven would tolerate this hardship. The question from a branding perspective is: what would cause someone to be this driven? What was the fuel that powered Paul's motor through all the things he endured? Certainly, Paul had faith in Christ, and the strength he derived from that drove him. As someone who has studied Paul's life, I often wonder if it might have been guilt for what he did to the church before his conversion. And that his drive was—in some small part—making up for those sins of the past. Biblical scholars will disagree with me and cite reasons why Paul would not have felt this way. But the obsessive manner in which he pursued his mission journeys, church planting, and writings feels like there is more at work than mere faith.

For the purposes of this book, let's say that Paul also demonstrated a brand attribute of *deep faith in Christ* as his Risen Savior and set about being a champion of that faith.

3. *Last Visit to Jerusalem and End of Life:* At the completion of his third missionary trip, Paul arrived in Jerusalem for his fifth and final visit with a collection of money for the local community. Before he got there though, while Paul was traveling in Caesarea, Philip the evangelist, took Paul's belt, tied his own hands and feet with it and said, "The Holy Spirit says, 'In this way the Jewish leaders in Jerusalem will bind the owner of this belt and will hand him over to the Gentiles.'" All the people there "pleaded with Paul not to go up to Jerusalem." (Acts 21:12)

Then Paul answered, "Why are you weeping and breaking my heart? I am ready not only to be bound, but also to die in Jerusalem for the name of the Lord Jesus." Paul did not die in Jerusalem. But his trip there set in motion the actions that would eventually lead to his death.

After his arrival, Paul was arrested by the Romans after being beaten by the people who were incited by "some Jews from the province of Asia." He was flogged and interrogated by a Roman centurion. After escaping a plot to kill him, Paul was transferred to Caesarea, delivering him over to Governor Felix. There, Paul remained in prison for two years, because the governor wanted to "grant a favor to the Jews." (Acts 24:27)

Eventually, Paul was brought before a new governor, Festus, then King Agrippa, to whom Festus sent Paul for examination. During his back and forth with the governor, Paul pulled the ultimate trump card and appealed to Caesar to hear his case. Paul was sent to Rome by boat. Along the way, he was shipwrecked on Malta, where he spent two years.

At last, Paul arrived in Rome, spending two years under house arrest and preaching to those who visited him. Acts 28:23 tells us that "he witnessed to them from morning till evening, explaining about the kingdom of God, and from the Law of Moses and from the Prophets he tried to persuade them about Jesus." During his time in Rome, Paul wrote four "prison epistles," which include Ephesians, Philippians, Colossians, and Philemon. Some years later, Paul was beheaded in Rome by order of Emperor Nero.

Paul's brand attributes evolved during his transition from missionary journeys to imprisonment in Jerusalem, Caesarea, then Rome. The years of wear and tear undoubtedly had taken a toll on him. He had a "thorn in his flesh" that troubled him for most of his adult life. Whether that thorn was failing vision, epilepsy, a speech impediment, a temptation to unbelief, his opponents, or some other ailment, he pleaded for God to remove it from him, but the Lord did not.

One wonders whether—when he left Philip and the followers in Caesarea for Jerusalem—he was tired and ready to meet his Lord. In his epistles, Paul spoke of the heavenly reward that he knew awaited him. He seemed to sum up his life as he wrote to Timothy in his second letter to him: "I have fought the good fight, I have finished the race, I have kept the faith." (4:7)

Paul's brand attributes at this point in his life transitioned. He still possessed a Pharisaical knowledge of Jewish law and his deep faith in Christ. But perhaps, he was a little less zealous, driven, or uncompromising, replaced by *tender loving* for the churches he planted and the followers at each of them. His imprisonment and late-in-life infirmities (e.g., he had to have someone write his letters for him) brought a measure of *humility* into his life. From Eph 6:19-20, "Pray also for me, that whenever I speak, words may be given me so that I will fearlessly make known the mystery of the gospel, for which I am an ambassador in chains. Pray that I may declare it fearlessly, as I should." At the end of the Book of Colossians, Paul asks the church there to "Remember my chains."

Paul's Godly brand evolved throughout his life. The real aspirational brand shift for Paul occurred after being commissioned by the Council of Jerusalem to be an apostle to the Gentiles. He clearly took that role very seriously and—along the way—his zealous, uncompromising, driven focus to fulfill his apostleship caused him great suffering and eventual execution. However, it also brought him immense joy to bring as many to Christ as he did. From 1 Cor 1:4-6, "I always thank my God for you because of his grace given you in Christ Jesus. For in him you have been enriched in every way—with all kinds of speech and with all knowledge—God thus confirming our testimony about Christ among you."

Why Companies Change Their Brand

Aspirational brand strategies are used by businesses and churches for a variety of reasons, but the most common ones are the following: 1) when a current brand image is either negative or no longer relevant; 2) when a company or individual wants to evolve their brand in response to opportunity, competition, or both; 3) when a crisis threatens to harm or already has harmed a brand; or 4) worldly or life circumstances impact a brand in such a way that it incrementally changes over time.

During the 1970s and 80s, American car manufacturers had to up their game in the face of foreign car manufacturers simply making better, more reliable, more fuel-efficient, more innovative, lesser-costing automobiles. At that time, except for those who were the most stalwart "buy American" types, domestic cars had a negative brand. Something had to happen, and it did. American auto manufacturers got competitive and slowly earned back their marketshare. In 2019, 4 of the 5 best-selling models are made in the U.S.: 1) Ford F-Series; 2) Ram pick-up; 3) Chevrolet Silverado; 4) Toyota RAV4; and Chevrolet Equinox. By the way, the 6th through 10th ranked models are all foreign-made.

Crisis can threaten the best of brands. British Petroleum (BP) rebounded in the Gulf States of the U.S. after an abominable handling of the Deep Water Horizon disaster. The company has made a lot of strides in the affected states with effective community outreach and investment programs.

Wells Fargo's account fraud scandal in 2016 involved the creation of millions of fraudulent savings and checking accounts on behalf of the bank's clients without their consent. The United States Consumer Financial Protection Bureau fined the company a combined US$185 million as a result of the illegal activity. The company faced additional civil and criminal suits reaching an estimated $2.7 billion by the end of 2018. To rebuild the beleaguered brand, Wells Fargo fired its CEO, changed its logo, and launched a marketing campaign that used the tagline *"Established 1852. Re-established 2018."* According to Wells Fargo CMO, Jamie Moldafsky, in an interview with *The Financial Brand*, the objective of the campaign is the "acquisition of new customers and retention of existing ones. 'This campaign obviously is intended to have legs.'"

Worldly or life circumstances can incrementally impact a brand in such small ways that—at some point—a company or person has drifted so far off course that it or he/she no longer recognizes where they are. This drifting occurs with people all the time. Little occasions of laziness, abuse, cheating, eating, sinning, etc. happen over time and, before you know it, you're divorced, fired from your job, sitting in jail, lying in a hospital bed, or worse—dead—and you don't even know how you got there. It's the "death by a thousand cuts" cliché. Each one wasn't that bad until you realize you're bleeding out from all of them.

With companies, it can begin with reducing their investments in training, customer service and support, marketing, employee benefits, research and development (R&D) of new products or services to keep up with the market, or any host of things that compromise the customer experience, cost them sales, and ultimately affect the bottom line.

The process to evolve your brand is similar to the process to identify and create one; however, there is one very important difference between the two. With aspirational branding, there is a pre-existing brand, and it has to be evaluated to see what customers liked and didn't like, what worked and what didn't, and which attributes should be preserved and which ones should evolve. The reason being is that you rarely will abandon all the aspects of the brand during a re-branding process, but rather reshape the brand through further building up of the strengths and repairing the weaknesses or eliminating them in favor of new brand attributes. Always remember, there was a reason why customers purchased your products or services at one point. You need to rediscover it. If you're an individual, there was a reason that people wanted to work with you, solicited your counsel, retained your services, became your friends, etc.

Companies that undertake an aspirational re-branding effort will perform research with their target customers to better understand their current perceptions about the brand and willingness to entertain it in the future. This type of research involves surveying or polling; focus group tests; A/B product or service tests where customers are asked to choose between two or more alternatives, including the brand's product or service; one-on-one meetings; and any other form of experiential customer feedback.

This intelligence gathering through research helps inform the re-branding process by identifying what brand attributes still resonate with your customers, which do not, and where new product or service opportunities reside.

How does this research portion of re-branding work if you're a small business or individual that does not have the money to hire an outside firm to help? Depending on the type of business you have, you can ask your top customers directly, either in-person or through a customer-satisfaction survey. If you're customers are retail consumers, a few options include in-store promotions that solicit feedback; social media, social media advertising, and direct marketing (e.g., e-newsletters) that send

Aspirational Branding: Evolving Your Godly Brand

customers to an online survey and promise an incentive for completing it; or special promotions at hyper-local events, like the city's 4th of July fireworks, AYSO soccer tournament, annual parade, etc. You need this feedback to determine how people feel about your brand, customer engagement, products or services, and more.

If you're an individual considering your own brand, you need to ask others who have had meaningful experiences with you at work, play, school, church, or any number of places where you're engaging with others. They should see you in circumstances that are not always ideal. Try to ask a people who have seen you experience some adversity and come through it.

Promoting a "Made-Up" Brand

I want to briefly touch on an element of aspirational branding that a very small number of you will consider, but does occur with personal branding of celebrities or marketing influencers. Earlier, I covered the evolution of Miley Cyrus' brand from her Hannah Montana days to what it is today. Her brand was deliberately, strategically changed to create and promote a new brand that—from all appearances—more or less correlates to who she is today.

Frequently among celebrities, their handlers and marketing representatives will make up a brand for them that does not correlate to who they are, but will sell their persona, show or movie, book, merchandise, or whatever he or she is hawking.

Even if you do not follow basketball, you probably know who LeBron James is from his playing career, movies (*Space Jam: A New Legacy*), shoes and apparel, video games, and more. When James decided to leave his hometown NBA (National Basketball Association) team, the Cleveland Cavaliers, back in 2010, he did so through a televised special called "The Decision." The show ran 75 minutes, at the end of which he announced that he was leaving Cleveland to go play for the Miami Heat. To evolve James' brand, his handlers and Nike (his shoe partner) ran a campaign to portray James as a villain for leaving the Cavaliers and his hometown (James grew up in nearby Akron, Ohio).

Then and now, the campaign felt hokey and dumb. It was just an attempt to make James more edgy and polarize fans for him or against him. But he wasn't a villain or bad guy. How did I know that, even though I do not have a personal relationship with James? The Decision was broadcast from the Boys and Girls Club of Greenwich, Connecticut, raising $2.5 million for the charity and an additional $3.5 million in advertising revenue that was donated to other nonprofit organizations. Villains keep that money, not donate it. Simple, right?

Plus, have you seen James' big, shiny smile on the court? Fortunately, the villain branding is a distant memory for James. Now, it's all about being the greatest basketball player of all time and strengthening his movie career.

Because their public persona is their primary asset for making money, smart celebrities will craft a brand image that does not match who they are as people. They will protect against things that would invalidate that image. Proper brand management by skilled marketing professionals and legal teams can ensure the preservation of a personal brand, despite actions or behavior by the celebrity that would harm it. Unless you're a celebrity or influencer who wants to brand "for effect," my recommendation is to align your brand with who you are and the value you deliver, and avoid anything that could cause a brand disconnect with your target audiences down the line.

Evolving Your Brand: How To Do It

As it pertains evolving your brand, you should not change your Core Purpose or Core Values except in very rare circumstances. In business, a change in ownership or complete overhaul in what the company does (product or service offerings) may entail switching one or both. Otherwise, a Core Purpose or Core Values should remain unchanged; they are meant to last decades. The same applies for individuals. It would take a monumental life change (e.g., marriage or divorce, diagnosis, career change) to consider a change to your Core Purpose or Core Values.

However, evolving your messaging (USP, tagline, elevator speech, and talking points) is where you want to start. Messaging is meant to be changed periodically to reflect broad new business initiatives. For individuals, evolved messaging can reflect new jobs or career focus, skills, volunteer involvement, and much more.

Whether you're a business or an individual, updating your messaging will involve the same process as described in chapter 17, Defining Your Brand Messaging, with one exception: you will not be starting from scratch. Updating doesn't mean abandoning. Review your current messaging, find what messaging elements you must preserve, ascertain which elements you need to revisit or adapt for your current business conditions, convene your leadership team, then begin the facilitated process of soliciting input that will eventually result in the writing of new messaging.

If you do need to update your Core Purpose or Core Values, refer to chapter 16, Defining Your Core Purpose and Core Values, to go through the processes outlined there. Like brand messaging, the key is updating, not abandoning. Unless you're performing a Miley Cyrus-like annihilation of your brand in favor of a new one, you will want to preserve most of your Core Purpose and Core Values.

Chapter 20

The Final Word

Walk the Walk and Pray

Now that you've defined your brand values, tagline, and elevator speech, you may be asking yourself, how do I make sure I follow and strengthen my own brand, which is hard enough, *and* adhere to all eight Godly brand attributes? It's difficult to remember all that stuff. It's even more difficult to live it out.

Actually, there is an "easy" way to do it. To live out your Godly brand and practice the foundational eight brand attributes for believers, you have to be in His Word, all the time, at least 5–6 days of the week. A daily devotional helps. The game-changer for me was getting a 365-day Bible where you read all of the Scriptures in a year. I've gone through the whole thing numerous times and large chunks of it in other years. Reading the Scriptures regularly helps you see examples of God's followers as recorded in the Bible, relate to them, and better enable you to internalize the eight brand attributes. I can't tell you how many times I've read the Scriptures and had God reveal a parallel in my daily life. It happens *constantly*.

If you feel like an outsider in your family, work, or community, read the book of Ruth. If you feel depressed to the point of not even eating, read the story of Hannah and her faithfulness to God through prayer at the beginning of 1 Samuel. The book of Psalms is woven with a fabric of fear, sadness, and desperation along with praise, adoration, and an understanding that God will always prevail and deliver you. The book of Job is the ultimate tail of faithfulness to God in the wake of literally losing everything: family, belongings and wealth, and health. You get the idea.

The Scriptures are filled with storytelling of everyday people just like you and me, who had to overcome life's challenges and turned to God for help. Many times, there was pain involved. But, through their journeys, we can see how we can walk with God.

Don't let the fact that they lived thousands of years ago fool you into thinking that their stories are not relevant to us today. Those figures dealt with many of the same issues that we do: abandonment, infertility, loss of a child or loved one, persecution, food scarcity, imprisonment, lies made against them, hopelessness, desperation, death, and more. They also experienced God's redemptive power, His glory, His forgiveness, His sacrifice, His salvation, and His awesome power at work in this world. Better understanding the living examples that these biblical figures offer and what they mean to us is the whole purpose of this book.

Yes, But How Do I Start?

If you agree that being in His word regularly is the way to adhere to the eight brand attributes of a believer and thereby live a more Godly life, you still may be struggling with how you do it. Maybe a 365-day devotional seems too intimidating. Where do you start, whether you're new to the Bible or not?

Attempt to make reading the Bible a habit. Maybe you've heard it said that it takes 21 days to form a habit. Some other studies say 18 days, another says 28, yet another says 66. No one is quite sure how long it takes. But, for the sake of this exercise, let's use 21 days. So, give yourself 21 days of habit-forming to do the following: Get to a quiet place, either at home, in your car, the office break room, wherever you can be by yourself. Read the Book of John. It's found in the New Testament and has exactly—you guessed it—21 chapters. Read one chapter per day, just one. At the end of each chapter, which you can read twice for good measure, turn to God in prayer and ask one simple question: Lord, what do you want me to learn from Your Word today? If you go to God in prayer, He will answer you.

If you get through the Book of John and you want to read more, read the Book of Romans. It's two books farther into the New Testament and is written by the Apostle Paul to the believers in Rome. The book is the clearest explanation of Christian doctrine in the Bible. It starts by relating how all people have been condemned due to their own sinfulness and rebellion against God. But, though His grace, God offers us justification by faith in His Son, Jesus Christ. With that justification by God, we receive salvation because Christ's blood redeems our sin.

Besides reading these two books, which can be accessed online at www.BibleGateway.com, if you do not own a Bible, pray every day to God. Praise Him. Ask Him for things like an understanding of the Scriptures that you're reading, help with difficult life decisions, help for friends and family members going through hard times, and guidance in your faith. Then watch how God will work in your life and see where He takes you to serve Him. If you let Him, God will transform your life and start you on a path toward living a Godly branded life for His purpose.

Final Blessing

It only seems fitting that the Lord should get the "last word" on Godly branding. From Num 6:24–26:

> The LORD bless you and keep you;
> the LORD make his face to shine upon you and be gracious to you;
> the LORD lift up his countenance upon you and give you peace.